D1745495

WITHDRAWN
FROM THE LIBRARY OF
UNIVERSITY OF ULSTER

100380393

Activity-based Costing in Financial Institutions

Activity-based Costing in Financial Institutions

JULIE MABBERLEY

FINANCIAL TIMES

PITMAN PUBLISHING

100380393   657·42
        MAB

Pitman Publishing
128 Long Acre, London WC2E 9AN

A division of Pearson Professional Limited

First published in 1992

© Julie Mabberley 1992

British Library Cataloguing in Publication Data
A CIP catalogue record for this book can be obtained
from the British Library

ISBN 0 273 03921 0

All rights reserved; no part of this publication may be reproduced,
stored in a retrieval system, or transmitted in any form or by any
means, electronic, mechanical, photocopying, recording, or otherwise
without either the prior written permission of the Publishers or a
licence permitting restricted copying issued by the Copyright
Licensing Agency, 90 Tottenham Court Road, London W1P 9HE.
This book may not be lent, resold, hired out or otherwise disposed of
by way of trade in any form of binding or cover other than that in which
it is published, without the prior consent of the Publishers.

10 9 8 7

Phototypeset in Linotron Times Roman by
Northern Phototypesetting Co. Ltd, Bolton
Printed and bound in Great Britain by
Biddles Ltd, Guildford and King's Lynn

CONTENTS

1 AN INTRODUCTION TO ACTIVITY-BASED COSTING

INTRODUCTION

Activity-based Costing is a new dimension of cost analysis that was first presented in a formal way by Professor Robert Kaplan, Robin Cooper and H. Thomas Johnson in Harvard in 1987. It has since been developed in many organisations, mainly in manufacturing industries. It has only recently been adopted by the financial sector as a useful tool for analysing costs in a way that encourages accountability and cost management in an industry which has experienced pressures to manage costs more effectively.

The concept behind Activity-based Costing is that costing should be much more than a financial system used by accountants; it should be a part of the profitmaking process of the business. Costs should be planned for and managed *before* they are incurred, rather than simply monitored and controlled after the event.

The traditional methods of allocating overhead costs to operating cost centres simply provides a means for focusing management attention on the large proportion of costs that are classified as overheads and which are effectively outside the control of the individual line manager. Over the past few years, it has become common practice to allocate all overhead costs back to operating functions on a variety of sophisticated bases. This practice has a tendency to focus attention on the allocation process, not on the management of the underlying costs. Activity-based Costing, however, concentrates on the analysis of activities and reviews overhead costs by means of direct cost management within the overhead function without the need to allocate costs to operations centres. It can also provide information to allocate costs to products and customers through the use of appropriate cost drivers if appropriate.

ACTIVITY-BASED COSTING DEFINED

Activity-based Costing analyses the activities of all departments within the organisation in order to provide focused information for the purpose of decision making. The goal of Activity-based Costing is to understand the behaviour of all costs within the organisation, linking operational and sustaining costs to the value chain in such a way that management can identify the factors that drive expenditure and, thus, manage these costs more effectively. The initial objective is to understand the activities that are performed throughout the organisation and be able to estimate the costs associated with delivering those activities. Then the costs of the activities can be identified, together with their causes, cost drivers, to produce more relevant information to help accurately fuel the process of decision making.

Activity-based Costing is a tool that can be used to bring about significant changes in the expenditure patterns, operational processes, overhead activities and organisational structure of a financial institution. It attempts to address the real issues of how and why costs are incurred and does not, therefore, simply record the expenditure and allocate it arbitrarily to cost centres or products. It provides a different dimension to cost information that focuses the attention of management on the underlying factors that can significantly affect the business.

Financial accounting provides external information to shareholders, regulatory authorities, creditors and other stakeholders, but it is unsuitable for making important internal decisions. Entirely different methods are required to provide managers with the information they require to manage the business and accurately assess the costs of doing business. Managers need rapid feedback on efficiency and performance, creating a requirement for the use of modern computer technology to handle large quantities of data in short periods of time. Some organisations have the data available but do not know how to use it effectively, while other organisations need information that they do not record.

Conventional costing techniques analyse profitability by department or cost centre and within each cost centre, analysing costs by category or type of expense. A high proportion of costs are normally allocated on a fixed basis from central or overhead functions using inappropriate allocation bases. This results in incorrect costing data and makes no attempt to establish links between expenditure and its cause.

Activity-based Costing is not a new technique, in essence, but the application of tried and tested techniques in a focused way that *is* new. The results can also be understood and interpreted by accountants and non-accountants alike. It is an approach to cost analysis that helps an organisation to analyse its cost base in a more meaningful way than does conventional departmental accounting. It analyses cost behaviour by activities, linking actions to the consumption of cost and enabling the identification of factors that cause the expenditure to be incurred. It enables management to utilise cost information for the purpose of decision making at all levels within the organisation, focusing on the factors that drive costs and the implications of changes in those factors on the company's overall profitability.

Many accountants will question how Activity-based Costing differs from more conventional types of costing and, in some ways, it is similar to traditional, process or job costing. It attempts to estimate the costs associated with the provision of a product or service. Process costing and job costing are also types of cost analysis based on activities, but traditional costing techniques do not relate the costs to the factors that cause the initial expenditure decision to be taken (cost drivers). The analysis of cost dynamics other than through the conventional techniques of variance analysis (rate and volume variances) can only be achieved by using Activity-based Costing. Activity-based Costs can, however, be based on standard or actual cost calculations in the same way as process or job costs.

The results of Activity-based Costing studies will rarely be precise. The nature of all cost allocation techniques are such that the estimation of costs by activity rarely takes account of capacity utilisation and, furthermore, assumes that the volume of activity remains relatively constant during the period to which the costs relate which, of course, they rarely do. This does not, however, detract from the value of the information provided by such a study. The results of the study will be meaningful in the context of the decisions being made because they link expenditure to the underlying factors that explain why the expenses are incurred and may, therefore, be considered with due reference to the volume-related capacity constraints.

ITS APPLICABILITY TO FINANCIAL INSTITUTIONS

Financial institutions have faced, and will continue to face, increased pressures on profitability due to increasing customer awareness, the increased risks of doing business and the economic environment that is likely to be prevalent in the foreseeable future.

All financial services organisations operate in an intensely competitive market with prices for products and services, generally, being determined by the competition. Margins are continuously being squeezed as competition increases, and it will continue to increase as communications become more global and, hence, the financial markets become more intermingled.

Banks are reporting significantly reduced profits due, mainly, to high levels of insolvency and large provisions for bad debts in Third World countries, Eastern Europe and domestic markets. This is compounded by the constraints on margins imposed by the high levels of competition in the lending markets.

Insurance companies are also, for the first time, reporting significant losses in their general insurance business as they have been subjected to continuously increasing numbers of claims, due mainly to bouts of bad weather throughout the world and an increase in both international and domestic crime rates. Even the Lloyd's market in London has experienced losses due to world-wide claims for catastrophes.

In such a competitive environment, the need to know the individual costs of products and services and to determine which of them are profitable, or at least make a contribution to overhead costs and ultimate profitability, is vital. In order to remain competitive, financial institutions are now looking for ways to reduce their cost bases without harming their businesses.

A financial institution can be viewed as a collection of activities that are performed to support the creation and delivery of its products and services. Competitive advantage is gained by performing activities at lower cost than competitors or by providing a differentiated product or service for which a customer is prepared to pay a higher price.

Financial services organisations are now attempting to make their managers accountable for income, costs and profitability. Historically, the level of management information in the financial sector has been surprisingly limited. Traditionally, managers have concentrated on the external information provided to the shareholders and regulators. Any internal information has been limited to conventional budgetary control by cost centre with full allocation of overhead costs, while measures of performance have focused on sales volumes and maintaining costs at budgeted levels.

The emphasis having shifted away from volumetric sales targets and towards profit-related objectives, managers are looking for guidance on where to concentrate their limited resources. This greater focus on profitability has resulted in the need to identify controllable costs and the factors that cause costs to be incurred (cost drivers), as well as the need to identify profitable product and customer relationships. Managers are concentrating their attention on the costs that they can manage and beginning to link the cost/benefit analysis to the value chain. Thus, they are focusing on those activities that add value and, hence, differentiate their products and services or delivery capability from that offered by the competition in a way that maximises the return to the organisation as a whole.

STRUCTURE AND CONTENT

This book explains the different uses of Activity-based Costing within financial institutions, suggests a standard approach to Activity-based Costing, discusses the problems most frequently encountered and provides examples in the form of case studies that demonstrate how Activity-based Costing has been used in practice within financial institutions.

Chapter 2 identifies four principal uses of Activity-based Costing and relates them to different types of financial institution. Chapter 3 explains the Activity-based Costing process in terms of 16 basic steps grouped into six broad phases. Chapters 4–7 address four aspects of the Activity-based Costing process where practical difficulties are most commonly encountered. Chapters 8–11 deal, in turn, with the four principal uses of

Activity-based Costing identified in Chapter 2 and provide examples in the form of case studies.

SUMMARY

Activity-based Costing is a tool that can be used to focus management attention on the costs within any organisation in a new way. It uses traditional costing techniques and links them to the factors that drive the expenditure in ways that enable managers to analyse the value chains within the company.

Activity-based Costing is a technique that can be used to bring about significant changes in management behaviour by focusing attention on expenditure patterns, operational processes, supporting activities and responsibilities throughout the organisation.

2 USES OF ACTIVITY-BASED COSTING

INTRODUCTION

Introduction of Activity-based Costing includes:

- providing a way of assessing why costs are incurred, rather than how much is incurred
- forming a basis for controlling costs by monitoring the underlying causes
- providing a basis for aligning costs with activities as a means of focusing attention on cost management.

Activity-based Costing is an approach to cost analysis that helps an organisation to analyse its cost base in a more meaningful way than conventional, departmental accounting. It analyses cost behaviour by activities, linking actions to the consumption of cost and enabling the identification of factors that cause the expenditure to be incurred. It enables management to utilise cost information for decision making at all levels within the organisation, focusing on the factors that drive costs and the implications of changes in those factors on the overall profitability of the institution or a specific section of it.

The results of Activity-based Costing studies will rarely be precise. This does not, however, detract from the value of the information provided by the Activity-based Costing study, as the results will be meaningful in the context of the decisions being made because they link expenditure to those underlying factors that explain *why* the expenses are incurred and may, therefore, be considered with due reference to the volume-related capacity constraints which inevitably exist.

WHY USE ACTIVITY-BASED COSTING?

Activity-based Costing was originally used in manufacturing organisations in order to:

- control and manage costs
- accurately relate costs to products and types of business
- set price and fee levels
- manage performance and analyse cost behaviour.

It has only been applied to the service sectors since the late 1980s. Key issues that may affect any organisation at any time include the need to understand the dynamics of profitability and resource utilisation and to be able to answer the questions shown in Figure 2.1.

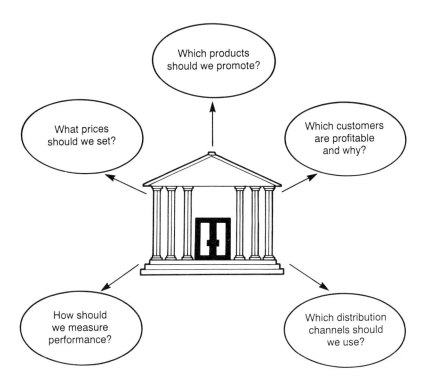

Figure 2.1   Profitability questions

The pressures on profitability in banking and insurance that applied in the late 1980s and early 1990s has meant that all financial institutions are focusing on managing and reducing costs to a much greater extent than in the relatively recent past. They are recognising that this type of costing technique is more appropriate to gaining competitive advantage by means of improving profits and managing costs rather than arbitrary price increases or cuts in the cost base, which could affect the basic structure of the business. It enables them to have more useful information on which to base key decisions relating to pricing, product promotion, customer profitability, performance management and use of distribution channels (see Figure 2.2).

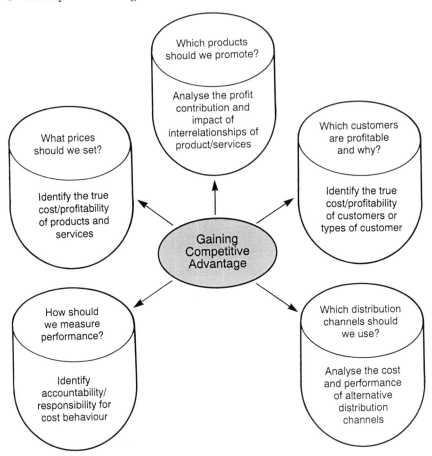

Figure 2.2 Key types of decisions

The following sections consider, in greater detail, how Activity-based Costing can be used to gain competitive advantage and its applicability to specific types of financial services, providing an overview of the practical application of this process in the financial sector.

USES OF ACTIVITY-BASED COSTING

Activity-based Costing can be used for a variety of purposes, as shown in Figure 2.3. It can form the basis of an ongoing cost and performance management system, which may incorporate activity-based budgeting and use activity analysis as a means of measuring and monitoring the cost, volume, value and quality of business processes. It leads to a better understanding of cost/resource management, emphasising the lag between spending and consumption, by analysing the factors that cause the initial expenditure and monitoring the consumption of resources and capacity utilisation. It does not control the business, but simply provides information that may influence the decision makers in the management process by providing indicators which help to demonstrate the cost utilisation within the organisation.

The uses of Activity-based Costing can be analysed in different ways. Generally, when using Activity-based Costing for strategic cost management, the exercise will include some form of 'what if' analysis. This will be true either in strategic planning or in resource management when the impact of investment in new or different products, markets or technical environments will require some form of modelling.

Alternatively, product and customer cost and profitability analysis will normally be based on existing knowledge of costs and behaviour and is likely to form the basis of regular reporting. Some modelling may be necessary,

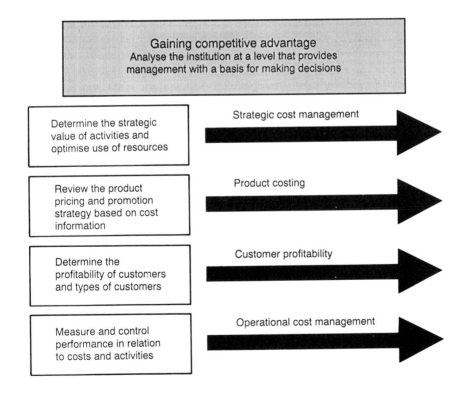

Figure 2.3 Gaining competitive advantage

however, in new product development in order to estimate the approximate cost of product delivery in advance of the product launch.

In operational cost management, Activity-based Costing can either be used as the basis of regular cost analysis through activity-based management, activity-based budgeting or performance management or be used as the basis of a one-off cost reduction exercise. Such a cost reduction exercise may result in the need for regular cost monitoring by activity in order to ensure that identified savings are realised.

Figure 2.4 shows the uses of Activity-based Costing as described above and discussed in more detail in the following paragraphs. Strategic cost management is generally more forward-looking and is likely to be performed less frequently than other types of Activity-based Costing. Reasons for undertaking Activity-based Costing for strategic cost management may include the need to review the overall direction of the company as the result of a merger, acquisition or takeover. It may be part of a strategic planning exercise or may simply be necessary as a major investment or divestment decision is to be made. It is unlikely to be performed more than once each year.

Product costing, customer profitability analysis and operational cost management are all management tools that are performed more regularly and on a consistent basis over time. Within operational cost management, however, cost reduction can be an exception to the regular reporting requirement as Activity-based Costing may form the basis of a single exercise to analyse the cost/benefits associated with discretionary expenditure and the effectiveness of the fundamental activities.

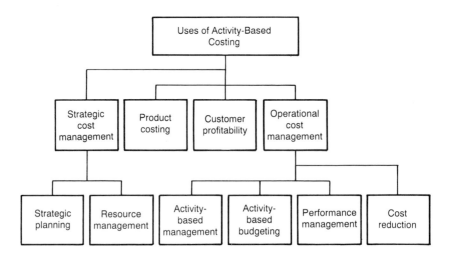

Figure 2.4 Uses of Activity-based Costing

Strategic cost management

Activity-based Costing has been put forward as one of the most powerful tools yet devised for improving the making of tactical and strategic decisions and for enhancing corporate cost control. It enables the directors in any organisation to recognise the factors that influence the cost dynamics in both the short and longer term.

Activity-based Costing provides information that emphasises the areas of high cost on which attention should be focused. It provides a tool with which the cost/benefits associated with investments in new products, markets, technology and so on can be measured and alternative investments prioritised in terms of value for money and impact on corporate performance. It also enables management to highlight areas within the institution that use up resource excessively.

The uses of Activity-based Costing in strategic cost management can be separated into two types: strategic planning and resource management.

Strategic planning

Activity-based Costing can be used to aid strategic planning by focusing attention on those factors that determine the expenditure on business activities, such as types of products or markets. It can help in prioritising business activities, because it can provide information relating to the cost/benefit to be derived from the particular businesses, geographic markets, products or customer groups and the potential benefit to be derived from future investment in particular strategic direction.

The main strategic focus of Activity-based Costing is that of influencing business strategy by providing information that identifies the flexibility within the cost base. This flexibility relates to the ability to utilise costs already incurred to gain competitive advantage and knowing what expenditure would be necessary to pursue a change in direction.

Activity-based Costing can also be used in the development of value chain analysis as a means of breaking down the strategically relevant activities in order to understand the behaviour of costs. The value chain involves a consideration of the cost/price relationship and ways in which value can be added to differentiate the products or maximise the price that can be realised.

Resource management

Resources within a financial institution include capital, costs and people. Management of capital is beyond the scope of this text; management of costs depends, to a large extent, on the management of staff costs (still more than half of the costs incurred by any financial institution); and management of people depends on motivation, which, in turn, depends on communication. Communication is assisted by knowledge of the underlying activities and focus of the business.

Activity-based Costing can be used to focus attention on those factors that determine the expenditure on key projects or activities and it can help in the cost/benefit analysis of individual initiatives and, hence, assist the prioritisation of alternatives to maximise the return on investment in line with the strategic direction of the company.

Also, because it identifies why costs are incurred and relates these to the activities that take place, it can be used to determine when costs should be incurred, such as whether/when to move to new premises. This enables management to manage costs on the basis of *spending* (the decision to buy/lease a new building) not *consumption* (the occupation of it).

Product costing

Product costing is the commonest use of Activity-based Costing and often forms the basis for product pricing and product profitability. This is primarily because activity cost analysis is similar to the standard costing technique and encourages organisations to extend existing cost analysis to review the underlying cost drivers in relation to the basic business processes and therefore gain a greater understanding of cost dynamics. This is of particular importance in the financial sector, where the increasingly competitive environment and the degree of product differentiation necessary to maintain or improve market share requires effective information relating to the costs of developing and providing such products and services.

Activity-based product costs generally include all costs affected by the cost drivers that are associated with the provision of the product or service. They usually exclude the basic sustaining costs of maintaining the overall organisation, although these can be apportioned back to individual products on an arbitrary basis in order to calculate a fully absorbed product cost.

Using Activity-based Costing as the basis of product costing is applicable in all types of financial institutions, although the importance of detailed analysis of operational costs by product may be less relevant in those organisations where a high percentage of costs are not related to activities but to interest or reinsurance cost.

Activity-based Costing as a basis for product costing is not only applicable to those products and services offered to the external market, but is also applicable to those internal services for which some form of transfer cost is required. It can be used as the basis of internal transfer pricing of products and services provided to other parts of the organisation and may focus management attention on the opportunity either to provide the service to other external organisations or to buy in the service from an external supplier at a lower cost. The most common form of internal transfer pricing in the financial sector is the internal charging for funds transferred to and from the treasury function and for IT facilities provided by a central support function.

Activity-based analysis can be used to improve the efficiency and effectiveness of a financial institution by analysing the activities performed and attributing them to individual products and services. Efficiency can be improved by eliminating duplication and unnecessary activities, improving work-flows and training staff. Effectiveness is dependent on undertaking the right activities, efficiently. By attributing costs to the activities, management can prioritise areas where effort should be focused to enable working practices to be made both more efficient and effective and where costs could be reduced or performance improved. The review of working practices can result in changes in processes and process management in terms of the automation of existing activities or a more dramatic re-engineering of the service provided.

Customer profitability

Activity-based Costing can be used as the basis for customer profitability analysis. The cost of providing the mix of products and services to a customer or type of customer is usually based on product cost information, but may be enhanced to reflect those costs that can be attributed directly to individual customers or customer groups. The income associated with the customer is normally available, although there are likely to be some types of fee or commission income that can only be identified by product or service. In these instances, the income per customer can only be estimated based on the level of activity.

Many financial institutions find it difficult to justify the cost of developing and maintaining customer profitability information for individual customers as this involves the capture and storage of individual transaction analysis from all automated and manual systems within the organisation, as well as the maintenance of up-to-date customer profiles. The value given to this information depends, to a large extent, on how it will be used and this generally reflects the importance of the individual customer relationship to the company. Some form of customer profitability analysis is important to all financial institutions, although the level of detail applied will vary depending on its type.

Operational cost management

Many organisations use Activity-based Costing as a basis for managing operational costs. This can be achieved in a variety of ways, including:

- activity-based management
- activity-based budgeting
- performance management
- cost reduction initiatives.

These management tools are described in outline below and discussed in more detail in Chapter 11, Using Activity-based Costing for operational cost management.

Activity-based management

Ways of managing the cost base depend on ongoing planning and control of all aspects of the business. Costs are an integral part of the business infrastructure and any decision made by management will inevitably involve expenditure in either the long or short term. The objective of activity-based management is to determine the importance and costs of activities within the value chain, giving management the opportunity to focus resources on adding value and on continuous improvement in effective use of costs. Activity-based management utilises Activity-based Costing as the basic component of financial management information that assists the operational control of the business by focusing attention on the key cost drivers and the factors that influence the day-to-day dynamics of the cost base. It can include the analysis of products and customers as described in Chapters 9 and 10, Using Activity-based Costing for product costing and customer profitability respectively, and can also form the basis of ongoing performance management.

It may include the need to set targets for activities or costs but tends to focus on long term improvements in the delivery of activities through monitoring productivity, capacity utilisation, efficiency and effectiveness.

Activity-based budgeting

Activity-based budgeting differs from traditional budgeting in that it concentrates on the factors that drive the costs, not just historical expenditure. Activity-based budgeting is often compared to zero-based budgeting and in some ways is based on similar concepts. Zero-based budgeting requires justification of expenditure from a zero base and requires costs to be estimated for differing levels of output and service. Activity-based budgeting, however, assumes an ongoing operation, justifying expenditure on the basis of activities performed in relation to the predetermined drivers and places responsibility for cost control on the manager with responsibility for the control of the driver. Activity-based budgeting differs from zero-based budgeting in that it assumes that activities exist and are related to the underlying cost drivers. Only if the cost driver can be eliminated, can the cost of the activity fall to zero.

Activity-based budgeting separates the analysis of cost/benefit and value of activities from the more mechanistic budgeting exercise, reducing the complexity of the budgetary process and concentrating attention on the management of the business not simply the costs incurred. It enables activities to be classified under two main headings: those costs that are incurred to sustain the basic fabric of the organisation and those costs that are driven by the levels of underlying business activity in some way. Sustaining costs may be analysed purely to ensure that the activities are both efficient and effective. The business-related costs, on the other hand, must be reviewed in relation to the factors that drive the costs and managed to ensure that spending remains in line with consumption, both in terms of the volume of activity and the quality of service provided.

This information can then be used as the basis of a regular reporting system, using activity-based budgeting to monitor and control the expenditure, efficiency and effectiveness of the activities performed in all parts of the organisation.

Performance management

Operational and financial performance can be managed by means of the measurement, monitoring and control of the costs, efficiency and effectiveness of the activities performed within the organisation. Activity-based Costing can form a key component of this type of reporting as it facilitates the classification of activities and the understanding of the causal relationships between costs and business activity.

Performance management combines objective setting, cost control and responsibility by setting people related targets or key performance indicators and monitoring activity against the indicators on a regular basis. Performance can be influenced by using these key performance indicators as the basis of regular reporting, identifying those areas where individual managers can control or influence behaviour towards the achievement of corporate objectives.

The control of cost is a key component of any performance measurement system and activity-based analysis can be used to focus attention on the areas of cost over which the individual has responsibility.

Cost-reduction initiatives

Activity-based Costing can be used in a variety of ways to assist in cost reduction initiatives. It can form the basis of an independent one-off review of the cost base. This type of review enables the organisation to investigate the activities performed throughout the organisation, undertake value analysis and explore opportunities for improvements in working methods. This could involve the identification of duplicate or extraneous activities across the various functional areas and usually highlights ways in which efficiency can be improved through the reorganisation and rationalisation of certain common activities.

Cost-reduction initiatives involve employing the Activity-based Costing approach to analyse the activities performed throughout the organisation and using this analysis as the basis for cost/benefit evaluation of the functions under review. The results of this exercise can then be used to identify areas where the benefits derived do not justify the costs incurred and hence where activities may be curtailed or eliminated.

The primary benefit of using Activity-based Costing rather than any other form of costing lies in the essence of the technique itself. Activity-based Costing focuses on activities not responsibilities and is therefore less threatening to the managers of the various functions under review. It depersonalises the cost review and enables management to value the activities undertaken in relation to the level and/or quality of service provided and factors that cause costs to be incurred.

Activity-based Costing is not restricted to an analysis of the direct costs associated with the delivery of a product or service, but also analyses the support costs that are incurred. This is particularly important in the financial sector as these costs may be as much as half of the cost base.

Activity-based Costing does not manage costs in its own right, but provides the analysis to enable management to focus on areas where costs are incurred and on which management attention should be focused. It is important, therefore, that management support the Activity-based Costing initiative and will implement the recommendations put forward as a result of the analysis.

SUMMARY

Activity-based costs can be used in a variety of ways, including:

- strategic cost management
- product costing
- customer profitability
- operational cost management.

Although many of the uses are equally applicable to all types of financial services, product costing and customer profitability may be more or less relevant depending on the services offered and the customer base.

Activity-based Costing can form the basis of an ongoing activity management system and may incorporate activity-based budgeting. It leads to a better understanding of cost/resource management, emphasising the lag between spending and consumption by analysing the factors that cause the initial expenditure and monitoring the consumption of resources and capacity utilisation. It does not *control* the business, but simply provides information that influences the decision makers in the management process by providing indicators that demonstrate the cost utilisation within the organisation.

3 THE ACTIVITY-BASED COSTING PROCESS

INTRODUCTION

Activity-based Costing can be used in a variety of ways and the process by which activity-based costs are derived may vary depending on how the information is used. The process of developing an Activity-based Costing system comprises six phases with a total of 16 steps. The use of the information will determine the definitions of products, activities and cost drivers that are appropriate.

The following paragraphs outline the process and then some of the practical issues are discussed. Subsequent chapters expand on the practical problems encountered in the implementation of Activity-based Costing using worked examples in the form of case studies.

THE PROCESS

Figure 3.1 shows the basic steps in the approach that are common to each way of using the information. The process will not change whether the approach is used for a one-off review of activities and cost or when a regular reporting system is being developed for either activity-based budgeting or activity-based cost analysis. The need to select appropriate software will be more important, however, when the system is to be used regularly.

Figure 3.2 attempts to provide some indication of the relative elapsed time of the various phases described in the following paragraphs. Obviously the man-days and total elapsed time for the project will depend on the scale of the exercise and the complexity of the requirements. Figure 3.2 does not provide a detailed work plan but simply illustrates the relative lengths of the various phases in a project. The time required for each phase will also be affected by the type of Activity-based Costing exercise and the experience of the team performing the analysis.

Review and confirm requirements

The first phase in the development of an Activity-based Costing system is to ensure that the terms of reference for the project are clearly understood. This should include interviewing key users, identifying information

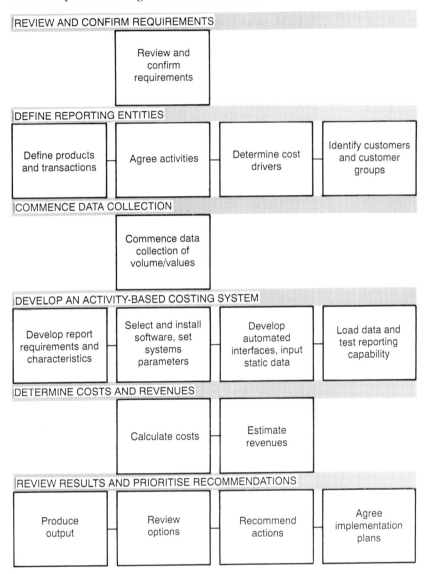

Figure 3.1   The Activity-based Costing process

requirements and taking account of best market practice and experience of the management information requirements in the industry. It is important to define the basic terms of reference to define the boundaries of the analysis and the data components that will need to be used. This will normally include a definition of the areas of activity to be analysed and the type of cost data (actual, budget, forecast, etc.) to be used.

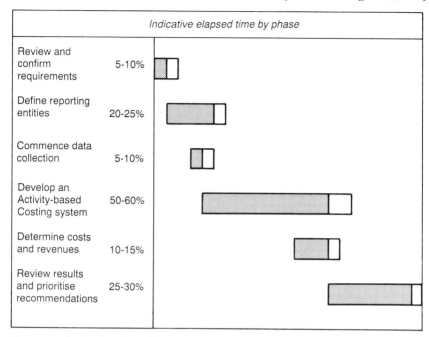

Figure 3.2   Indicative elapsed times

Define reporting entities

The reporting entities for an Activity-based Costing system will vary with the use of the system. The uses of the system are described in Chapter 2, Uses of Activity-based Costing. Products or types of business, activities, cost drivers and customers may be defined and agreed.

In strategic cost management, the core definitions will relate to types of business. Cost drivers will be required, focusing on the strategic value chain.

In product and customer cost and profitability management, products and customers must be defined and agreed, activities identified and analysed and classified by type of activity. Cost drivers can be identified relating the volume, value and quality of the delivery of products and services to external and internal customers.

Operational cost management requires a focus on the principal and sub-activities. The activities will be classified as fundamental or discretionary and opportunities may then be identified to improve efficiency and effectiveness through business process re-engineering.

Define products and transactions
In order to ensure consistent data collection and understanding of the information produced by the management information system, it is

important to define and agree the product and transaction definitions and to ensure that these are understood throughout the organisation.

Agree activities

It is important that common activities are defined and agreed prior to any analysis, otherwise different definitions will be used in each department and making comparisons will be more difficult. Activities should be defined at a low enough level to allow the operations within a department to be related to the various products and services agreed above. They can then be linked to products and/or customers and classified as fundamental or discretionary and sustaining or operational as discussed in Chapter 4, Agreeing activities.

Determine cost drivers

When the products and activities have been agreed, then the cost drivers can be identified. Too many costing systems assume that responsibility for costs coincides with the organisation structure. Cost drivers, however, recognise that this is not the case and focus instead on the decisions that give rise to costs being incurred. Cost drivers generally relate to volume, quality, time and level of service.

Identify customers and customer groups

If Activity-based Costing is being used as the basis of customer profitability, then it is necessary to ensure that common definitions of customers and customer groups exist throughout the organisation. Customers can be classified into types or analysed individually. They may also be grouped for summary analysis, but the classifications and groupings must be agreed prior to any data collection.

Commence data collection

It is important to begin data collection as soon as the data requirements have been defined. The data requirements will be derived from the definition of reporting entities agreed and must be translated into detailed data components for which sources can be identified. Although most data should be available from financial accounts, transaction processing systems, accounting systems and customer information files, there is likely to be some data that must be gathered manually. Procedures and data collection forms will, therefore, be required.

When the means of data gathering have been identified and agreed, the data can be accumulated and stored until it is required for analysis and reporting. Also any data that is not readily available can be identified and a means of collection determined. Missing data can cause serious delays to the project as all other activities can be held up while it is located.

Develop an Activity-based Costing system

Even when Activity-based Cost analysis is used as an *ad-hoc* exercise, some form of system will be required to evaluate the data. The system could be limited to a simple spreadsheet but the discipline of identification of reporting requirements, identification of static and variable data, and system and report testing should still be required.

Develop reporting requirements and system characteristics

In my experience, it is rare to find users who know exactly what format of reporting they wish to use until they are presented with alternatives. To this end it may be necessary to develop a range of reports that can be used as a catalyst to focus the users on their own reporting requirements. When the requirements (level of detail, degree of comparative data, frequency and style of reporting, etc.) have been agreed in outline, then the appropriate system's characteristics can be defined.

The characteristics of systems that need to be defined normally include:

- the hardware platform to be used
- the degree of integration to other systems
- types of reporting
- types of activity analysis required
- types of apportionment for support and sustaining costs
- system capacity
- complexity of maintenance.

Select and install appropriate software and set system parameters

There are several software packages on the market that can be used to produce multidimensional profitability analyses on either mainframe or personal computers. The packages can differ quite significantly one from the other in terms of the features and facilities they offer. Before selecting a package, therefore, it is very important to ensure that its features will provide the analysis required.

When the appropriate package has been identified, it can be installed and the system parameters can be set. This is very important, as the base parameters set within the system will determine how the system will store and report the data. Any changes later in the project may involve a significant amount of effort reworking reporting and data analysis so decisions need to be made at this point rather than later if at all possible.

Develop automated interfaces and input static data

Most systems have standard input formats that must be used to load data into the system, either by means of automated downloads or manual input. The volume and complexity of the data collection will determine the mode of input used. Any automated downloads will inevitably involve some development of a bridge between existing applications (such as the transaction processing or administration system) and the management information system.

When the basic parameters have been set up on the system, it is possible to load the static data. By static data I mean the standard definitions of products, transactions and cost drivers and the interrelationships between them. The system should relate the regular variable data to this base data to ensure consistent reporting and summarisation. It will also define report layouts and reporting hierarchies.

Load data and test reporting capability

Once the static data has been loaded and verified, the first variable data can be input and the first test reports produced. Normally, in a systems implementation, test data is used for input and report testing, but in practice users will only review the reports and comment on data accuracy when real data is used. It is therefore more practical to use a subset of actual data for the basic system tests that can be verified against expected results and presented to the users as test results.

It is important that the project team be fully satisfied with the results of the systems tests before any reports are shown to users. This is because the credibility of the whole project depends on the reporting capability and the users must have confidence in the reports produced. They usually identify errors in the accuracy of data used but should not be able to question the way the reports are produced.

When the users have accepted the reports from the system, the remaining data can be loaded. Most systems require data to be loaded and processed by period and so this may take some time to input into the system if the data relates to several periods. Clearly, if the system is to be used on an ongoing basis, it is necessary to document operator and user procedures to enable the system to be controlled and operated in the future.

As the project team has been loading the year-to-date data, it should have been developing user procedures. These procedures should refer to (not duplicate) the system user manuals but should also provide step-by-step instructions for the operation of the system. Without this type of documentation, the organisation is dependent on the project team members to operate the system in perpetuity.

Determine costs and revenues

When the first activity and driver data has been analysed, the associated costs and revenues can be estimated and the validity of the product definitions and cost drivers confirmed. This is important as only when real costs and revenues are utilised will the users be able to focus on the definitions and sample reports and, hence, review and agree them in detail.

Calculate costs

Costs can be calculated as the system is developed, by confirming the definitions of activities and the relative time or cost spent on each activity. Costs can be standard or actual costs and could be based on historical, or current costs, budgets, forecasts or long-term expenditure projections. They should, however, be reconcilable to existing reports to ensure data consistency and integrity.

Estimate revenues

When Activity-based Costing is used as the basis of profitability analysis, it is also necessary to estimate the revenue generated by products or types of business, or by customers or types of customers. It is vary rare to be able to identify revenue by individual activity. In general, activities must be summarised to products for which interest, fees, or commissions are paid or received. Customer profitability analysis should also include analysis of actual revenues received as it is common in the financial sector for fees and commissions to be discounted or waived for particular customers or types of customers.

Review results and prioritise recommendations

It is very important not to stop the analysis of activity-based costs with the production of the reports. Reports, in their own right, are of little use unless actions are identified and implemented.

Produce output

Reports should be produced and presented to the users. Managers cannot be expected to understand reports in isolation and should have the content explained and the information put into context.

Review options

When the output has been produced and explained to the users, the information can be put to use and the options for improving cost control and profitability can be identified.

When the system is designed to be used for cost reduction or resource allocation, it is necessary to identify the benefits associated with the delivery of each activity or group of activities. The cost/benefit of any activity should enable it to be ranked in relation to other activities in terms of the value of each activity to the organisation. This involves obtaining consensus within the organisation as to the value placed on each activity in relation to the strategic goals of the organisation as a whole (for example, whether the organisation values customer marketing more than new product development). When the value of the individual activities has been completed, a cost/benefit matrix can be completed and a review of the activities undertaken in a more focused way, (see Chapter 11, Using Activity-based Costing for operational cost management).

Recommend actions

Any Activity-based Costing exercise is likely to identify opportunities for improvements in the way in which activities are performed. These must be evaluated, agreed and prioritised to ensure that they are accepted and the necessary action can be recommended.

Although it is important to involve the management and staff in any Activity-based Costing exercise, it is absolutely essential that they be involved in any analysis of opportunities for cost reduction or efficiency improvement. They should be involved in the identification of opportunities to eliminate, curtail or improve the efficiency or effectiveness of activities undertaken. This is usually done by means of interviews with those involved in the activities, as well as thorough discussions between the managers responsible for the activities and their peers or users.

Agree implementation plans

The final task in any Activity-based Costing exercise, regardless of whether it is a one-off exercise or the development of an ongoing system, is the agreement of priorities and the implementation plan. Even when a regular reporting system has been developed for product costing, customer profitability, activity-based management, activity-based budgeting and/or performance management, it is necessary to ensure that the reports are used and actions taken as a result of the analysis. Without this, the exercise loses all meaning. Users of reports should be trained in the interpretation of the information to ensure that information is not used out of context and to maximise the benefit obtained from the exercise.

PRACTICAL ISSUES

There are many practical issues that may be encountered in the development of Activity-based Costing systems. The most complex are discussed in detail in succeeding chapters and are:

- agreeing activities
- determining cost drivers
- calculating costs
- implementation issues.

Other issues are addressed below and include:

- confirming requirements
- definitions of products and services

- identifying benefits
- searching for opportunities for improvement.

Let us look at these in turn.

Confirming requirements

Activity-based Costing is, fundamentally, an analytical approach to the study of activities undertaken within an organisation and their associated cost/benefits. Its relevance to the management of the business depends, to a large extent, on the presentation and understanding of the use of the information. It is very important that management use the information in context and understand the approach on which the analysis has been based. The presentation of the results is therefore considered in the context of how the information is to be used and is discussed in Chapters 8 to 11, where the use of the Activity-based Costing technique and the resulting information is explained with worked examples.

Activity-based Costing reports differ from more conventional financial reporting as they relate cost consumption to expenditure decisions and enable management to focus on improvements in profitability in the long and short term. The calculation of activity-based costs provides the information necessary to provide strategic cost evaluation and product costing. Product and customer profitability reporting requires not only activity-based cost analysis but also revenue data (the capture and analysis of revenue data is considered further in Chapter 6, Calculating Costs).

Cost reduction and efficiency improvement require the activity-based cost information to form the base data for the evaluation of the cost/benefit associated with the current level of expenditure on the activities identified. Management can then perform the opportunity search exercise and identify the areas where costs can be curtailed or eliminated, where activities can be made more efficient or effective or where further investment should be made to maximise the benefits received.

Definitions of products and services

The initial tasks in any Activity-based Costing exercise include achieving agreement on the definitions of products, activities and cost drivers that will be used in the analysis. These definitions must be carefully worded and documented to minimise confusion within the organisation and to ensure common understanding of the results of the analysis.

The importance of these tasks cannot be overstated. Unless the appropriate definitions are used, the analysis may not provide sufficient information to identify the true cost issues or, alternatively, it may provide too much detail and cloud the real issues that should be addressed.

The definition and classification of activities is discussed in Chapter 4, Agreeing activities. The determination of cost drivers is addressed in Chapter 5, Determining cost drivers.

The first definitions that need to be agreed on are, however, those of the products or services for which Activity-based Costs are required. One unfortunate feature of the financial sector is that, as a service industry, many of the products and services offered are difficult to define. A service may be defined as any activity that one party can offer to another that is essentially intangible and does not result in the ownership of anything. Definitions of products and services will depend on the assistance provided to various types of client and may depend on the quality of service provided. The definitions of products and/or services may differ depending on how the information is used. If, say, the resulting reports are to be used for strategic purposes, the products defined will generally be at a higher level than those defined for product and customer profitability analysis.

For strategic cost management, the products and services are likely to be generic product groups, such as lending, deposit taking, transmission services, trade finance, foreign exchange, corporate finance, life assurance and health, marine and motor insurance. They may be differentiated by customer type (corporate, retail, etc.) or by geographic area (country, region, etc.).

For product costing and customer profitability, the products and services defined are normally those to which revenue can be attributed or which the customers will identify as being different from each other (for detailed examples, see Chapters 9, Using Activity-based Costing for product costing and 10, Using Activity-based Costing for customer profitability).

For cost reduction and efficiency improvement, products and services are less important. The emphasis of the Activity-based Costing normally shifts to concentrate on the analysis of activities and opportunities to reduce, eliminate or improve the individual activities performed. Products and services are only necessary as a means of differentiating between similar activities from which disparate benefits are derived.

Identifying benefits

When the activity-based costs have been derived, it is then necessary to evaluate the benefits obtained from performing the activity. The evaluation should consider the level of service or benefit provided and evaluate the incremental costs associated with the provision of a different level of service. This may be a higher quality of service and, hence, there would be an increase in cost, but could alternatively be a reduction in quality and, hence, a reduction in its cost. The benefits identified will not all be *quantifiable* but could be *qualitative*. For instance, the objective of customer service training is to train staff to provide improved customer service and although this does not provide an immediately quantifiable benefit, it should be measurable in terms of reduced customer complaints in the future.

Searching for opportunities for improvement

Cost reduction, resource management and efficiency improvement depend on the activity-based cost and benefit information as this forms the base data for the identification of areas where costs can be curtailed or eliminated, where activities can be made more efficient or effective or where further investment should be made to maximise the benefits received.

This opportunity search can be performed in one of two ways: either by interviewing those involved in performing the activities or discussions between groups of senior or middle management within the organisation. The manager responsible for the delivery of the activity or group of activities should discuss with his peers the value of the activity and the benefits derived. The group may decide that the level of service provided is too high and should be reduced, therefore resulting in reduced costs. Alternatively it may decide that the activity can be undertaken more efficiently in another manner. One should not underestimate the value of asking the individuals undertaking the activities themselves to suggest ways in which efficiency or effectiveness could be improved. These individuals are closer to the tasks and so often have good ideas that have never been voiced.

When all opportunities have been identified, they should be classified by cost/benefit and priority to enable an implementation plan to be produced. It is very easy to develop the opportunities in theory, but it is important that the exercise be completed and the benefits achieved in practice. The plan must, therefore, be agreed and its implementation monitored against the plan on a regular basis.

SUMMARY

Activity-based Costing can be used in a variety of ways and the process by which activity-based costs are derived can vary according to how the information is used. The use of the information will determine how products, activities and cost drivers are defined, as these need to be appropriate, and the additional steps that need to be added to the basic approach.

The process of developing and implementing an Activity-based Costing system comprises six phases with a total of 16 steps. These are:

- *review and confirm requirements*
  – review and confirm requirements
- *define reporting entities*
  – define products and transactions

  - agree activities
  - determine cost drivers
  - identify customers and customer groups
- *commence data collection of volumes and values*
  - commence data collection of volumes and values
- *develop an Activity-based Costing system*
  - develop reporting requirements and system characteristics
  - select and install appropriate software and set system parameters
  - develop automated interfaces and input static data
  - load data and test reporting capability
- *determine costs and revenues*
  - calculate costs
  - estimate revenues
- *review results and prioritise recommendations*
  - produce output
  - review options
  - recommend action
  - agree implementation plans.

There are many practical problems that may be encountered in the process, the most complicated are:

- agreeing activities
- determining cost drivers
- calculating costs
- implementation issues.

Subsequent chapters analyse these problems and use worked examples that relate the problems to how the information is used. Other issues that may be encountered include:

- confirming requirements
- definition of products and services
- identifying benefits
- searching for opportunities for improvement.

4 AGREEING ACTIVITIES

INTRODUCTION

As we saw in the last chapter, the first phase in any Activity-based Costing exercise is 'review and confirm requirements'. This is necessary to ensure that the terms of reference of the project are clearly understood by both the sponsors and the project team. The detailed scope and extent of the project will then be further confirmed in the second phase 'define reporting entities' in Figure 4.1. The reporting entities for an Activity-based Costing system will vary with the use of the system, but will require the agreement on common definitions of products, activities and cost drivers that will be used in the analysis. These very important definitions must be carefully worded and documented so as not to generate confusion and so that the results of the analysis can be readily understood by everyone.

A financial institution can be viewed as a collection of activities that are performed to support the creation and delivery of its products and services. Competitive advantage is gained by performing activities at lower cost than competitors or by providing a differentiated product or service for which a customer is prepared to pay a higher price.

Activities are generally performed for a purpose. They result in an output. If the output can be assessed in terms of benefit, then a cost/benefit relationship can be derived and used to value the activity. Activities are often undertaken on behalf of another part of the organisation. They may, therefore, confer benefits to one part of the organisation by incurring cost in another part of it. This creates interorganisational conflict when attempting to evaluate activities within part of the company. Activity-based costs can best be applied across the whole company or at least within a stand-alone

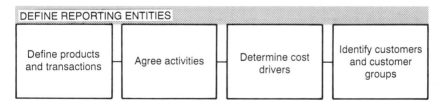

Figure 4.1   The Activity-based Costing process – Phase two: define reporting entities

entity that is not heavily reliant on services provided by other parts of the organisation.

When the principal activities across the organisation have been defined, the detailed activities performed within each department can then be identified and agreed. All activities identified by the departments must then be categorised as fundamental or discretionary and sustaining or operational and be capable of linkage to measure cost drivers that may be product- or service-related. This chapter details this process together with examples.

Activities	Strategic cost management	Product costing	Customer profitability	Cost management
Customer loan enquiry			Enquiry	Complete application [f]
Complete loan application form		Loan application	Loan application	[f]
Enter application into system				[f]
Check credit rating	Secured			
Authorise facility (Account Manager)	Lending	★	Obtain authorisation	Authorise credit facility
Authorise facility (Branch Manager)		★		
Authorise facility (Regional Manager)		★		
Authorise facility (General Manager)		★		[f]
Authorise facility (Credit committee)		★		
Notify customer of acceptance		Notification		
Review security provided		Open loan account		Open loan account
Open loan account			Accept loan facility	
Set up repayment standing order				
Credit current account		Drawdown		[f]
Monitor repayments		★		[f]
Close loan account on maturity		★		[f]
Supervise lending staff		+		[f]
Maintenance of on-line system	+	+		[f]
Management reporting	+	+	+	[d]
Loan service training	+	+		[d]
Maintenance of customer information	+	+		[d]

Key
★ Separate activity   + Allocated over related activities   [f] Fundamental activity   [d] Discretionary activity

Table 4.1 Sample activities and their usage

DEFINING ACTIVITIES

It is important that common activities are defined and agreed prior to any analysis being undertaken, otherwise different definitions will be used in each department and comparisons will be made more difficult. Definitions of activities will vary depending how the information will be used. In all instances, however, detailed activities should be defined at a low enough level to allow the operations within a department to be related to the level of decision making for which the analysis is focused.

The process of definition should be undertaken at two levels. First, for the principal activities that are performed in the department (normally no more than 12 in each department) and, second, for the detailed activities that are the components of the principal activities which relate to different products or are affected by different cost drivers. Depending on how the information is to be used, this may only require one or two activities to be defined within operating departments for strategic cost management purposes, but, alternatively, may require approximately ten principal activities and several detailed activities below each principal activity to be defined in order to cost the product or improve efficiency. Table 4.1 shows some sample activities defined at the lowest levels and identifies the levels that are appropriate for the various uses described.

For strategic cost management, the activities defined are likely to be high level and may relate to the operation of a whole department such as credit authorisation, loan administration, etc. The activities typically identified within financial institutions for the purposes of strategic cost management are:

- life assurance
- property and accident insurance
- health insurance
- reinsurance
- investment management
- lending
- deposit taking
- trade finance
- foreign exchange
- payments transmission
- correspondent banking
- corporate banking
- retail banking
- card services
- private banking
- asset management
- corporate finance
- stockbroking
- registrar services
- development capital
- capital markets
- treasury management
- sales and marketing
- compliance
- information technology
- personnel
- financial control
- office services
- planning
- general management.

For product costing and customer profitability, the activities defined are normally those to which costs or volumes can be attributed and, hence, to

Foreign exchange department	Documentary services department
Travellers' cheques purchased	Documentary/clean collections
Travellers' cheques sold	Payment of collections
Telegraphic transfer	Discount of bills
Inward remittance	Sterling advance against bill/cheque
Mail transfer	purchased
Journal entries (intercurrency account	Sterling advance repaid
transfer)	Negotiation of exchange
Journal entries (single-currency account	Negotiation repayments
transfer)	Currency loan against bill
Issue of sterling/dollar bankers' payments/	Outward documentary/clean collection
cheques	Collection proceeds paid away
Set up forward deal	Confirmation of letter of credit
Set up spot deal	Advising letter of credit without confirmation
	Amendment to inward letter of credit
Payment services department	Pay/check documentation presented under
Effect payment by bankers' payment/	letter of credit
cheque	Payment of bills at maturity drawn on opening
Effect payment by CHAPS	bank
Receive payment by CHAPS	Credit bills negotiated (advances under
In-house funds transfer	acceptances)
Receipt of payments over £10 000	Clean reimbursements
Effect cover payment, etc. by bankers'	Opening/issuing letter of credit
payment	Amendment to outward letter of credit
Telegraphic transfer	Check documentation presented under letter
Mail transfer	of credit
Issue of draft	Despatch documentation presented under
Effect payment by BACS	letter of credit
	Accept draft in respect of documents
	presented
	Payment against documents presented
	under letter of credit
Counter services	**Loan services department**
Issue of personal cheque books	Open account
Issue of cheque cards	Set up direct debit
Interview customer	Input loan application
Personal – sterling pay in	Obtain credit authorisation
Personal – cash dispenser	Obtain/verify security
Personal – sterling withdrawal	Review facility
Personal – currency pay in	Monitor repayments
Personal – currency withdrawal	Debit account for loan fees
Commercial – sterling pay in	Close account
Commercial – sterling withdrawal	Issue of special corporate cheque books
Commercial – currency pay in	Lodgement of safe custody items
Commercial – currency withdrawal	Withdrawal of safe custody items
	Temporary withdrawal of safe custody items
	Provision of lists of securities held
	Provision of valuations of holdings
	Registration of death/probates, etc.
	Auditors' certificates
	Rental charge – per annum

Personnel	Management
Recruitment	General management
Training	Membership of external committees
Industrial relations	Strategic planning
Appraisals/counselling	Contingency planning
Payroll	Marketing
Pensions management	Public relations
Employee relations	Product development
Finance	Relationship management
Accounts payable	Legal
Bank reconciliations	Security
Financial accounting	Organisation and methods
Statutory and regulatory reporting	**Systems**
Consolidations	Systems planning
Tax management	General management
Property management	Contingency planning
Management reporting	Capacity planning
Budgeting and forecasting	Computer operations
Capital appraisals	Systems maintenance
Internal audit	Systems development
Credit management	Communications management
Cash management	Storage management
Asset and liability management	PC support
	Network support

Table 4.2   Typical activities included in product costing and customer profitability analyses

which different cost drivers will be attributed. As the products and services are agreed at a lower level, then the definitions of the activities will also be more detailed. For example, in bank lending, each type of loan product may require a variety of operations for which the frequency of occurrence will differ, that is, loan set-up, credit authorisation (within branch limit), credit authorisation (within area limit), loan repayment, loan renewal, loan maturity and so on. The activities defined should, therefore, allow the costs of the individual operations to be calculated and the different product costs to be analysed. Table 4.2 lists the activities often identified within corporate and personal banking for the purposes of product costing and customer profitability analysis.

These typical activities may be applied to individual products, types of business, customers or groups of customers. They may be specific to a particular product or customer. Alternatively, they may be equally applicable to a range of products, although the frequency of occurrence may vary with the individual products or customers to which they apply. In a letter of credit, for example, the number of amendments may vary by customer, the complexity of the amendment may also differ and hence, the time and cost of processing will be different, the number of payments made may also differ, but the process of making a payment is likely to be common.

For cost reduction, the definition of activities is key to the analysis. The emphasis of the Activity-based Costing here is normally concentrated on the analysis of common activities throughout the organisation and opportunities to reduce, eliminate or improve the individual activities undertaken. The activities identified tend to provide more detailed analysis of common activities, such as training, secretarial support, management reporting, etc., and to place less emphasis on the operational activities.

Alternatively, activity definitions for improving efficiency must be at a level that enables the improvements to be identified. This is likely to require a lower level of detail than that required for any other use of Activity-based Costing. This type of analysis can be compared to the work measurement activities performed in many financial institutions in the 1970s, although Activity-based Costing tends to be one level higher and therefore less onerous to perform.

Table 4.3 lists the activities typically identified within financial institutions for the purpose of operational cost management. The activities are grouped together as this makes analysis easier, but this may not necessarily reflect their location within the organisation.

This level of detail is likely to be required for any type of operational cost management whether the information is used for activity-based management, activity-based budgeting, performance management or cost reduction, although the emphasis on particular types of activities may differ.

When using Activity-based Costing for cost reduction initiatives, the analysis tends to provide details about such common activities as training, secretarial support, management reporting, etc. and moves the focus away from the operational activities. Alternatively, definitions of activities for performance management and improving efficiency may initially be at the level shown in Table 4.3, but may require further analysis to identify a level that enables improvements in efficiency to be identified.

AGREEING ACTIVITIES

When the common definitions have been agreed, then it is necessary to identify and agree on which of the principal and detailed activities are undertaken in each department and what the unit of measure is to be for the activity. Some activities will be specific to individual departments (for example, review loan application, complete credit check, approve borrowing limit, authorise payment, set up standing order for repayments, etc.). Others will be common at either the principal or detailed level and may occur in a number of departments (such as strategic planning, management reporting, recruitment, training, staff appraisals and counselling, secretarial support, customer liaison, etc.).

After the activities undertaken have been identified, the staff cost or time

General management	**Claims**
General management	Claims enquiries
Membership of external industry-related committees	Claims recording
	Claims reserving
Membership of professional and technical bodies	Claims investigating
	Claims case management
Internal committees	Claims settlement
Project management	Claims recoveries
	Litigation
Planning	
Strategic planning	**Premium accounting**
Tactical planning/budgeting/forecasting	Billing
Operational planning	Collections
Contingency/disaster recovery planning	Credit control
	Agency remuneration
Sales/marketing	
Market research	**Treasury management**
Market strategy	Cash management
Public relations	Accounts payable
Product development	Accounts receivable
Competitor analysis	Foreign currency management
Advertising/promotion	Asset and liability management
Distribution network management (insurance)	
	Dealing
Product distribution	Money market dealing
Sales support	Foreign exchange dealing
Direct sales (insurance)	Futures and options trading
Client relationship management	Equity trading
	Bonds/securities trading
Underwriting	Commodities trading
Risk assessment and quotation	Position management
Policy issue	
Policy renewal	**Investment management**
Policy administration	Research and analysis
Reinsurance	Property management
	Fixed asset management
Actuarial	Portfolio management
Rating	
Fund valuation (reserve calculation)	**Management information**
Bonus calculation	Tactical planning/budgeting/forecasting
Surrender/maturity calculation	Regular management reporting
	Ad-hoc management reporting
Lending	
Loan application	**Personnel**
Credit review	Recruitment
Loan opening	Training – general
Loan administration	Training – technical
Loan closure	Industrial relations
Credit management	Career development/appraisals/counselling
	Remuneration/benefits
Deposit taking	Outplacement
Deposit taking	
Deposit administration	
Withdrawal	

Table 4.3   Activities typically identified for operational cost management

Trade finance	Information technology
Letters of credit	Systems planning
Collections	Capacity planning
Guarantees	Computer operations
Acceptances	Systems maintenance
	Systems development
Corporate finance	Research and development
Mergers and acquisitions	Communications management
Management buy-outs	Storage management
Corporate reconstructions	
	Compliance
Payments transmission	Audit
Incoming payments	Taxation management
Outgoing payments	
Queries	**Office services**
	Secretarial support
Card services	Office supply management
Card issuance	Filing
Merchant acquiring	Organisation and methods
Transaction processing	Legal services
	Environmental management
Financial accounting	Catering
Statutory and regulatory reporting	Transport
Consolidation of accounts	Security
Bank reconciliations	Internal communication
	Insurance

Table 4.3 contd.

spent within each department can be apportioned to the activities. This can be done in a number of ways. These activity analysis techniques include self-logging, historical averaging, Relative Values, Activity Sampling, stop-watch and pre-determined time standards.

Activity analysis or work measurement techniques have formed the basis of standard costing and productivity measurement in manufacturing for many years and have also been used as the basis of clerical work measurement in some financial institutions. There are several individual techniques that can be applied, ranging from simple historical averaging to more complex methods such as pre-determined time standards.

Which technique is chosen is dependent on:

- the complexity of the activities
- the level of detail required
- how the data collected is to be used
- the cost/benefit perceived from the study
- the culture of the organisation
- the type of costing system required.

Although it would be usual for one technique to be applied to all the areas to be measured, there will often be instances when particular departments or activities require a different approach. However, the main considerations are likely to be the level of detail required and the usefulness of the data produced.

There is a divergence of opinion within financial institutions as to just how much detail is required. The administration of work measurement can be costly. Automation and the use of relative values allow financial institutions to approximate standards without incurring major costs. Conversely, increased competitive pressure has led to many organisations feeling the need for a fairly detailed breakdown of each cost component. Each situation is unique, however, and should be approached as such, because the degree of detail entered into in the activity analysis phase dictates the type and nature of information used in future Activity-based Costing exercises.

Whichever technique is chosen, it will facilitate the staff-related costs to be related to the activities within the department. It should also serve as a check that all activities have been identified by verifying that the total of all time allocated equals the available man time.

The following sections give a brief overview of the main work measurement techniques that are used, together with an indication of their limitations and possible applications. It should be remembered throughout that while work measurement enables the labour costs to be identified, the cost of other resources (equipment, materials, computer time, etc.) may not be allocated to activities on the same basis, so separate analysis is often required to attribute these costs.

Self-logging (time ladders)

Self-logging, also called time ladders, relies on workers to each account for the time they have spent on activities in segments, such as 5–15 minutes each. At the end of each time period, they are required to make a note of what they have just been doing on a prepared reporting sheet, which usually has the working day broken down into the select segments on a vertical axis. A horizontal axis will often contain the major categories of work of the department.

There are several variants of this method, including the use of pre-defined codes for the different activities which facilitates the use of computers in analysing the data. A further variation is the use of a special clock with a random prompting alarm, whereby workers log what they are doing at the time the alarm sounds.

Any self-logging study needs to be carried out for a representative period of time – which may be several weeks – and the usefulness of the data is dependent on all the sheets being fully and accurately completed. It is very difficult to collate the results without a computer. When the representative period has finished, the results are taken from each sheet and the percentage of time spent on each task is then calculated as a function of the total time taken.

Self-logging can be useful where no previous work measurement has been carried out or where there is a wide variety of products and/or services being handled, many of which are low in volume. Its main practical advantage is that it does not require the valuable resources of senior staff, specialists or consultants to carry out the actual data collection.

The disadvantages are that it is quite tempting to interpret what has been done in the most favourable light. Even in the best cases, there are always problems caused by inconsistency in interpretation of what activities are actually being performed. It can also further distort the inaccuracy of product times inherent in all methods that measure what *is* happening as opposed to what *should* be happening, by failing to identify slack time or the under-utilisation of capacity.

Historical averaging

Historical averaging involves comparing relationships of previously recorded data in order to develop time estimates. This method is the least complicated of all and usually only applies to situations where the area being costed involves few activities.

The net staff hours worked are divided by the output volume to arrive at a time standard. Net staff hours can be taken as the total paid hours, but, if the information is to be used for detailed productivity measurement, holidays, absences and training should be deducted. The figure is only an estimate as one cannot ascertain idle time and other such factors. There may, therefore, be distortions in the time standard. Other limitations are that the time values derived could be obsolete and the performance of the workers cannot be rated as it can in other methods of work measurement. Due to these inherent limitations, this method is usually applied on an interim basis, prior to using a more comprehensive method.

The only advantage of this method is that the work can usually be done quite rapidly. The disadvantages are that, as it is volume sensitive and takes no account of other activities in the service centre, its outcome is likely to be little better than an approximation. Also it is really only applicable to areas that have just one product, so appropriate occasions for its use are rare.

Relative Values

The Relative Values method works on the principle of weighting tasks or activities relative to each other based on their consumption of resources.

For the purpose of the following examples, let us assume that the service centre consists of direct people costs and overheads that are to be absorbed equally over the whole spectrum of activities of the centre and that it may be necessary to assign a second set of figures to these activities that reflects their use of these resources.

Usually, the activity that takes the least time is given the lowest value and is assigned a weight of 1.0. All other weights are constructed from their resource usage relative to this value. Under normal circumstances the relative weighting provided will be per activity. For example, it takes three times as long to perform one task X as one task Y. However, in some instances, the information provided may be in terms of total time, that is, we need three people to perform task X and one person to perform task Y. From this it can be seen that an activity with the same weighting as another will have the same unit cost.

The major advantage of this method is that it takes much less time to arrive at cost indicators than most other methods. In addition, it is easy to use and does not disrupt the work of the service centres.

The big disadvantage is that its accuracy relies almost totally upon the relative value selected. Sometimes this can be reasonably relied upon, but in many instances these estimates have been shown to be very inaccurate. This is often caused by attributing the weighting of staff positions within the service centre, but not taking account of any over- or under-capacity in these positions, nor of the fact that some of the staff spend part of their time on administrative or housekeeping activities.

Activity Sampling

Activity Sampling is a direct observation method of work measurement that uses random sampling to identify the proportion of time spent on the various products, services or activities in an organisation. From these random samples, statistically significant results can be obtained that show how the time was used in the group being studied, allocating this time to the activities and functions performed. Relating these proportions of time to the people costs of the group, costs per activity can then be calculated.

Activity sampling can be used to collect as much (or as little) detail about the work being performed as is required, but in order to ensure the accuracy of the results, it must be carried out over a representative period of time, which, say, in an insurance company can often be a month. It can be used to obtain base information for unit costing (products and services) cost allocations and capacity planning for cost reductions.

It is usually carried out by the supervisors of the sections being studied. The supervisors make a pre-determined number of observations each day, at randomly selected times. At these times the observer will walk around and note down, in coded form, exactly what each member of staff is doing. This process is repeated every day until the end of the sampling period. When all the observations have been completed, the time spent on each of the activities is calculated by taking the number of observations of each activity and working this out as a percentage of the total number of valid observations.

Activity Sampling has some major advantages. It can provide a lot of detailed information, including the identification of direct and indirect activities for various costing purposes, and it is easy to learn and to apply without disrupting the work of an organisation.

The disadvantages are that it only identifies how time and costs *are* used, rather than how they *should* be used. There is the potential, therefore, for bad work practices to be compounded, although this is the case with all methods that do not have pre-determined time standards. In addition, it may have to be repeated if organisational or environmental factors change dramatically. The total time required for one comprehensive study would be about eight to ten weeks.

Stop-watch

Sample observations of activities are measured with a stop-watch in order to determine standard times. This methodology should only be used for the derivation of standard costs, the calculation of times for commonly performed functions or to capture times for low-volume activities, even though the actual time spent on them may be quite short.

Stop-watch observations should be undertaken after thorough preparation work. This includes a detailed definition of the activity to be measured, listing the steps or functions involved and then measuring the time taken to perform each activity several times. The average time taken can then be calculated.

The biggest difficulty with using a stop-watch is that, in many instances, it can be culturally unacceptable and may actually lead to a distorting of the performance being observed because of the artificial climate it creates. It is also very time consuming if it is the only technique being used.

The advantage of this methodology is that it enables a measurement to be obtained of activities that are difficult to capture using many of the other methods, either because they do not occur very often or because they are fragmented. Its most appropriate application is for key activities where several functions that are spread out across an organisation need to be measured to produce a total time and cost for a product or project.

Pre-determined time standards

Pre-determined time standards methods use systems that classify body movements into time values. They therefore save the analyst from having to actually measure tasks afresh each time, such as is necessary in the stop-watch method, for example.

Three techniques in common use are Methods Time Measurement (MTM), Modular Arrangement of Pre-determined Time Standards (MODAPTS) and Integrated Business Control (IBC). Using any of these three methods requires special training and the methods themselves are time consuming and costly to maintain. The standards also need to be carefully aligned for costing purposes and sometimes this linkage is difficult to achieve. This kind of measurement only applies to highly repetitive and routine work.

Methods Time Measurement (MTM) expresses values as Time Measurement Units (TMUs). Body movements are classified into major categories and TMU values are assigned to each. Some body movements are specific to particular activities and may, or may not be included in standard measurements. One TMU is 0.00001 hours.

Modular Arrangement of Pre-determined Time Standards (MODAPTS) classifies specific anatomical body movements. It relies on pre-determined standards for 'gets' and 'puts'. Basic movements are called MODS and one MOD is 0.129 seconds. MOD values are assigned to 21 types of body movements, such as by the hands, arms, feet and eyes. This may be more applicable to physical activities than the more clerical and intellectual activities carried out in the financial sector.

The major steps that are followed when using pre-determined standards include:

- observing work activity and recording a sequence of motions
- classifying the motions to conform to pre-determined standards
- assigning pre-determined time values
- applying frequency factors where needed
- adjusting and/or levelling values where necessary (this includes adjustments for personal needs, fatigue and delays).

The amount of detail that these techniques can go into is so great and the amount of training required to use them so extensive that they are almost certainly inappropriate for costing purposes in financial institutions. They could be used as a basis for standard costs, but really only for very repetitive work and, as there are other methods available for this area, there seems little advantage in using these techniques. There are also problems when applying them to computer-related work, where the number and types of key strokes may be less relevant than the response time taken by the computer in the verification and acceptance of data.

The basic concept of the Integrated Business Control (IBC) system of clerical work measurement is that every procedure (activity) can be broken down into a series of events or 'data blocks' for which pre-determined time standards exist, together with appropriate allowances for environmental factors. Examples of data blocks include 'Read', 'Write', 'File', 'Fasten' (and their equivalents in machine operations) each of which can be further categorised.

The simplicity of the vocabulary used means that it is easy to train staff how to use this method themselves and, therefore, the system does not require too much input from a specialist after the early stages.

The major steps involved when using IBC are:

- reviewing each procedure step by step
- translating these steps into IBC terminology
- inputing this data, plus allowances, into the software
- analysing output in the context of volumes and percentage of available time
- setting targets for phased reductions in terms of method, system and environmental improvement.

The advantages of IBC are that it can be undertaken fairly by internal staff and does not have to be done all at one time. It is probably the most culturally acceptable, pre-determined time standard methodology and the most appropriate for developing standard times. An added benefit is that it identifies areas appropriate for cost reduction and productivity improvement and makes proposals for how to get costs down to the standard level.

The disadvantages are that it does not reflect how costs are currently being generated nor provide the kind of detail necessary for detailed cost studies or cost allocations.

The emphasis of IBC is very much on cost reduction and it could be applied as part of an overall cost management review and for target setting in conjunction with budgetary techniques.

ANALYSING ACTIVITIES

All principal activities identified by any department should be identifiable as fundamental or discretionary and, within these basic boundaries, be further classified as sustaining or operational. Table 4.4 shows how such analysis is done.

This analysis is only necessary when Activity-based Costing is being used with the aims of reducing costs or improving efficiency. Fundamental activities must be performed at some level and management must decide at what level the effort and associated expenditure is necessary.

Discretionary activities, however, can be eliminated without affecting the basic fabric of the organisation. Table 4.4 gives examples of these kinds of activities that can help to reduce costs and highlights the fundamental, discretionary, sustaining and operational classifications which may apply. It is important to stress that the classification is subjective and is used only as an aid to the search for opportunities for cost reduction or efficiency improvement. The classification of an activity is an art not a science and so may vary

Example activities	Sustaining activities	Operational activities
Fundamental activities	Statutory reporting Remuneration/benefits Health and safety General management Compliance	Lending services Life assurance FX trading Reinsurance Investment management
Discretionary activities	Strategic planning Market research Public relations Management accounting Treasury management	Systems development Customer marketing Sales New product development Product costing

Table 4.4 Classifying activities

in different companies. For example, client relationship management may be viewed as absolutely fundamental in one organisation but be discretionary in another.

Finding fundamental activities

A fundamental activity is one that must be done, either because it is a legal requirement (such as filing statutory accounts) or because the business will cease to function if the activity is not performed (for example, current account processing in a retail bank). This generally includes all operations directly related to the provision of products and services and those activities that are necessary to maintain the basic infrastructure of the business.

It is easy to classify all activities as fundamental, but the object of the exercise is to identify those non-essential activities that are discretionary and should therefore be justifiable in terms of value added. Fundamental activities will still be reviewed in any cost reduction or efficiency improvement exercise, but the focus will be on ways of making operations more effective through some form of business process re-engineering.

Determining discretionary activities

Discretionary activities are those activities that are not fundamental and may not vary with the level of business undertaken. Principal activities defined by any department are likely to include at least one or two discretionary activities and the administration functions may only be able to identify one or two fundamental activities and the rest will be discretionary.

One way of identifying whether or not an activity is discretionary is to assess whether products and services could still be supplied for the forthcoming year if the activity was curtailed. Activities that may fall into this category include strategic planning, management accounting, training, new systems development, new product development, premises refurbishment and so on.

Selecting sustaining activities

Sustaining activities are those non-product-related activities that are performed in order to stay in business (such as regulatory reporting). These activities are generally fundamental in nature but can include such discretionary activities as corporate advertising. These are not related to a product or product group but are undertaken to maintain the corporate image in the market-place. Any discretionary sustaining activities should be discussed critically to see whether they are justified in terms of their cost/benefits during the opportunity search exercise.

Indicating operational activities

As can be seen in Table 4.4, operational activities can be classified as either fundamental or discretionary. In which column they are placed will determine, to some extent, the effects of the analysis. Where Activity-based Costing is used as the basis for cost reduction or improving efficiency, how the activities are classified will facilitate the search for ways in which these improvements can be made (see Chapter 11, Using Activity-based Costing for operational cost management).

PRACTICAL PROBLEMS

Defining activities and agreeing which of them are to be undertaken where in the company is fraught with practical problems. Several of the commonest problems may be overcome by carefully designing and operating an effective Activity-based Costing system, including:

- clarity of activity definition
- level of detail
- maintenance of the data.

Clarity of activity definition

It is important that the definitions of the activities used are clear and unambiguous. Departmental managers need to be able to recognise and apply the definitions to their own organisational unit and feel comfortable that all activities performed there have been included in them. Definitions must, therefore, be general enough to apply across organisational boundaries when necessary, but still specific enough to ensure that the managers can recognise the activity within their own operation.

Property management may be one activity that should be carefully defined. It may relate to either of two very different activities – either the management of a property portfolio for investment purposes, including the purchase, leasing, development and sale of properties, the maintenance of existing properties within the portfolio, the selection of tenants and collection of rents or the management of the properties occupied by the company, including the acquisition and disposal of appropriate accommodation and management of the infrastructure necessary to relocate departments and divisions within properties to optimise the use of space within the organisation. The former definition indicates an activity that should be considered within a strategic cost review as a product which is offered within the investment management portfolio and for which a product cost may be required. The latter may be defined as a sustaining activity that is part of the basic infrastructure of the organisation. If the information is used as part of an efficiency review, then the acquisition, maintenance and disposal of property should be considered as a common activity for which economies of scale may be achieved by either combining investment management with internal property management or at least ensuring that both activities are handled in the most effective manner.

Level of detail

The level of detail required in the activity analysis depends, to a large extent, on how the information is to be used (see Defining activities at the beginning of this chapter). It may be tempting to perform the analysis at a lower level of detail than is required for the current purpose. This way data may be collected that will serve a variety of uses but it can create discontentment among the staff responsible for data collection if they have to amass data for which there is no apparent use. This is a greater problem where Activity-based Costing forms part of a regular reporting system than where it forms the basis of an isolated exercise. An isolated exercise may, however, be a good way of developing a prototype for the development of a system that will be used regularly in the longer term.

When Activity-based Costing forms the basis of a regular product costing or customer profitability system then the level of detail in the definitions of the activities will form the essence of the system. Judging the level correctly is important because as shown in Chapter 10, Using Activity-based Costing for customer profitability, the analysis is framed on activity-based costs within departments that can be related to cost drivers. The cost drivers, in turn, determine the allocation of costs to each product or customer and must therefore be measured on a regular basis (this data may be available from automated sources but generally changes will need to be made to the systems). Consequently, it is important that the detailed data requirements are agreed at the correct level of detail when the systems enhancements are specified to ensure that the data is made available as required.

The number of activities identified will also determine the size of the database required to perform the analysis (this is discussed in more detail in Chapter 7, Implementation issues).

Maintenance of the data

Maintenance of the data will only be a problem in a regular reporting system. Where Activity-based Costing is used for an isolated exercise, maintenance will not be necessary. The complexity of maintenance depends, to some extent, on how frequently reports are required. A system that produces information monthly or quarterly will require more frequent updating but will generate a greater interest in the accuracy of data by the users. However, when a system produces reports semi-annually or annually, the users tend to be less motivated to maintain the data because its importance has been diluted in their memories.

The accuracy of data in any management information system tends to increase when users begin to use the information. As they start to depend on the reports, they are motivated to focus on the accuracy of the base data and to instigate improvements in data quality.

SUMMARY

The second phase of an Activity-based Costing exercise is 'define reporting entities'. The reporting entities for an Activity-based Costing system will vary with the use the system is put to, but will require the agreement of common definitions of products, activities and cost drivers that will be used in the analysis. These definitions must be carefully agreed and documented to minimise confusion within the organisation and to ensure common understanding of the results of the analysis.

In summary, defining, identifying and agreeing the activities throughout the organisation can be a time-consuming exercise. Activity-based costs can best be applied across the whole institution or at least within a stand-alone entity that is not heavily reliant on services provided by other parts of the organisation.

Definitions of activities will differ depending on how the information is to be used. It is important to match the use of the information to the level of detail of activity analysis required and then to agree common definitions for at least the principal activities before analysing the departmental activities in detail. Otherwise different definitions will be used in other departments and comparisons will be difficult. Also one may only require one or two activities to be defined within operating departments for strategic cost management purposes, but alternatively approximately ten principal activities and several detailed activities below each principal activity may be required for product costing or improvements in efficiency.

After the activities have been identified, the staff cost or time spent within each department can be apportioned among the activities. This can be done in a number of ways – self-logging, historical averaging, Relative Values, Activity Sampling, stop-watch and pre-determined time standards. Which technique is chosen depends on:

- the complexity of the activities
- the level of detail required
- the use of the data collected
- the cost/benefit perceived from the study
- the culture of the organisation
- the type of costing system required.

However, the main considerations are likely to be the level of detail required and the usefulness of the data. The administration of work measurement can be time consuming and costly so automation and the use of Relative Values can be used to allow financial institutions to approximate standards without incurring major costs. Conversely, increased competitive pressure has led to many organisations wanting a fairly detailed breakdown of each cost component. Each situation, however, is unique and should be treated as such, because the degree of detail worked to in the activity analysis phase dictates the type and nature of information used in future Activity-based Costing exercises.

These techniques will facilitate the allocation of the staff-related costs to the activities within the department. It should also serve as a check that all activities have been identified in that the total of all time allocated should equal the available man time.

All activities may also be classified as being fundamental or discretionary and sustaining or operational. This analysis is useful because, in the process of identifying which activities are fundamental (those that must be performed), opportunities for improving efficiency or effectiveness may be discovered. All other activities must be discretionary and therefore could be eliminated without affecting the basic fabric of the business. Operational activities, both fundamental and discretionary, can normally be linked to measurable cost drivers, which relate to the products and services offered by the institution. Sustaining activities are generally related to the overall business management and may be linked to cost drivers that are more strategic in nature and are linked to the business policy of the organisation.

5 DETERMINING COST DRIVERS

INTRODUCTION

As we have seen, in the previous chapter, the second phase of the Activity-based Costing process is 'define reporting entities', (see Figure 4.1). The reporting entities for an Activity-based Costing system will vary depending on how the system is to be used, but will require agreement on common definitions of several of the basic components of Activity-based Costing. These include products, transactions, activities, cost drivers, customers and customer groups. The definitions that will be used in the analysis must be carefully agreed and documented to minimise confusion within the organisation and to ensure common understanding of the results of the analysis.

The use of cost drivers is the nucleus of Activity-based Costing. This is the key difference between the traditional approaches of standard costing or average costing and Activity-based Costing. All three approaches analyse activities and calculate costs by activity and product. Traditional costing methodologies are unit based and use allocation criteria that are based on unit-level characteristics of the products, such as product volume, staff time, square footage and number of staff. An Activity-based Costing system, however, uses cost drivers, which focuses attention on the factors that give rise to the cost and hence assists the decision-making process by concentrating on these factors without clouding the issue with irrelevant or arbitrary allocations.

Costs can be controlled in various ways, at diverse levels and over differing time frames, but, ultimately, can only be controlled by the management responsible for the initial investment decision. Other managers may then be responsible for controlling the day-to-day expenditure in line with the initial plans. Cost drivers, therefore, enable the management of the organisation to link expenditure to the factors that affect the value and frequency of the expense and hence, to control it in a more focused way.

The concept of assigning cost drivers to activities and other cost types as an integral part of the process provides a means of linking cost behaviour to decision making as well as providing a means of handling joint costs. The emphasis given to the type of cost driver will depend on the objectives of the analysis. Activity-based Costing systems tend to be more complicated than traditional unit-based cost accounting systems, because of the need to include the dimension of cost drivers when identifying the ways in which costs can be managed. Unfortunately, the costs are rarely driven by one single factor and, hence, the identification of appropriate cost drivers is not always easy. It is important, therefore, to involve the line managers in the identification process in order to understand as much as possible the key driver that is most instrumental in a particular activity or cost type. Cost drivers generally relate to volume, value, quality, time and level of service. In general, short-term variable costs can be traced to products using volume-related cost drivers, but these are inappropriate for most long-term costs because they are driven by complexity and diversity not volume.

In practice, the identification of cost drivers in an Activity-based Costing system calls for both judgement and analytical skills. The first principle is to identify those activities with large time or cost values and consider the relationship between the diversity of products, services and customers supported by the activity and the degree of variation in the performance of the activity for each product, service or customer. This will determine the level of accuracy that is necessary to maximise the value of the exercise (a larger variation in the activity between products, services or customers will suggest that greater accuracy is necessary and that activities must be defined at a lower level). Second, identify the balance-related costs and ascertain the drivers to be attributed to interest income and expense to take account of the rates and risks associated with the products and counterparties. Finally, consider the non-activity-related costs and the drivers necessary to analyse how and why the costs arise.

The minimum number of cost drivers that an Activity-based Costing system operates on will depend on the desired accuracy of the information produced and the complexity of the products and services offered by the organisation. The desired accuracy plays an important part – as the number of cost drivers increase, the accuracy of the resulting information should also increase. In general, the higher the relative cost of an activity, the greater the distortion caused by using an imperfectly correlated cost driver to trace the cost of the activity to products or customers. This must, however, be balanced by the availability of the information and the cost of obtaining and processing it. This latter cost of Activity-based Costing systems development and operation must be justified by the benefit of the information obtained and its usefulness.

Cost information is required for two types of decisions: first, for the strategic or tactical product or market decision and, second, for cost control. The following sections consider the types of drivers relevant to the decisions discussed above and then examine the drivers that are most appropriate to the activity types in financial services.

PRODUCT OR MARKET DECISIONS

Cost analysis for product or market decisions tends to relate to strategic costing, product costing or customer profitability. This requires cost drivers to be identified that allow for all appropriate costs to be linked to the product or market and the exclusion of the costs which remain unaffected by this type of decision, such as the central administrative costs. Cost drivers for central costs tend to separate the basic sustaining costs of the business (general management, regulatory reporting, etc.), which may be affected by the size and complexity of the financial institution, from the administrative costs of running the day-to-day business (personnel, premises management, etc.), which may be driven by the number of staff, staff turnover, geographic location or age and condition of properties.

For product- or market-related decisions, it is necessary to identify all costs that are driven by factors that are linked to products or services, or at least to groups of products or services by market or geographic areas. The contribution to sustaining costs and profitability can be estimated by means of the analysis of the direct product- or customer-related revenues and costs. This involves the identification of all direct or operational activities (see Chapter 4, Agreeing activities) and the definition of associated cost drivers, as well as the determination of drivers relating to the non-activity-related costs, such as premises, marketing and information technology. This highlights the need for drivers that may not be related to the volume of products or customers. Cost drivers generally relate to volume, value, quality, time and level of service.

For the support or overhead functions, the goal of Activity-based Costing is to understand what activities are being performed and why. All activities must, in some way, support the delivery of products and services, but the actual link between the support activities and the customer may be difficult to identify. There will be fundamental activities for which the cost drivers will relate to the need to meet regulatory or statutory requirements, but the reasons *why* these requirements exist is because of the types of products and services offered and the environment in which they are provided.

Indirect or sustaining costs must not be ignored either in the overall decision-making process but will be recognised as having different behaviour patterns and being unaffected by the product or market-related activity. They may be apportioned to products or services to provide a fully absorbed product cost that may form the basis of the strategic or tactical decision-making process (see Chapter 6, Calculating costs).

COST CONTROL

For cost control, costs, and hence activities, must be traced back to the point of *expenditure* rather than the point of *consumption*, which is usually shown in the financial accounts. This is because costs can only be managed at the point of initiation and the role of the cost driver is to identify when and why the expenditure takes place. Cooper and Kaplan have developed this Activity-based Costing approach, which relates overhead costs to the forces behind them. Too many costing systems make the assumption that expenditure coincides with organisation, but this is not generally true. Costs can only be controlled by the management responsible for the factors that affect expenditure, which are the cost drivers.

Managers need feedback on both the cost incurred and the underlying factors that caused it. They need to understand the reasons for the existence of the cost. This can only be achieved by measuring and monitoring the factors that drive the cost.

For most operating or administrative departments, cost drivers will tend to relate to the volume and variety of products and services offered. Such factors will be readily measurable and such information may already be reported regularly. Activity-based Costing simply relates the expense analysis to the business behaviour that influences the expenditure.

For overhead or support functions, cost drivers relevant for cost control will generally relate to the level of service provided and the efficiency and effectiveness of its delivery.

DETERMINING COST DRIVERS

When the products and activities have been agreed, then the cost drivers can be identified. As noted earlier, too many costing systems assume that responsibility for costs coincides with the organisation structure. The process of identifying cost drivers, however, recognises that this is not the case and focuses instead on the decisions that give rise to costs being incurred.

The key decision that must be taken at this stage of the exercise is how many and what type of cost drivers should be used? The complexity of the activities performed in any financial institution is virtually endless, but experience has proven that the major drivers are such factors as:

- the number and diversity of products or services offered
- the rate of new product launches
- the number or variety of distribution channels used
- the quality of service
- the number and diversity of customers serviced
- the value and risk associated with the product offered
- the number of transactions performed.

Typically the number of major drivers utilised within an organisation is fewer than 15. These will be the generic drivers, such as volumes (transactions, products, number of accounts, number of staff, etc.), values, quality of service and variety (products, instruments, customers, currencies, time, etc.). This will then be complicated by the number of products and activities to be included in the analysis. Let us look at an example.

Before a loan can be granted, an application must be completed, reviewed and authorised, securities reviewed and accepted, accounts opened, facilities agreed, repayment schedules agreed and payments paid. Despite this complexity, the drivers associated with the approval of a loan in a well-designed Activity-based Costing system might be limited to 'the number of applications made', 'size of facility' and 'term of the loan'.

Short-term variable costs can be traced to products using volume-related cost drivers, but these are inappropriate for most long-term costs because they are driven by complexity and diversity not volume. Consider, for example, the cost of an insurance operation. The number of systems and staff required will be driven by a combination of the number of new and renewed policies and the variety of policies offered. A system may be maintained for many years to service a life or pensions policy that has been withdrawn from the market but for which policies have not yet matured.

The minimum number of cost drivers that an Activity-based Costing system uses depends on how accurate the information produced needs to be and the complexity of the products and services offered by the organisation. This former factor plays an important part because, as the number of cost drivers increases, the accuracy of the resulting information should also increase. The complexity of the products and services offered by the organisation will also affect the number of drivers.

All financial institutions have a large number of 'joint costs' (costs and activities that support more than one product or service). Where Activity-based Costing is used to support product or customer cost and profitability analysis, the joint costs must be assigned to products, customers or product groups. This may require additional cost drivers. Account relationship management, for example, may relate to a range of products and services offered to particular customers or customer groups. It may be possible to use a single cost driver such as 'relationship management hours' that can then be attributed to individual products, services and/or customers in different proportions without introducing unacceptable levels of distortion. Several factors determine if a single driver is acceptable. These include the diversity of weighting to products and services and the relative costs of the activities included in the principal activity to which the driver is applied. If, for example, the costs of 'account relationship management' comprise 20 per cent of the cost base, then more detailed analysis of the activities within it and the identification of individual drivers relating to 'relationship maintenance', 'new account development', 'new product development' and 'sales of products and services' may be necessary. In general, the higher the relative cost of an activity, the greater the distortion caused by using an imperfectly correlated cost driver to trace the cost of the activity to products or customers. This must, however, be balanced by the availability of the information and the cost of obtaining and processing it. This cost of Activity-based Costing systems development and operation must be justified by the usefulness of the information.

Drivers can be assigned to all cost types, not just those costs that are incurred due to the execution of operational or sustaining activities. There are many cost types in financial institutions that are not related to activities. The key cost types that must be considered when determining cost drivers, therefore, include operational activities, interest costs, claims, premises costs, marketing costs, information technology and support or overhead activities. Many organisations use arbitrary allocation bases such as staff time as a means of allocating premises, marketing, IT and support activities to products and/or customers. This may be misleading. The drivers that are appropriate to each cost type are considered in more detail in the following sections.

Operational activities

Activities that can be directly identified with products and services are generally the easiest to assign cost drivers to. Table 5.1 shows the activities and drivers applicable to a securities trading operation. Here it can be seen that drivers relate not only to the number of trades performed, but also to the diversity of trades, the number of customer accounts, the value and diversity of stocks held and the need to meet regulatory requirements.

Transaction volumes or direct labour will not be an appropriate cost driver for many types of activity, yet it remains the most common cost driver in any financial institution.

Interest costs

The primary business of banking and insurance revolves around obtaining funds from policy holders, depositors, the money markets and other sources and investing these funds in loans, securities and investment funds. The sources of funds equal the uses of funds for the total organisation. However, when the organisation is subdivided into organisational units, products or customer relationships, the sources and uses will frequently not be in balance. Some units, products or customers are net providers of funds (liabilities exceed assets) and some are net users of funds (assets exceed liabilities).

When a financial institution measures costs and profitability performance of its organisational units, products or customer relationships, a mechanism is required to ensure that the interest cost associated with being a net

Activities	Cost drivers
Securities trading:	
Trading	Number of trades/type of instrument
Confirmation	Number of trades/type of instrument
Domestic settlement	Number of domestic trades/type of instrument
Foreign settlement	Number of foreign trades/type of instrument
Stock lending	Number of trades/type of instrument
Dividend collection	Number/variety of holdings
Tax reclaim	Number/variety of holdings
Corporate advisory	Number/variety of holdings
Research:	
Research and analysis	Variety of instruments traded
Relationship management:	
Customer liaison	Number of accounts/level of service
Customer reporting	Number of accounts/level of service
Balance sheet management:	
Cash management	Number of accounts
Position management	Variety of instruments traded
Regulatory reporting:	
Regulatory reporting	Variety of instruments traded
Management reporting:	
Regular management reporting	Level of detail required
Staff management:	
Supervision	Number of securities staff
Recruitment	Securities staff turnover
Career development/appraisals/ counselling	Number of securities staff
Internal communication	Number of securities staff
Training:	
Training – general	Number of securities staff
Training – technical	Experience of securities staff
Administration:	
Secretarial support	Number of accounts/level of service
Filing	Number of accounts/trades

Table 5.1   Activities and cost drivers in securities trading

provider or user is taken into account. This mechanism is referred to as funds transfer pricing (see Chapter 6, Calculating costs).

The application of funds transfer pricing involves placing a value on the organisation's funds by paying or crediting providers (an imputed interest income) and charging users of funds (an imputed interest expense). The drivers associated with the imputed interest income or expense relate to the type of product (floating-rate loan, fixed-rate deposit, one-year motor policy, ten-year life policy or pension), the average balance of the asset or liability and the risk associated with the product and counterparty. Drivers may not be necessary for each product, balance and risk mix; products can be pooled by profile, which takes account of the rate, maturity and risk character of the product being offered and the driver will then relate to the product pool. The analysis of funding cost for interest-related products can be complicated and so a separate exercise.

Premises

Premises costs relate to the acquisition and maintenance of the premises occupied by the financial institution. The factors that give rise to the expenditure relate to the need to purchase or sell premises or maintain existing buildings. This tends to be driven by organisational decisions at a strategic or tactical level, such as mergers, acquisitions, restructures or reorganisations, as well as the need to repair ordinary wear and tear. Allocating premises costs to products and services as a means of cost control is counter-productive, unless the need for the expenditure is as a result of changes to the product or service offered.

Premises should, therefore, be treated as a sustaining cost unless they form part of the decision-making process. For example, if the financial institution is extending its range of products or services and will require new or renovated premises, such as a new trading room, this should be identified as the cost driver associated with the premises expenditure and this activity will then form part of the investment appraisal.

Marketing

Marketing costs may be allocated to products or customers on the basis of product volumes or value, which generally bear little relationship to the *actual* factors that drive the expenditure. Marketing costs tend to be driven by three key factors: first, the need to maintain the corporate image, second, the need to reinforce market perception of the range of products and services offered by the institution and, finally, the need to notify customers of a new product or service.

The drivers associated with each type of expenditure may be different. The need to maintain the corporate image may be considered a sustaining cost and driven by the importance of a universal corporate image to the marketing policy of the institution. The need to reinforce market perception of the range of products and services offered by the institution may be driven partially by the degree of competition for the products and services in the market-place, partially by the buying patterns of the consumers and, also, by the amount of differentiation between competing products. Finally, the need to notify customers of a new product or service will be driven by the number of new products and services launched by the institution and the need to create demand for the particular products and services offered by one institution against those offered by the competition.

The focus on marketing policy and market position created by the cost driver approach allows management to make decisions based on the true factors that drive the expenditure. Identifying new product launch costs to the appropriate product ensures that the incremental costs of the development and launch are recognised and included in the decision-making process, which is a big improvement.

Information technology

Allocating systems costs on the basis of staff time will encourage staff to reduce time taken as a means of reducing the allocation of IT costs. This may be a good incentive to reduce labour costs, but it is likely to increase the automated systems costs as reducing time tends to involve further automation and, hence, higher systems costs. Many systems-related costs vary with the diversity of products offered *not* with the volume of transactions. In foreign exchange, for example, the application system must be available when the markets are open for trade even if only *one* contract is agreed but its capacity must be able to cope with the maximum number of deals that could be performed at any one time.

The factors that give rise to expenditure on IT will relate much more to the initial capital expenditure decisions on new applications, new central processing units (CPUs), additional storage or communication links. The only variable costs will relate to the production of output (print, microfiche, etc.) and the maintenance of the existing systems. Systems costs, therefore, tend to be driven by:

- capacity requirements (both processing and storage capacity)
- diversity of applications required
- volume of output
- transaction volumes.

Overhead/support activities

As with premises, overhead or support activities should only be related to products or customer-related drivers where they affect the investment decision. Determining the cause of many types of overhead or supporting activities in financial institutions (that is, the cost drivers) will not be easy. It involves talking to each department and finding out what creates work for that department. This is particularly difficult in support functions, where, at the detailed level, each week will be different but, at the higher level, they should be able to identify the activities (as described in the previous chapter) and to determine the cause of the activity.

For example, the finance department, on a day-to-day basis, may find it difficult to determine the core activities within the department, but looking at it from a slightly different angle it will be seen that certain activities must be undertaken each month, quarter or at least once each year. These include the principal and detailed activities shown in Table 5.2.

Management reporting Tactical planning/budgeting/forecasting Regular management reporting *Ad hoc* management reporting
Financial accounting Statutory and regulatory reporting Financial accounting Fixed asset accounting Payroll – remuneration/benefits Bank reconciliations
Staff management Supervision Career development/appraisals/counselling Recruitment Internal communication
Training Training – general Training – technical
Audit Audit liaison
Taxation Taxation management
Administration Secretarial support Filing

Table 5.2   The principal and detailed activities in a finance department

A cost driver can be identified for each of these activities, as shown in Table 5.3. Those activities identified as sustaining activities tend to be more difficult to associate with a cost driver. It is difficult, for example, to determine the driver associated with the annual audit or review of the taxation position. However, it is possible to determine the costs associated with doing these activities to the current quality or service level.

Activities	Cost drivers
Management reporting	
Tactical planning/budgeting/forecasting	Level of detail required
Regular management reporting	Level of detail required
Ad hoc management reporting	Number/variety of requests for reports
Financial accounting	
Statutory and regulatory reporting	Regulatory requirement
Financial accounting	Number of items to be accounted for
Fixed asset accounting	Number of items to be accounted for
Payroll – remuneration/benefits	Number of staff
Bank reconciliations	Number of transactions to be reconciled
Staff management	
Supervision	Number of finance staff
Career development/appraisals/ counselling	Number of finance staff
Recruitment	Finance staff turnover
Internal communication	Number of finance staff
Training	
Training – general	Number of finance staff
Training – technical	Experience of finance staff
Audit	
Audit liaison	Quality of audit team
Taxation	
Taxation management	Complexity of tax environment
Administration	
Secretarial support	Degree of automation/computer literacy of finance staff
Filing	Number of reports produced

Table 5.3 Activities and cost drivers in a finance department

SUMMARY

In summary, costs can only be controlled by the management responsible for the expenditure. The cost driver approach looks for the factors that give rise to the cost. Experience has proven that the major drivers are such factors as:

- the number and diversity of products or services offered
- the rate of new product launches
- the number or variety of distribution channels used
- the quality of service
- the number and diversity of customers serviced
- the value and risk associated with the product offered
- the number of transactions performed.

Too many costing systems assume that responsibility for costs coincide with the organisation structure, but in the process of locating cost drivers, it is recognised that this may not be the case and, instead, the focus is on the decisions that give rise to costs being incurred. These decisions may take place in other parts of the organisation and may simply be implemented within a particular department or division.

Cost drivers generally relate to volume, value, quality, time and level of service. Short-term variable costs can be traced to products using volume-related cost drivers, but these are inappropriate for most long-term costs because they are driven by complexity and diversity, not volume.

In practice, identification of cost drivers in an Activity-based Costing system calls for both judgement and careful analysis. The first principle is to identify those activity costs with large values and consider the relationship between the diversity of products, services and customers supported by the activity and the variety within the activity for each product, service or customer. This will determine the level of accuracy that is necessary in order to maximise the value of the exercise. Second, identify the balance-related costs and ascertain the drivers to be attributed to interest income and expense to take account of the rates and risks associated with the products and counterparties. Finally, consider the non-activity-related costs and the drivers necessary to analyse how the costs arose.

The minimum number of cost drivers that an Activity-based Costing system requires to operate effectively will depend on how accurate the information produced needs to be and the complexity of the products and services offered by the organisation. This factor plays an important part because, as the number of cost drivers increase, the accuracy of the resulting information should also increase. In general, the higher the relative cost of an activity, the greater the distortion caused by using an imperfectly correlated cost driver to trace the cost of the activity to products or customers. This must, however, be balanced by the availability of the information and the cost of obtaining and processing it. This cost of Activity-based Costing systems development and operation must be justified by the usefulness of the information produced.

6 CALCULATING COSTS

INTRODUCTION

There are three basic components of Activity-based Costing: activities, cost drivers and costs. Activities and the associated cost drivers have been discussed in the two preceding chapters; this chapter concentrates on the costs themselves and on the associated revenues.

The fifth phase of the Activity-based Costing process is 'determine costs and revenues' (see Figure 6.1). Although the basic concepts behind Activity-based Costing relate purely to cost analysis, it is important not to forget revenues. Without being able to relate costs and revenues for reporting entities the analysis can only be used to monitor and control costs in isolation. Revenues provide the input necessary to monitor and control return on investment and profitability.

Costing is the process of identifying, measuring, assigning and analysing the expenses associated with items that are to be costed. The items to be costed may vary from activities to lines of business, individual products, customers, organisational units or any definable output.

Cost accounting concepts have primarily been developed for and applied to manufacturing companies. Indeed, the development of the cost of goods in process and finished goods inventories required for financial accounting in manufacturing is accomplished by means of cost accounting. The obvious difference between costing in manufacturing and in financial institutions is that a variety of raw materials are required by manufacturing companies to produce tangible finished goods for sale. In financial services, however, the only 'raw materials' are the funds offered or borrowed by the customer.

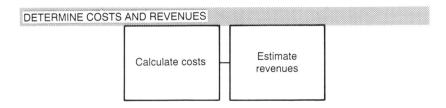

Figure 6.1 The Activity-based Costing process – Phase five: determine costs and revenues

Both financial services and manufacturing operations utilise labour, equipment and facilities, but financial institutions do not produce a tangible product. Products and services offered by financial institutions to their customers may be the provision of assurance, insurance, financial management, lending or deposit facilities and financial advice. There are, however, other characteristics of financial institutions that make costing within these environments different to that within manufacturing companies. For example, the speed at which services or products are provided has an impact on cost and profitability due to the time value of money and to the customer service level component of a service or product. As interest expense is a principal component of the cost of funds, only a portion of the unit cost of providing a service can be reduced by operating more efficiently. Interest costs cannot be managed and controlled by traditional cost management techniques. The 'raw materials' a financial institution handles are the funds obtained from deposits, premiums or borrowings. Even if the cost of obtaining these funds can be worked out, it is difficult to identify the specific depositary balance and associated interest rate that was the resource for a specific product, such as a loan. Most financial institutions have high volumes of transactions that fluctuate widely, due both to peak or slack business times and to economic conditions. They tend to have high fixed costs, due to unavoidably idle or underutilised capacity, partially due to the high and fluctuating volume of transactions.

Table 6.1 summarises the characteristics of management accounting, including cost and profitability measurement and reporting, as it is applied to manufacturing and financial institutions.

COST TYPES

Costs within a financial institution can be classified into several basic types:

- interest costs
- claims
- commissions paid
- operating costs
- overhead or support costs.

For Activity-based Costing, it is also useful to separate the fixed and variable elements within each classification as these generally relate to different cost drivers.

Interest costs, for example, are usually variable costs within financial institutions that can be attributed directly to an account and hence, to a product. Interest costs can be analysed as net or gross. Net interest is defined as interest income net of funding cost. This requires some means of estimating the cost of funds to be attributed to the product and is discussed in more detail below.

Costs/revenue	Financial institutions	Manufacturing companies
Products	Loans Fee-based financial services	Tangible finished goods
Raw materials	Deposits Premiums Borrowings Labour	Tangible raw materials Labour
Cost components	Funds Labour Equipment Facilities	Raw materials Labour Equipment Facilities
Revenue components	Interest margin Fee-based income Trading income Investment income	Sale of goods
Identification of cost and revenue streams by: organisational unit, product, and customer	Interest cost and revenue are accounted for by product and unit while non-interest costs and revenues are accounted for only by unit. Complex adjustments are required to associate all costs and revenues to all three dimensions.	Costs and revenues are accounted for on a product basis, which can generally be associated with units and customers.
Traditional cost accounting for: – organisational unit – product – customer	Yes, if any cost accounting at all Limited cost analysis Rarely costed	Yes, almost always Yes, always Limited, generally through product analysis
Traditional profit measurement for: – total operation – organisational unit – product – customer	Yes, always Yes, if any internal analysis Yes, possible Unlikely	Yes, always Yes, almost always Yes, always Limited

Table 6.1 Characteristics of management accounting

Claims costs are also variable costs that can be attributed to a particular policy or type of policy.

Commissions paid are variable costs that relate to services purchased by the company. Services purchased are generally advisory or brokerage and can be linked directly to types of business if not to individual products.

Operating costs and overhead or support costs will include both fixed and variable elements. Staff costs, for example, will be semi-variable and will relate directly to the activities identified. They can therefore be classified by activity as direct or indirect. The truly variable staff costs (overtime, etc.) are usually related to the volume of particular activities and can be accurately attributed. Premises costs are generally fixed costs that may be apportioned to products or services on the basis of utilisation (the trading room is attributed directly to the foreign exchange products, say), but there may be a significant proportion of administrative areas that must be treated separately. Information technology and communications costs are mainly fixed costs although there will be some variable components that will relate to the volume of activity. Other expenses will include marketing and advertising, travel and entertainment, stationery, public relations, catering and distribution. These cost classifications are generally variable costs that may be directly attributable to products and services but may also be indirect costs which form part of the general overhead, which must be analysed in more detail.

Interest costs

Interest costs are generally the largest cost components in any financial institution and will, therefore, have a significant impact on the decision making of the managers of organisational units, products and customer relationships. Managers will want to maximise the profitability of their individual responsibilities so funds transfer pricing systems, that are used to estimate the net interest payable or receivable, need to function in a manner that motivates managers to improve the profits of their units, products or customers while simultaneously improving the overall profits of the bank.

The application of funds transfer pricing involves assigning a value to the organisation's funds by paying or crediting providers (an imputed interest income) and charging users of funds (an imputed interest expense). The cost drivers associated with the imputed interest income or expense relate to the type of product (floating-rate loan, fixed-rate deposit, one-year motor policy, ten-year life policy or pension), the average balance of the asset or liability and the risk associated with the product and counterparty. Cost drivers may not be necessary for each product, balance and risk mix; products can be pooled by profile, which takes account of the rate, maturity and risk character of the product being offered and the driver will then relate to the product pool. The process of analysing the costs of funding interest-related products can be complicated and so this can be carried out as a separate exercise.

In addition to enabling segments of the bank's profitability to be measured, funds transfer pricing allows the evaluation of the earnings contribution of funds gathering functions (deposit taking, etc.) as well as funds placement functions. Without funds transfer pricing earnings credits, funds gathering represents only the cost of borrowing and the associated operating expense and does not have any income against which to offset these costs.

Asset pricing decisions should incorporate the costs of funds as well as the costs of obtaining and carrying the asset and desired profit margins. The funds transfer pricing charge made for the costs of funds may affect the pricing decision.

Asset and liability management objectives are frequently supported by building incentives and disincentives into funds transfer pricing, therefore asset and liability decisions throughout the organisation can be influenced. Financial institutions utilise a wide variety of methods to accomplish funds transfer pricing and, due to the numerous alternatives, there are virtually unlimited combinations and, therefore, different funds transfer pricing systems.

The remainder of this section outlines the key characteristics, advantages and disadvantages, primary considerations and sample calculations for each of the three main forms of funds transfer pricing, which are:

- single pool
- multiple pool
- matched funding.

Single pool method

In single pool funds transfer pricing, *one* funds transfer pricing rate is used. The assets and liabilities of any organisational unit, product or customer are netted to produce either a net funds used or provided position. The funds transfer pricing rate is multiplied by the net funds position to calculate the cost-of-funds charge for users and the earnings credit for providers. Cost-of-funds charges and earnings credits will balance in total, thereby not presenting reconciliation problems.

The advantages of single pool funds transfer pricing are that it is simple, easy to use and to understand. It cannot, however, reflect the varying characteristics of an organisation's assets and liabilities. It is most appropriate for unsophisticated situations or homogeneous situations where assets and liabilities tend to have similar characteristics (maturity, interest sensitivity and liquidity) or situations where measured entities (centres, products, customers) have similar mixes of characteristics. Depending on the single rate chosen, only one set of characteristics (maturity or interest sensitivity) will be represented and so distortions in profitability measurement and decision making can result for assets and liabilities with different characteristics. For example, use of an internal rate reflects the rates at which the assets and liabilities were acquired and may be most appropriate for measuring historical costs, but this would not reflect the true economic value or cost of new funds and may not be appropriate as a basis for current decision making. Conversely, the use of external rates may reflect more closely the incremental cost of obtaining or investing new funds and may, therefore, be more appropriate in current decision making but may not reflect the actual costs of the products and services offered where positions have been covered at actual rates.

The single pool method produces no particular data or systems problems. For the measured entity, the net funds position is required (preferably an average balance) and the rate. The balance will usually be required for the profitability reporting regardless of funds transfer pricing and, therefore, not require additional resources. Single-rate computations will, therefore, be simple to implement.

Multiple pool method

In the multiple pool method of funds transfer pricing, two or more funds transfer pricing rates are used. Pools are established on the characteristics of the assets and liabilities, such as maturity, liquidity, interest rate sensitivity, currency and domicile.

Asset and liability pools may or may not parallel each other and, if they do match, a net funds position within each pool may or may not be calculated. Cost of funds and earnings credits will frequently not net out, thus requiring monitoring and reconciliation.

The advantages of multiple funding pools are that they can be established to reflect the varying characteristics (maturity, interest sensitivity, etc.) of the assets and liabilities. They are also more flexible in that they are capable of reflecting both short-term market conditions for short-date products and the longer term nature of other assets and liabilities.

They are, however, more complicated to use and understand. As more pools are established to reflect more characteristics, the system becomes increasingly difficult to develop and implement. As more than one pool exists, there is likely to be a residual cost of funds or earnings credits due to mismatches among pools. This type of funds transfer pricing is most appropriate for the measurement of situations with diverse asset and liability characteristics.

Multiple pools range in sophistication from ones with only two pools (one for assets and one for liabilities) to ones with so many pools, the system approaches virtual matched funding for all combinations of characteristics. If pools are defined in a way that requires individual assets or liabilities to be tracked, identification of assets and liabilities in manners not captured in the general ledger or in the application systems or the use of complicated rates, then funds transfer pricing will require substantial resources. The more complicated specifications require a separate funds transfer pricing system that accesses data from the application systems perhaps more frequently than reporting.

A balance must be established between complexity and accuracy.

Frequently complex systems will not be understood and, therefore, will not have the intended effect on its users.

Matched funding

When an asset is booked using the matched funding method, a quoted rate or spread is established and remains with the asset throughout its life. This is commonly used for large commercial loans in conjunction with multiple pool funding for other smaller transactions. The rate or spread assigned is estimated based on the maturity and pricing structure of the asset or liability to be matched. This method generally requires a treasury or funds administration function, which can take responsibility for assigning funding rates to the assets and liabilities to be matched funded.

Matching rates to large transactions parallels market reality most closely. This method has the advantage of linking the rate or spread to the asset or liability to maturity, hence providing stability and equity in performance measurement and accuracy in cost analysis. The increased flexibility provided by this method also enables the rate or spread used to reflect the characteristics (maturity, interest sensitivity, value and currency) of the transaction. It does, however, require the facility to track the funding rate by transaction and is, therefore, more difficult to administer. It also requires more complicated monitoring and reconciliation to the operating and financial systems to ensure that consistency and integrity are maintained.

Claims

The principle elements of cost within an insurance company are the claims paid to policy holders for losses they have suffered. Claims are usually recorded as gross and net (of reinsurance recoveries). At any point in time, a claim may be either paid/payable, outstanding or incurred but not reported and these are described in more detail below.

The claims reserves of a general insurance company principally comprise the total of notified outstanding claims (as adjusted) and a provision for claims incurred but not reported. Insurance companies prepare various statistics to monitor their performance on claims and it generally falls into two categories:

- contract profitability
- settlement performance.

Each insurance company will have its own particular method of monitoring the performance of its claims department. The prompt settlement of claims can be a key factor in customer service and, accordingly, may be an area of focus in the settlement statistics.

Claims paid/payable

Claims paid/payable are claims that have been agreed by the insurance company as valid and, accordingly, have been passed for payment. These represent a cost to the insurance company and can therefore be aligned with the relevant policy type for Activity-based Costing. The claim may relate to a policy that was issued in previous accounting periods, for which provisions have been made. It is important that any double counting is avoided and that the cost of claims is reported as accurately as possible by policy type.

Notified outstanding claims

Notified outstanding claims are those claims that have been reported to the insurance company as losses but for which payment of the claim has not yet been agreed by the insurance company. The total of the notified outstanding claims at any point in time represents a reasonable estimate of the liability to the insurance company of notified claims and the movement on the total of notified outstanding is an adjustment to cost.

Claims incurred but not yet reported

Claims incurred but not reported relate to losses that are covered by insurance contracts that have not yet been notified as losses to the insurance company. The insurance company will usually establish a provision for claims incurred but not reported and movement in this provision will affect the cost of claims. The calculation of the provision for claims incurred but not reported is obviously a subjective process and generally calls for actuarial techniques. The insurance company will usually perform a detailed exercise at the year end to calculate this provision, but it is sometimes updated on a more frequent basis for management accounting purposes.

Commissions paid

Commissions are paid by financial institutions to other organisations for services they provide. These may include insurance commissions paid to agents and brokers, trading commissions paid to securities or foreign exchange traders or brokers, payments or commissions paid to members of the clearing organisations, commissions paid to credit agencies and commissions or fees paid to research organisations who specialise in economic or industrial research.

The two principle types of expense, apart from claims, for an insurance company are commissions and administration expenses. Commissions are paid to individuals or companies by the insurance company, principally for services rendered in acquiring business for the insurance company. They form the major part of acquisition costs, for example. Commissions are generally paid up front for new business and the insurance company may match these costs against the respective policy term and, hence, not as an expense for the full amount of these costs in the period in which they are incurred. An amount is therefore carried forward as deferred costs.

Trading, payments and credit commissions tend to relate to individual transactions, although there may be a basic annual charge associated with the maintenance of the relationship with the supplier. These costs can be assigned accurately to the activities, products and services to which they relate. Research costs, however, rarely relate to individual activities and may be incurred to support the general activity of trading in a particular market. In this instance, the cost would be assigned to the product *group*, not to *individual* products or activities.

Operating costs

Operating costs within a financial institution will normally include all direct costs relating to the provision of products and services to customers or other parts of the organisation. These costs may be identifiable by organisational unit as direct costs before the allocation of overheads. Activities are identifiable in each cost centre at the detailed level and will normally be reported by expense type.

Types of expense shown in management reporting vary by organisation. They generally include, as a minimum, staff, premises, IT and other direct costs. They may detail individual expense lines, as shown in the financial accounting system. Alternatively they may ignore conventional accounting and analyse costs by business line, product or service.

For Activity-based Costing, it is necessary to separate the controllable costs from those costs that are normally allocated to the operating areas. Premises costs, for example, are rarely controllable by operating area, although the area may be able to control the amount of space that it occupies. IT costs may also be difficult to control by operating area. Costs may be allocated to operating areas on the basis of system utilisation, but the unit cost assigned to the system may not be controllable by the operating unit. Other direct costs may include both controllable and non-controllable items. These should be separated for the purposes of Activity-based Costing if they represent a material value in relation to the overall exercise. Stationery, travel and entertainment costs are normally controllable, but marketing and advertising costs are rarely controllable by the operating area, unless a specific campaign is initiated in relation to the products or services offered.

Overhead or support costs

Overhead or support costs may include all costs that are not directly attributable to products or services and which traditional cost accounting would apportion to products and services according to some standard allocation basis. The use of activity analysis and cost drivers allows for the factors that cause the expenditure to be incurred to be identified and, hence, for the costs to be aligned, which is very helpful to the decision-making process. In the same way that activities are identifiable in each operational unit, activities should be agreed for each overhead or support function. Each cost centre will normally receive cost analysis reported by expense type.

For Activity-based Costing, it is necessary to separate the controllable costs from those costs allocated to the cost centre. The controllable costs in a support function may include the same expense types that are controllable by the operating areas. It may also include other costs that are controllable at the more tactical or strategic level, such as premises, systems development, capital expenditure and marketing, which form part of the core responsibility of that particular support centre. All costs are ultimately controllable by someone within the organisation, although it may not always be easy to identify the relevant manager.

REVIEWING REVENUES

In order to calculate profitability or return on investment, it is important to be able to measure revenue and cost by business activity, product, customer or responsibility depending on the use of the analysis. Revenue in financial institutions can arise in five ways – interest income, fee or commission income, premiums, trading and investment income.

Interest income

Interest is the charge made by the lender to the borrower for the use of the lender's funds over time. Interest is normally shown as two separate items – interest revenue (the gross interest charged to the borrower for the funds placed or the loan made for the reporting period) and interest expense (the gross interest paid to the depositor for the funds borrowed or deposits taken for the reporting period).

The net interest income is the difference between interest revenue and interest expense and is the spread or contribution to profits and operating costs made by the asset- and liability-related products.

Where products and services need to be identified separately, interest revenue should usually be adjusted for the cost of funds figure. In summary, lending products have gross interest revenue, calculated as the interest received from the customer on the loan, but the funds had to be obtained from a depositor before they could be lent and, consequently, interest expense had to be paid to the depositor for those funds. As loans and deposits can rarely be matched in value and term, the cost of funds figure attributed to the loan is normally estimated by using an internal cost of funds rate. The internal cost of funds rate is generally a mid-rate between the average lending and deposit rates so that revenue and cost can be attributed to the lending and deposit product types.

Interest income is calculated in relation to the balance on the account. The balance is, however, likely to vary during the reporting period and, hence, the interest should reflect the actual balances as they change. In practice, most financial institutions calculate interest on the transaction processing systems daily, but may not keep records of the daily balances or calculate the internal funding cost at the same time. Balances are generally stored in financial accounting systems as actual balances at the end of the period. In order to calculate a more accurate interest margin, it is therefore necessary to calculate the average balance. This should be calculated by accumulating daily balances and calculating a daily average debit or credit balance to the end of the reporting period. Some institutions, however, may still use an average of the current and prior period end. This ignores any fluctuation between reporting dates and so may misrepresent the margins reported as return on assets. This generally provides more favourable margins as many customers may try to reduce their borrowing at the period end for reporting purposes. The interest paid by the customer may, therefore, reflect higher balances during the period, but be reported against the lower actual balance at the period end.

Current accounts can be more difficult to analyse as they may fluctuate between debit and credit balances. In order to calculate the interest payable and receivable and the associated cost of funds, it is, therefore, necessary to maintain and report both average debit and credit balances for any account that may fluctuate and to calculate the interest payable and receivable on both balances.

Fee- or commission-based income

Fee- or commission-based income is the revenue that is generated by means of charges levied for products or services provided. These services include most credit advisory, foreign exchange and transmission, documentary, advisory and broking services. The increase or decrease in revenue is generally related to the volume of services provided and can be analysed in detail by means of product and customer reporting. Fees or commissions differ from interest income in that they are not usually assessed as a percentage of balances outstanding, although they may relate to the value of the loan or facility offered.

Fees or commissions are also payable by customers for the initiation and management of most funded products in the form of loan, new issue underwriting and arrangement fees. This revenue could be identified separately and reported in conjunction with the spread or yield made on the product.

Fee- or commission-based revenue is usually related to the agreed fee structure of the organisation and is predetermined. Exceptions arise when fees are waived or discounted for particular customers. Customer profitability reporting must take account of the reduced fees for those customers and the sources of data capture must identify the transactions to which these relate.

Premium income

Insurance premiums are generally stated gross and net of reinsurance and may represent single premiums (to create an annuity, for example) or recurring annual premiums that may be paid weekly, monthly, quarterly or annually. In order to accurately project the future liabilities, the premiums will be split by policy type, at least, and will frequently be further subdivided so as to ensure that the actuary has access to full analysis information concerning the policyholder and the risks accepted. Premiums are usually accumulated within the insurance company's management information system by policy type, contract or grouping of contracts and reviewed by the respective business underwriters on a regular basis.

Trading income

Trading income is that revenue made by speculative trading in the money markets and exchanges on behalf of the company. Speculative trading can take place in any negotiable instruments including foreign exchange, certificates of deposit, Eurocurrency, futures, options, stocks, bonds and other securities.

Accounting for securities and other negotiable instruments purchased for trading purposes, readily realisable and held with the intention of resale in the short term, requires that they should all be included in financial statements at market value. This involves a periodic revaluation of the securities held to the current market price and the identification of the unrealised gains and/or losses that this generates.

Trading income is generated when there are changes in the perceived value of securities. Changes may be due to perceived changes in any combination of the following factors: interest rates, exchange rates, the time value of money, economic environment, political environment, market activity or availability of the particular commodity.

Investment income

Investment income is the revenue made by holding any negotiable instrument with the intention of gaining financial advantage in the longer term. The principal source of profit for a life assurance office is the earnings obtained directly or indirectly from investment income. Insurance companies accumulate vast sums of money on behalf of their policyholders and, in addition, the proprietary companies hold considerable amounts on their shareholders' behalf in the form of capital and reserves. Naturally, the companies must employ this money usefully and profitably and, taking into account the possible need to draw on the money to pay out claims, they invest the money in various ways.

Substantial investment returns are essential to a long-term fund. Indeed, the track record of a life office's investment management in comparison with its rivals is of paramount importance, overshadowing even its underwriting performance. A life office is vulnerable to large losses if a significantly large number of cases lapse in the early years before the initial expenses and commissions can be recovered. The effect of lapses is a major factor affecting the capital required for a life office and the overall profitability of the business.

In traditional policies, like whole life and endowment assurances, the office, when fixing its premium terms, gives a long-term interest rate guarantee to the policyholder. The office will record a profit or loss if it can achieve, over the policies' lifetime, investment earnings above or below the guaranteed rate. Surpluses from investments are related to the size of assets and reserves and hence the bulk of the surpluses are earned towards the end of the contract when the reserves have built up.

In unit-linked business, the policyholders directly benefit from the investment performance and the life office normally receives a management fee defined as a percentage of the fund. The management fee is the principal source of profit on these contracts, though the office will receive jobbing profits if a bid/offer spread is built into the unit price.

The rate of interest guaranteed to policyholders is very high on non-profit policies, but on with-profit policies a substantially increased premium is charged and the underlying rate of interest guaranteed to the policyholder is low (the difference between a with-profit premium and the equivalent non-profit premium is commonly called the 'bonus loading').

Consequently on with-profit business, large surpluses arise almost automatically, as, in addition to the investment earnings, all the bonus loadings collected over the period accentuate the surplus. How this large surplus is shared between shareholders and policyholders' bonuses, and the form of the bonus, has significant consequences on the financing required for new business and the profitability of the office.

Investment income is also very important to a general insurance fund, especially where underwriting losses and inflation otherwise deplete reserves. With operating losses (combining underwriting results, business acquisition and administration costs), now the norm among non-life insurers, there is increasing reliance on investment performance to produce a bottom-line profit.

TIME FRAMES

Costs can be calculated on a variety of time frames. Historical costs generally relate to the actual costs for the previous period, which is usually the previous year. Actual costs are generally the costs of the current period and may need to be annualised for comparative purposes. Budgeted costs are the cost plans that are normally agreed prior to the period to which they relate. Forecast costs are the re-planned figures, which are revised estimates of the projected expenditure. Long-term expenditure projections are estimates of future expenditure beyond the period covered by the budget or forecast. Activity-based Costing can be based on any of these cost types. Long-term expenditure projections are most useful, though, in strategic cost analysis and capital appraisals. Actual, budget or forecast costs are more normally used for product costing, customer profitability and operational cost management. Whatever basis is used, it is important that the volume of activities identified relate to the *same* time frame and are based on the *same* assumptions.

Costs are usually available within the organisation at a cost centre level and may include allocated costs from central support or service areas. It is necessary for Activity-based Costing purposes that costs are returned to the point of origination. This enables the analysis to be performed on direct costs which can be more accurately attributed to cost drivers.

When the activity analysis and cost drivers have been analysed, the associated costs and revenues can be estimated and the validity of the product definitions and cost drivers confirmed. Only when real costs and revenues are utilised will the users be able to focus on the definitions and hence, review and agree them in detail.

It is important to agree the type of cost information to be used in advance of beginning the analysis. Where budgets and/or forecasts are available at sufficient level of detail and where they can be associated with defined levels of activity and transaction volume, these may be the most appropriate costs on which to base the analysis. If the budgets have not been approved or recognised as accurate by the individual line managers, then it may be more appropriate to use actual costs for a defined period over which the levels of activity and transaction volumes can be collected.

TOTALS AND SUB-TOTALS

Any cost analysis should include all the costs of doing business, in order to demonstrate that integrity of the cost base has been maintained. It is important, however, not to cloud the analysis by arbitrary allocation of costs *just* to ensure reconciliation to the financial accounts. The balance between the need to include all costs and the requirements of the decision-making process can be achieved by using reconciling statements and sub-totals that highlight the key results.

There are several definitions of Activity-based costs that can be used as the basis of management decision making. They can be reported as marginal costs, direct costs or fully-absorbed costs. How a financial institution defines costs in relation to strategic cost management or product costing is essentially a function of its management philosophy. Some managers prefer costs to be reported as fully absorbed, that is, all fixed and variable costs being included in the reporting. Other organisations prefer costs to be reported with only those items that relate directly to the product or product group being analysed.

Marginal costs are defined as those costs incurred by the production of an additional unit of an activity, product or service that are also variable. Due to the relatively fixed nature of operating costs in most financial institutions, marginal costs are rarely relevant as, generally, they will only include interest, claims, commissions paid and sundry direct expenses (stationery, etc.). Marginal costs do not normally include the activity costs as staff costs tend to be fixed costs, at least in the short term. There are, however, always exceptions to the norm. Some financial institutions employ operational staff on a piece-work basis, where payment is related directly to the availability of work. This is particularly relevant in retail financial services in high-volume activities, such as cheque or credit card processing, where volumes fluctuate with customer demand.

Direct costs are defined as those prime costs incurred by the operating functions and exclude all indirect or overhead costs. Direct costs form the nucleus of Activity-based Costing. They generally include all costs that can be legitimately assigned to the activity, product or customer. This would include interest, claims, commission paid and all direct operating costs as well as those support costs that can be assigned to an individual activity, product or customer. These costs therefore exclude those items that can only be assigned to product groups or are classified as sustaining costs. Care must be taken to ensure that managers understand the definition of direct costs and the proportions of overhead or support costs that are excluded otherwise they may assume that *all* costs have been apportioned and therefore that any income level which exceeds direct costs creates profit.

Fully absorbed costs are defined as a total of all fixed and variable costs that can be allotted to cost units. They are the basis of most traditional cost accounting systems and are easily reconcilable to the financial accounts as all costs are allocated to activities, products or customers. They cloud the analysis performed in an Activity-based Costing exercise, however, in that they ignore the analysis of cost behaviour and assume that all costs can be aligned with products and customers.

The most appropriate cost will vary depending on how the information is to be used. In strategic cost management, for example, where Activity-based Costing is used to identify the costs associated with a particular business activity or market, it is important to include *all* costs that can be attributed to the activity or market. The costs will, therefore, include all product-related expenditure and any sustaining costs that would change as a result of the strategic decision.

In product costing and customer profitability analysis, only the direct costs that relate to the provision of the product or service should be included in the analysis. Although it is important to highlight the sustaining costs, to ensure that pricing decisions cover the full costs of the organisation, these costs can be shown as a percentage increase in direct cost.

In operational cost management, all activity-related costs will be analysed. This will include all sustaining costs. Costs will be classified as fundamental and discretionary and attention may be focused on the discretionary activities to a greater extent than on the fundamental activities, but no costs should be excluded from the analysis and the allocation of costs will not be necessary.

ASSIGNING COSTS TO ACTIVITIES

Assigning interest, claims, commissions and staff costs to the activities identified above should be relatively easy, but assigning IT and communication systems costs can be much more difficult. Other costs will either be directly attributable to products, services or customers (marketing costs, travel and entertainment, stationery, etc.) or will be analysed according to the use that will be made of the information resulting from the exercise. For example, premises costs can be attributed to products on the basis of staff utilisation, but, if premises costs are to be reduced, then any apportionment may be counter-productive.

In some organisations, cost centres may be organised according to the support of particular products and services and, therefore, may then be easy to analyse. Branches, however, generally support a range of products and services and so must be analysed in more detail. The following sections consider the alternative techniques for assigning the various cost types to activities or cost drivers.

Assigning staff costs

Staff costs are normally assigned to the activities performed within the department or cost centre on the basis of the time they take to perform.

As discussed in Chapter 4, Agreeing activities, the activity analysis techniques of self-logging, historical averaging, Relative Values, Activity Sampling, stop-watch and pre-determined time standards have different characteristics and so a choice has to be made. Which technique is chosen will depend on:

- the complexity of the activities
- the level of detail required
- how the data collected is to be used
- the cost/benefit perceived from the study
- the culture of the organisation
- the type of costing system required.

All the activity analysis techniques will facilitate the staff-related costs of the activities within the department to be broken down. The process should also serve as a check that all activities have been identified in that it should verify that the total of all time allocated equals the available man time.

Most financial institutions are likely to use at least two techniques to analyse the use of staff time by activity. They may also wish to use some form of statistical measurement to estimate the time associated with operational activities, where there is a larger volume of the more repetitive tasks. They may also use some form of relative value analysis to estimate the man time appertaining to support or overhead activities, which could be more difficult to analyse using statistical measurement techniques.

The results of Relative Value analysis can be used to calculate unit costs by using the departmental staff cost as the basis of the calculation. Relative Value analysis normally expresses activity times as proportions of a man year. The annualised departmental staff cost can therefore be divided by the total number of man years available within the department to calculate what the cost is per man year. Using this figure, the cost of the individual activities can be calculated. This type of costing assumes that all man years within the department have the same value and that staffing remains constant throughout the period to which the costs relate. It does, however, provide a quick and simple means of assigning costs to activities at a departmental level.

The costs of the activities for which minute values have been identified can be calculated in two ways – either by estimating the value of a minute in the relevant department by taking the cost of the department divided by the total available staff time and, thus, calculating the value of the time taken to perform the activity, or by taking the normal volume of activity within the department and calculating the number of productive minutes within the department before estimating the value of a minute on which to base the cost of each activity.

Using total available staff time as the basis of the calculation of the cost per minute does not include any idle time allowance in the calculation of an activity value. If the time taken to perform the total volume of activities does not equate to the total available staff time, there will be unallocated staff costs. These costs will relate to the unutilised capacity in the department. Alternatively, using the normal volume of activity as the basis for estimating the number of productive minutes assumes that the department is working at full capacity and will allocate all departmental costs to the activities identified.

Assigning systems costs

Many IT- and communication systems-related costs vary with the diversity of products offered, not with the volume of transactions. The system must have sufficient available capacity, however, to cope with the maximum number of transactions that could be performed. It will not be sufficient to apportion the activities within the systems department to the products because many of the costs incurred are not related to activities but to other types of cost. Thus, in these circumstances, costs will be assigned to cost drivers not to activities.

Cost drivers associated with IT and communications include the number of hardware platforms and systems applications maintained, the number of transactions processed, the level of service provided, the number and complexity of communication channels, the amount of storage required, the number of terminals supported and the size and complexity of the network. The use of Activity-based Costing will determine the level of detail required for the analysis of the systems-related costs. In most organisations, costs can be assigned to a business area or product group but are unlikely to be assigned to individual products or services unless a particular system or machine is only used by that product or service (automated teller machines for example, are only used for credit and debit card-related cash transactions and, in some instances, balance enquiries and statement requests). Most costs, therefore, must be analysed in a matrix, as shown in Table 6.2.

There are still costs within the systems department that may be classified as sustaining costs. These would include the maintenance of supporting systems, such as the financial control systems and the operational control programmes. The estimation of costs of duplicate facilities, system back-up and spare capacity remains an issue in Activity-based Costing, as in any other form of cost analysis, but they can be isolated as sustaining costs and any attempt to apportion these costs to products and services can be eliminated.

Assigning other direct costs

Other direct costs will include marketing and advertising, travel and entertainment, stationery, public relations, catering and distribution costs. For product and customer analysis, some of these costs may be assigned directly to individual products, customers or product groups.

Marketing, advertising and public relations expenditure, for example, may appertain to campaigns that support particular products or product

Current account services	Payment system	Account maintenance	Card Management	ATM	Interbank clearing
Cash withdrawals		▓		▓	
Cash deposits		▓			
Cheque deposits		▓			▓
Balance requests		▓		▓	
Statement requests		▓			
Credit card issuance			▓		
Debit card issuance			▓		
Cheque card issuance			▓		
Credit card usage	▓		▓		▓
Debit card usage	▓	▓	▓		▓
Cheque usage	▓	▓			▓
Standing order payment	▓	▓			▓
Set up standing order		▓			
Set up direct debit		▓			
Direct debit payment	▓	▓			▓
Account transfer		▓			

Table 6.2   Analysis of current account related systems costs

groups. There may, however, be some marketing and advertising costs that are classified as sustaining costs and cannot be assigned to specific products or business areas.

Travel and entertainment expenses can, if necessary, be assigned to products or customer relationships. This level of detailed analysis can be undertaken for individual product and customer profitability but, unless the costs are material, they are normally included in staff costs and assigned to activities on the basis of time utilisation.

Stationery costs can also be assigned to particular products or services, but, once again, unless the costs are material, they are normally included in staff costs and assigned to activities on the basis of time utilisation. Distribution costs could also be product-related – the distribution of cheques, drafts, letters of credit and securities, for example. Catering costs, however, are rarely product specific and may be treated as overhead costs, as discussed below.

Overhead and support costs

In the same way that activity-related costs are identifiable in each operational unit, they should also be agreed for each overhead or support function. Overhead and support functions could include premises, catering, security, systems development, financial control, personnel, strategic planning, executive management, public relations and marketing.

In a traditional cost accounting system, premises and security costs are normally calculated centrally and allocated to individual cost centres on the basis of floor utilisation. In Activity-based Costing, these costs are monitored and controlled in relation to property management activities. They may be apportioned to product groups or business areas, where this is relevant to the use of the information. The cost of a retail branch network, for example, may be included in an analysis of the retail banking activity within a financial institution. It would be difficult, however, to attribute this cost to individual retail products.

Financial control, personnel, strategic planning, executive management, public relations and corporate marketing are all activities that are part of the overall management of the business. Costs may be monitored and controlled by activity within the individual departments, but should only be assigned to products, customers or business areas where they are relevant to the business decision, as discussed above.

SUMMARY

In summary, costing is the process of identifying, measuring, assigning and analysing the expenses associated with items that are to be costed. These items may vary from activities to lines of business, individual products, customers, organisational units or any definable output.

Costs within a financial institution can be classified into several basic types, including interest costs, claims, commissions paid, operating costs and overhead or support costs. Interest costs, for example, are usually costs within financial institutions that can be attributed directly to a product. Claims costs are also costs that can be attributed to a particular policy type. Commissions may include insurance commissions paid to agents and brokers, trading commissions paid to securities or foreign exchange traders or brokers, payments commissions paid to members of the clearing organisations, commissions paid to credit agencies and commissions or fees paid to research organisations who specialise in economic or industrial research. In general, all commissions paid can be assigned to products or product groups. Operating costs within a financial institution will normally include all direct costs relating to the provision of products and services to customers or other parts of the organisation. These costs may be identifiable by organisational unit and can then be assigned to the activities performed within the operational area. Overhead or support costs may include all costs that are not directly attributable to products or services and which traditional cost accounting would apportion to products and services according to some standard allocation criterion. The use of activity analysis and cost drivers allows the factors that cause the expenditure to be incurred to be identified and, hence, the costs to be aligned for the purpose of decision making. In the same way that activities are identifiable in each operational unit, activities should be agreed for each overhead or support function and costs assigned in the same way.

In order to calculate profitability or return on investment, it is important to be able to measure revenue as well as cost by type of business, product, customer or responsibility depending on the use of the analysis. Revenue in financial institutions can arise in a variety of ways – interest income, fee or commission income, premiums, trading and investment income. Interest can be shown as two separate items – interest revenue (the gross interest charged to the borrower for the funds placed or the loan made for the reporting period) and interest expense (the gross interest paid to the depositor for the funds borrowed or deposits taken for the reporting period), or as net interest income. Net interest income is the difference between interest revenue and interest expense and is the spread or contribution to profits and operating costs made by the asset- and liability-related products. Fee-based income is the revenue that is generated through charges levied for products or services provided. Insurance premiums are generally stated gross and net of reinsurance and may represent single premiums (to create an annuity, for example) or recurring annual premiums which may be paid weekly, monthly, quarterly or annually. Trading income is that revenue made by speculative trading through the money markets and exchanges on behalf of the institution. Speculative trading can take place in any negotiable instruments including foreign exchange, certificates of deposit, eurocurrency, futures, options, stocks, bonds and other securities. Investment income is the revenue made by holding any negotiable instrument held with the intention of gaining financial advantage in the longer term. The principal source of profit for a life insurance office is the earnings obtained directly or indirectly from investment income.

Costs and revenues can be based on a variety of time frames. Historical, actual, budgeted and forecast costs, and long-term expenditure projections are all cost bases that may be used in Activity-based Costing.

Any cost analysis should include all the costs of doing business in order to demonstrate that the integrity of the cost base has been maintained. It is important, however, not to cloud the analysis by arbitrarily allocating costs just to ensure reconciliation to the financial accounts. The balance between the need to include all costs and the requirements of the decision-making process can be achieved by means of reconciling statements and sub-totals that highlight the key results.

Assigning interest, claims, commissions and staff costs to activities should be relatively easy, but assigning IT and communication systems costs can be much more difficult. Other costs will either be directly attributable to products, services or customers (marketing, travel and entertainment, stationery, etc.) or will be analysed by cost driver and included in the reporting according to the use that will be made of the information resulting from the exercise.

7 IMPLEMENTATION ISSUES

INTRODUCTION

Although there are many complicated issues associated with the definition and calculation of activity-based costs in any financial institution, the key to any successful system lies in its effective design and implementation. Previous chapters have concentrated on the definition of activities and cost drivers and the estimation of costs and revenues linking issues to the tasks included in Phase two, 'define reporting entities', and Phase five, 'determine costs and revenues'. This chapter therefore concentrates on the practical issues relating to Phase three, 'commence data collection', and Phase four, 'develop an Activity-based Costing system' (see Figure 7.1). It considers the types, sources and availability of data, the systems solutions, likely modules and operational considerations.

The key requirement for all data in Activity-based Costing is that it be available at the lowest level at which reporting is to occur. Whether Activity-based Costing is to be used for strategic cost management, product or customer cost and profitability analysis or operational cost management, the cost and usage data must either be originally captured or be allocated to the lowest level of analysis required (that is, activity). The primary sources of

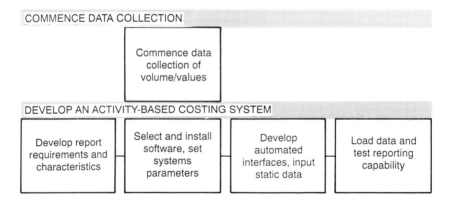

Figure 7.1   The Activity-based Costing process – Phases three and four

data required for Activity-based Costing and profitability reporting are likely to include the general ledger system, the cost accounting system, the budgeting and forecasting systems. It is unlikely, however, that all the data requirements will be able to be met by these systems. The transaction processing systems, accounting applications (payroll, fixed assets, etc.), customer information file and to a lesser extent, the administration systems, risk management systems and trading systems may also provide information that relates to more detailed analysis of usage and direct operating income and balances by product and customer. In addition, the accounting systems in different organisations carry varying degrees of information. Therefore, data that one institution receives from its general ledger, another institution must obtain from the application systems. Although it is preferable to avoid manual capture and entry of data into an Activity-based Costing system as much as possible, some data requirements may not be able to be met in any other way. Care must be taken to ensure that all data sources used are compatible and that the data will eventually be able to be reconciled to the financial results.

In addition to the specific data required for profitability reporting to take place at the lowest level, a reporting system will require for there to be various calculation, accumulation and history retention capabilities. The contents of a specific report often require calculations of sub-totals, differences, ratios, averages, etc. from the data. As part of the basic requirements of the system, it is important to ensure that all reporting characteristics and needs have been considered.

Just as there is no one correct approach to using Activity-based Costing information, there is no one system that will provide that information. This situation exists not because software vendors are uninterested in developing such packages, but because of the complexity and individuality of a good Activity-based Costing system and the need to obtain data from transaction processing applications, customer databases and financial systems.

Any package or bespoke Activity-based Costing system should include several features, which fall into two essential categories: cost accounting features relating to the Activity-based Costing requirements and profitability measurement and reporting features, which add the income, balance and usage information to the activity-based cost analysis. While the requirements for a particular company will obviously be specific to them, it is possible to consider the basic functional modules of cost and profitability reporting systems. The features may be modules of a separate cost and profitability system or may represent features of other systems that are accessed to pull together the data required for cost and profitability reporting.

As part of the implementation of an Activity-based Costing system, some operations and maintenance factors also need to be considered. On a generic level, it is not possible to estimate the cost of these various factors, but in a specific situation the cost involved in operating and maintaining a system should be one of the factors that is weighed up alongside the value of the information to the institution. Personnel, data processing and maintenance costs of the system may or may not be material to the decision to begin the operation of a system, but there will be an upper limit as to the value of activity-based cost and profitability information.

DATA REQUIREMENTS

The key requirement for all data in Activity-based Costing is that it be available at the lowest level at which reporting is to occur. Whether Activity-based Costing is being used for strategic cost management, product or customer cost and profitability analysis or operational cost management, the cost and usage data must either be originally captured or be allocated to the lowest level of analysis required (that is, activity). This requirement is more frequently satisfied when Activity-based Costing is used as a cost control tool than it is with product or customer reporting. This is because most organisations utilise a form of responsibility reporting that subdivides it into units, often called cost centres or profit centres.

In general, the data required for product and customer reporting is more difficult to obtain by activity than is the data for cost control. Although the basic data that is reported in product or customer reporting is the same, this data will need to be available with the desired product and/or customer identification. Cost data must, therefore, be analysed below responsibility centres into individual activities performed to support defined products and services. Interest income, interest expense and most other forms of revenue may be identifiable by product within the general ledger, but volumes and customer usage information will probably come from the transaction processing systems.

The data required for comprehensive customer reporting is the most difficult to obtain. Customer reporting, generally, is dependent upon a customer information system that links all pieces of a customer's relationship with the institution together or, at least, upon some common customer identification number. The normal financial accounting system plays virtually no role in customer reporting as virtually no data within it can be associated with an individual customer as it is normally accumulated at a summary level prior to capture by the accounting system.

The characteristics of the data that are required within an Activity-based Costing system do not simply relate to the basic components of cost, income, balance and usage data necessary to calculate the activity-based costs, but will also include the *way* in which information is summarised and reported. These characteristics will therefore include:

- the definitions of profitability used (controllable profits, marginal profits, fully absorbed profits)
- the components of income included
- the components of cost and definitions to be used
- the comparative data used (historical data, budgets, forecasts, other units, competitors)
- the definitions of ratios used
- the specification of items included in sub-totals and totals.

Types of data

Data may be financial or statistical. Financial data includes interest income, premium income, fees and commissions, trading income, investment income, claims and operating expense and asset and liability balances. Statistical information may include volume and qualitative data by cost driver and usage data by product and customer. It may also include staff numbers, occupancy details and other operational statistics to assist in the basic Activity-based Costing calculation. Whether data is financial or statistical, it may be reported as historical actual data or as projected data. Projected data is sometimes classified as budget, forecast, outlook or plan data. Budget data is generally set at a point in time for a fixed future period of time. Forecast or outlook data tends to be dynamic and may be constantly revised to reflect what has taken place as well as the latest predications for the future. Plan data, in the current year, should remain fixed.

Financial data

Financial data includes interest income, premium income, fees and commissions, trading income, investment income, claims and operating expenses and asset and liability balances and forms the core of most reports. Interest income is earned primarily from loans and deposits to and from customers. Premium income is earned from the monies received for the policies written by the company. Fees and commissions are earned from a variety of sources, including loan arrangement, service charges, documentary services, foreign exchange and advisory services. Trading and investment income is earned from investment and trading securities.

Expenses within a financial institution fall into several basic groups: interest costs, claims, commissions paid, operating costs and overhead or support costs. Interest costs, for example, are usually costs within a financial institution that can be attributed directly to a product. Claims costs are also costs that can be attributed to a particular policy type. Commissions may include insurance commissions paid to agents and brokers, trading commissions paid to securities or foreign exchange traders or brokers, payments commissions paid to members of the clearing organisations, commissions paid to credit agencies and commissions or fees paid to research organisations who specialise in economic or industrial research. In general, all commissions paid can be assigned to products or product groups. Operating costs within a financial institution will normally include all direct costs relating to the provision of products and services to customers or other parts of the organisation. These costs may be identifiable by organisational unit and can be assigned to the activities performed within the operational area. Overhead or support costs may include all costs that are not directly attributable to products or services and which traditional cost accounting would apportion to products and services according to some standard allocation basis. The use of activity analysis and cost drivers identifies the factors that cause the expenditure to be incurred and, hence, provides the alignment of costs for the process of decision making. In the same way that activities are identifiable in each operational unit, activities may be agreed for each overhead or support function and costs assigned in the same way.

Assets and liabilities are reported either as average balances over a period of time or balances at a particular point in time. Due to the calculation of interest rates and yields, average balances are often preferred. Asset balances may be categorised as earning (such as interest income) or non-earning (fixed assets, etc). Further distinctions are often made according to product type (loans, investments) and other sub-categories.

Liability balances are usually reported by type and/or sensitivity. Several balance sheet accounts are frequently not captured at the lowest organisational product or customer level and may or may not be allocated. These include statutory reserves, equity and loss reserves.

Statistical data

Statistical data is a key component of most Activity-based Costing reports. The statistical information may represent data at a point in time (number of accounts at month end), accumulated data (number of policies written during the month) or average information (number of activities performed per day). Some reports require that statistical information be expressed in financial terms but not be part of the financial results of the organisation, such as waived fees or uncollected premiums.

SOURCES OF DATA

The primary sources of data required for Activity-based Costing and profitability reporting are the general ledger, cost accounting, budgeting and forecasting and numerous product and special application systems. These application systems include the transaction processing, accounting systems, executive information (if present) and many others.

The general ledger in different companies carries varying degrees of information. Therefore, data that one company obtains from its general ledger, another must obtain from the application systems. Although it is preferable to avoid manual capture and entry of data into an Activity-based Costing system as much as possible, some data requirements may not be able to be met by any other means.

Systems that must be accessed

There are several main types of systems that must be accessed to provide the basic components of data for any Activity-based Costing system (see Figure 7.3, later).

Financial accounting

The capturing of income, expense and balances data is the basic function of all general ledgers. This same data is the primary component of all cost and profitability measurement and reporting, but additional components are necessary to allow the analysis to be performed.

Transaction processing

These systems include the deposit, loan, trading, investment management, claim (life, disability, health, property), benefit payment (annuities, pensions), collection, investment trading and policy management systems as well as numerous transactions and various internal transactions. Financial data generally interfaces from the systems with the general ledger and, therefore, when the level of data carried in the general ledger is not sufficient for cost and profitability reporting, transactions processing systems must be accessed. The types of data normally extracted from these systems may include rates, average balances, income, waived and discounted fees and commissions, product volumes and customer activity levels.

Some organisations may use work measurement techniques to provide detailed costing, which may then be extended to produce activity-based costs for each product. However, this degree of detail is useless if revenues cannot be allocated as accurately and revenue data is usually available in most detail from the transaction processing systems. Reports are only as accurate as the least accurate data within them.

Product volumes are not usually included in the financial database unless it also generates sales or productivity data. This information can be collected by using transaction processing systems or sampling.

Accounting applications

These systems include the payroll and fixed assets systems, accounts payable, accounts receivable and risk management. They represent the initial capture and processing point for various internal transactions not normally related to financial services activity. Financial data generally interfaces from these systems with the general ledger and, therefore, when the level of data carried in the general ledger is not sufficient for cost and profitability reporting, accounting application systems must be accessed. The types of data normally extracted from these systems may include payroll expenses by responsibility centre, staff numbers and availability, allocation of fixed assets and direct expenditures relating to products and customers.

Although the fundamental data that is reported for Activity-based Costing by product is the same as in the organisation as a whole, generally the level of detail required for product reporting precludes use of the general ledger, cost accounting, budgeting and forecasting systems as the primary sources of data. Much of the information required for product costs and profitability reporting, can be obtained from a comprehensive financial database that holds items with some form of product indicator. This type of system is becoming much more common. Where this is not the case, however, data must be analysed outside the normal accounting framework, either manually or using other systems. In general, transaction processing systems are the primary source for statistical information and the sources of income, balances and cost data for product reporting could include the general ledger, cost accounting, budgeting and forecasting systems but will require statistical and balance data to enable the activity-based costs to be calculated. Care must be taken to ensure that all data sources used are compatible and that data will eventually reconcile with the financial results.

The core accounting system should include transaction records, which allow income to be captured or analysed by product. Without such a system, the identification of income by product can only be achieved by capturing income from the operational systems and feeding this data directly into the Activity-based Costing system. When this cannot be achieved, data can be obtained by means of statistical sampling techniques and is usually performed on a less regular basis. The information produced by these techniques is likely to be concentrated on the major products and services.

Customer information files

Although customer identification is generally available in transaction processing systems it is rarely, if ever, carried over to general ledgers. In addition, as transaction processing systems are rarely required to interface with each other, customer data is not related between the systems unless a customer information file system is in place. The existence of a customer information file is a key component in regular customer profitability reporting of any substantial magnitude. Some customer information file systems also have profitability reporting features.

As the data required for customer reporting is the most difficult to obtain – primarily because of the level of detail – the main sources of data required for customer reporting tend to be the customer information or operational application systems. Few, if any, cost accounting, budgeting and forecasting or general ledger systems maintain customer-level detail. Some sub-systems (direct billing systems) may contain customer-level information, but this data will be limited to those products and services for which direct billing takes place. Although it is always preferable to avoid manual data capture, some data requirements may preclude other means.

Customer profitability reporting normally relies on accurate product information and the availability of additional information by customer. This information is rarely available in any accounting system. The most accurate approach is normally to use product costs that have been amended by adding in those cost elements that can be directly attributed to individual customers. As such, reliable customer reporting may only be achieved if product costs have been calculated and it is possible to incorporate the customer-specific income and cost information with standard product costs based on usage statistics.

DATA AVAILABILITY

When initiating any Activity-based Costing system, rarely will all requested data be available exactly as the user wants. Therefore, compromises, assumptions and allocations may have to be made to attain the desired form of reporting. Sometimes, these will be permanent if it is deemed to be too expensive to obtain the desired level of accuracy. Often, even if the budget does allow for the necessary changes in the long term, temporary solutions must be found while system changes or other procedures are put in place that will capture the necessary data.

One common data availability issue arising in connection with an Activity-based Costing system is that data within the general ledger does not contain adequate detail. For example, general ledger accounts are generally established to reflect some categorisation of the organisation's assets and liabilities. It is unlikely, therefore, that the accounts will also reflect every other way in which it might be meaningful to report. More often than not, one will have to interrogate a particular application system for information at a more detailed level.

Another common data availability problem occurs when, within the application system, the data is not accumulated in a form that makes it easy to retrieve. For example, although information may be available in the particular application system with a certain value, the information is generally not passed to the general ledger in the level of detail required. The data may not even be accumulated in the system in the appropriate manner. To overcome this limitation permanently, system modifications would be required that may not be cost effective.

If data is to be reported for both actual and budget purposes, it is generally useful to have information at the same level of detail. Generally, budget figures are recorded at a higher level than is needed for reporting of actual costs. The budget may be prepared for key cost and income items within each cost centre and so may not incorporate sufficient detail to allow analysis by activity or cost driver. There are two solutions that enable reporting to be done at the same level of detail. First, budgeting can be carried out at the activity level. Several financial institutions are now considering moving towards activity-based budgeting. Second, the budgeted costs and income can be apportioned to the lower level of detail required according to some criterion, such as last period's actual data.

Two more substantial data limitations are when an institution does not have a responsibility reporting system and when balance sheet items are only reported with balances as of a point in time instead of averages over a time period. The lack of a responsibility reporting system can be overcome if allocations are based on samples, statistics, etc. This, however, will only be satisfactory for a once only or special analysis and will rarely be adequate for on-going reporting. In practice, most financial institutions now have some form of financial accounting or management information system by responsibility or cost centre. Some banks still do control all performance using the banking system, which will produce trial balance reports of operating income, costs and balances. Administrative costs in these circumstances are normally controlled by a separate purchase ledger, which may be operated by a finance or purchasing department. The lack of average balances in such a system substantially limits the reasonableness of rate and yield calculations. To obtain average balances in these organisations, major system changes would be necessary but these may or may not be justified.

The most common problem with regard to customer analysis is that all parts of the customer's relationship with the financial institution are not identified and therefore not linked together in a way that will facilitate reporting. This is not only a problem when reporting is initiated, but is an ongoing maintenance problem as the customer establishes new facilities and uses other products or services. Sometimes organisations have a customer information system, but it may not hold data on all the relationships that the customer has with every part of the organisation.

Although customer identification exists within most application systems, the information may be difficult to retrieve. Additionally, certain identifying factors, such as customer segment, may not be readily available or may require conversion routines to make it meaningful. As substantial systems changes are often called for in order to report needed information from the application systems, the solution frequently involves the development of a customer information file or other form of customer database.

REPORTING REQUIREMENTS

In addition to the specific data required for profitability reporting at the lowest level, a reporting system will require various calculation, accumulation and history retention capabilities. The contents of a specific report often require calculations of sub-totals, differences, ratios, averages, etc. from the data. In addition to the lowest level of activity, product or customer reports will usually require the accumulation of several tiers within one or more hierarchies, either at the detail or summary level. Reports may present data from any of the following: current period, prior period, year-to-date, same period last year, or rolling month or period (3-month moving, 12-month moving) basis. As part of the basic design of the system, it is important to ensure that all reporting characteristics have been considered. These should include consideration of the following:

- the level of reporting provided
- the definitions of reporting units used
- the level of detail used for reporting
- the degree to which sustaining or indirect costs are allocated to direct activity costs for reporting purposes
- the users of the reports
- the frequency of reporting
- the acceptable lead time to produce the reports after close of business for data collection
- the activity and cost driver definitions
- the need for summary reports
- any multicurrency reporting requirements
- integrity of actual data
- the report formats (the amount of information per page, the narrative, graphic and numeric presentation style)
- the maximum number of columns of numerical information shown on a report
- the reporting media used (paper, on-line reporting, floppy disc or microfiche).

In practice, users of the Activity-based Costing data should feel that the integrity of the reports is acceptable and should be able to reconcile the figures to the financial results. The reports may need to balance the need to be produced accurately with the need to have timely information, early enough after close of business. Indeed, it may be preferable to produce less accurate but adequate information in a more timely manner than completely accurate information too late to be useful.

It is important that the revenues, costs and balances reported reflect the same level of activity, in terms of the timing of cost and income flows. Income may, for example, be received on a quarterly or semi-annual basis, while costs are incurred on a regular basis. If data is reported quarterly, any fees or commissions charged less frequently should be included as accrued or notional figures in the reports.

SYSTEMS SOLUTIONS

Just as there is no one correct approach to using Activity-based Costing information, there is no one system that will provide that information. This situation exists not because software vendors are not interested in developing such packages, but because of the complexity and individuality of a good Activity-based Costing system and the need to obtain data from transaction processing applications, customer databases and financial systems. As with most profitability systems the two implementation options are the in-house bespoke development or the purchase of a package solution.

The main advantage of bespoke systems is that they can be constructed to closely match business requirements, both now and in the future. This usually implies a strong knowledge of costing techniques and systems analysis and is likely to require an extensive development period.

Software packages do exist but must be implemented and used in the most appropriate way to meet the specific needs of the institution. There are only a handful of suppliers who currently actively market Activity-based Costing systems that are not aimed exclusively at manufacturing companies, although this is changing all the time. Packages are available that can operate on mainframes and personal computers with varying levels of complexity and diversity of functions. The largest number of packages are produced for personal computer usage and offer fairly basic ranges of functions. Alternatively, there are large embedded, advanced costing systems that form modules within complex manufacturing and accounting systems, which are used in several large, international financial institutions. Package solutions are likely to mean compromises in terms of the functions you want and the functions available or paying for costly amendments to the standard system, but an advantage is that shorter development and implementation timetables can be achieved.

SYSTEMS MODULES

Any package or bespoke Activity-based Costing system should include several features. The following section contains a discussion of the features that may be included in an Activity-based Costing system and the modules in which these features may be found.

Features are of two basic types: cost accounting features relating to the

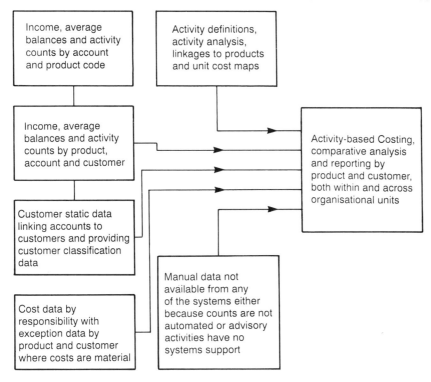

Figure 7.2 Systems solutions

Activity-based Costing requirements and profitability measurement and reporting features that add the income, balance and usage information to the activity-based cost analysis. While the requirements for a particular company will obviously be specific to it, it is possible to consider the basic functional modules of cost and profitability reporting systems. All requirements for cost measurement and reporting generally require some form of systems solution, as shown in Figure 7.2.

The features shown in Figure 7.2 may be modules of a separate cost and profitability system or may represent features of other systems that are accessed to pull together the data required for cost and profitability reporting. A general ledger system may be the key component of an Activity-based Costing system but will be unlikely to contain all data required for product and will be even less likely to contain the data required for customer reporting. Further, as there is an increasing need for more sophisticated features, the possibility that all of the capabilities will be found in a general ledger system decreases. The options at that point include either developing separate modules to accomplish the special processing for pro-

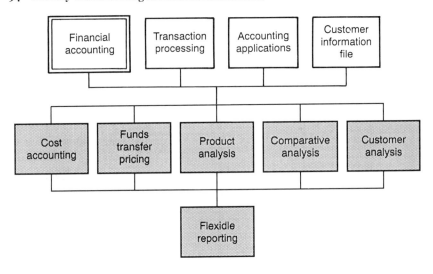

Figure 7.3 Modules to enhance general ledgers

ducts and customers not possible within the general ledger while continuing to use the general ledger for basic profitability reporting or developing a separate profitability reporting system that not only performs some of the special processing but is the primary reporting tool relegating the general ledger to the role of one of the principal data sources.

The modules required to enhance or amend a general ledger system will increase with the complexity of the required reporting. Each module identified in Figure 7.3 is discussed below. Those modules that perform processing activities are discussed in sufficient detail to establish their input, process and output operations.

Cost accounting

The cost accounting module may include the funds transfer pricing, transfer and allocation modules (discussed below) or may be a separate module that analyses the support and overhead costs to identify the unit costs to be transferred or the values to be apportioned through the allocation module. Inputs to this module could include, support and overhead costs, activity levels, definitions of activities and cost components to be included in activity-based costs. Processes to be completed within this module may comprise calculation of activity-based costs and identification of sustaining costs that may be allocated. Outputs from the module may include activity-based costs accumulated as necessary to meet reporting needs.

Funds transfer pricing system

The transfer of the costs associated with the use of funds and the credits associated with the providing of funds is one type of transfer that can become very sophisticated and complicated and, as a result, require a special system to handle it.

Inputs to this module normally include, interest rates used in transaction processing systems, balances by pool, activity, responsibility centre, product or customer, to which the rates should be applied and internal transfer rates to be used for each pool. The processes that take place within the module may include the calculation of the cost of funds and earnings credits, which should be applied to each balance.

Outputs from this module normally are the cost of funds and earnings credits that have been transferred and the activities, products or customers to which the debits and credits relate.

Product analysis

Product data is normally available either from the general ledger or directly from the transaction processing systems. The raw data must be analysed by product using the Activity-based indicators that link the core costs and activities to products and services by using cost drivers. This analysis must be performed and stored to enable further analysis and duplication of data relating to differing time periods.

The result of all data modules listed above will provide data by activity within responsibility centre or product that must be consolidated or stored. The information should, ideally, be stored separately so that the direct activity costs of fundamental and discretionary activities and the sustaining costs can be itemised on reports for the individual managers responsible for the cost or profitability. Depending on the number of components required, this may require a large storage capacity.

Inputs to the product analysis module normally include income, expenses, balances, volumes and interrelationships by product or activity. The process that takes place within the module is the quantification and calculation of costs and income by product or type of business. Outputs from the module are the standard or actual costs and revenues by product or type of business.

Comparative data

The most common comparative data used in cost and profitability reporting is budget data. Budgeting systems may be part of the general ledger or a separate system. Budget information is most frequently developed along the lines of organisation or responsibility centres and based on historical information. Budgeting systems for product and customer data are less common.

Inputs to a budgeting module normally include historical income, expenses, balances, volumes, assumptions and projections. The process that takes place within the module is the quantification and calculation of plans and budgets by activity within organisational unit or product. Outputs from the module are the budgets by activity within responsibility centre and/or product.

Another common form of comparative data is historical information. This information may be retained in the general ledger if originally captured there or may be maintained in separate historical data files. As with other data not in the general ledger, historical data may be maintained in the transaction processing or application systems.

Customer analysis

Where customer profitability reporting is required, the data by product must be further analysed by customer or customer group and must be consolidated and stored. As with other activity-based information by product and responsibility centre, it should ideally be stored separately so that the direct activity costs of fundamental and discretionary activities and the sustaining costs can be itemised on reports for the individual managers responsible for the customers concerned. Depending on the number of customers or customer groups reported, this may require a large storage capacity.

Flexible reporting module

The ability to report the results of cost and profitability measurement with desired flexibility and frequency and through the desired media will be required of any system to some degree. The degree of flexibility available will depend on the amount of information accumulated and stored in the modules discussed above and on the accessibility of the information.

OPERATIONAL CONSIDERATIONS

This section addresses the operations and maintenance factors that should be considered in developing or evaluating a system for cost and profitability reporting in financial institutions. Generically, it is not possible to estimate the cost of these various factors, but, in a specific situation the cost of operating and maintaining a system should be one of the factors that are considered, together with the value of the information to the company. Personnel costs, data processing costs and the cost of maintaining a system may or may not be material to the decision to begin its operation but whatever its cost there will be a limit as to the value of the cost and profitability information it produces. The following discussion of operational considerations is divided into three sections: ongoing operational considerations, special or periodic maintenance considerations and maintenance of information.

Operational cost implications

Whether a cost and profitability measurement and reporting system is mainframe computer-based, microcomputer-based, manual or any combination of these, data must be input into the system, processed and output produced, analysed and distributed.

For data to be input into a system, it must be accumulated either within automated systems or manually. If accumulated within an automated system, such as an operational processing system or the general ledger, there is the expense within the computer of accumulating, storing and, in some manner, reporting or interfacing the data. If accumulated manually, the costs of staff, including salaries, benefits, etc. must be considered.

Data may be entered into a system in several ways. It may be automatically interfaced or manually entered. Both cost and control factors associated with data entry must be considered. Costs would include those of computer terminals, telecommunications, computer storage and run time and people costs. As the level of manual data collection and input into a system increases, the risk of errors also increase. Balancing procedures and controls must be established to ensure the continued accuracy and integrity of both manual and automated data capture. They will generally be more extensive and even more so if the procedures are manual.

Unless a system is entirely manual, most processing costs are computer related. Depending on the amount of data to be processed, the efficiency of the system and the frequency with which the system is processed, the costs associated with the system will vary extensively. If a system is mainframe computer-based there may be times when access is limited or the ability to process the system will be controlled by other priorities. One advantage of the smaller computer systems is that they are often under the full control of the system's user.

Output from a system may take several forms. Traditionally, the most common form has been printed paper reports, with the associated costs of printers, paper and report distribution. The trend is towards more on-line access to the output or results of cost and profitability reporting systems. This access may be provided in many different ways with different costs, access and control implications.

There are generally staff responsible for the maintenance and analysis of any cost and profitability reporting system. Immediately after the generation of output from the system, these staff will spend some time reviewing the output and perhaps conducting additional analysis of the results. In order to be integrated into the decision-making process of the company, the results of the system must be available to be reviewed by appropriate managers throughout the organisation. All of these steps require time and therefore generate expense.

Frequency

Other concerns that affect the operation of a system are the frequency with which the system is run and the time constraints under which results must be produced. Obviously it is more expensive to operate a system monthly than annually, although it will probably not be 12 times as expensive. Additionally, if the results are required within two days of period end instead of, for instance, ten days, the operation of the system may be more expensive and there may also be a greater risk of errors. Regardless of the time constraints or frequency, the logistics of operating a system that relies on data from numerous sources must be thoroughly documented, including what data is needed, where that data comes from and where it goes, who is responsible for the data and the sequence in which the steps in the system's operation are supposed to occur.

Maintenance considerations

Companies and the systems that support the decision making in the company do not remain constant. Not only has the financial industry been changing over the past few years, but advances in technology are so fast that they have made systems of just a few years ago obsolete.

Several recurring causes of maintenance of cost and profitability reporting systems include changes to the definitions of activities, revisions to Activity-based Costing assumptions, changes within the organisational structure, new systems and products and growth within the organisation.

Regardless of the uses for or level of detail within the Activity-based Costing system, the data will have to be updated periodically. Maintenance of cost accounting data will depend on the level of detail required, the frequency of updates and the availability of data needed for the updates. After cost accounting data is revised, the entry into the system and confirmation of the data will require resources.

Changes within the organisation can take many forms and may affect the staff time required to generate cost and profitability reporting and may also require system maintenance. Often sufficient time is not available to make the needed changes to the system prior to the implementation of the change and so temporary solutions must be found. The most common change is that a company will reorganise itself and so require its cost and profitability reporting to reflect the new organisation. A system must be flexible enough to accept organisational changes. Sometimes historical data may be requested but must take into account the new organisational reporting structure and, in other instances, the historical data may need to retain the former reporting structure. Organisational changes are often effected with a new budget cycle and so the system must maintain two structures – one for actual and another for budget accounts.

When new application systems are installed, the impact on the existing cost and profitability reporting system must be considered. The continued availability of current data, the possibility of obtaining new, previously unavailable data and the maintenance or expansion of interfaces, downloading and uploading capabilities and so on must be examined.

In addition to new systems, new products will be offered by the company. The system should be flexible enough that the new products can be integrated into the system. As most cost and profitability systems interface closely with the general ledger system, the ability to recognise and handle new general ledger systems, the ability to recognise and handle new general ledger account numbers and responsibility centres should be available. The inability of the system to adapt to any of these changes will require substantial human intervention and, potentially, expensive maintenance to the system. Growth within the institution can mean that the system requires maintenance from several directions. First, size constraints may appear – numbers of units, products, activities, customers; levels and hierarchies for pyramiding of reporting; absolute size of data fields both for statistical and financial information. Second, as the company grows and as time passes, the retention of historical data may become impossible or very expensive. Growth of the company because of mergers and acquisitions can put pressure on a system and require considerable maintenance. Indeed, this may result in the integration of different and multiple charts of accounts and application systems.

There are other operations and maintenance considerations, too, but each situation will have unique characteristics that deserve careful evaluation at the outset. The important things to remember are that the development and installation of a cost and profitability measurement and reporting system are not the only factors to consider; the ongoing operation of that system and its future maintenance also affect the design and success of such a system.

SUMMARY

To summarise, the key requirement for all data in Activity-based Costing is that it be available at the lowest level at which reporting is to occur. The primary sources of data required for Activity-based Costing and profitability reporting are likely to include the general ledger, cost accounting and budgeting and forecasting systems, although it is unlikely that *all* data requirements can be met from these systems alone. The transaction processing, administration, risk management and trading systems may also provide information that will provide a more detailed analysis of usage and direct operating income and balances by product and customer. Care must be taken to ensure that all data sources used are compatible and that data will eventually reconcile to the financial results.

In addition to the specific data required for activity-based cost analysis, a reporting system will require various calculation, accumulation and history retention capabilities. The contents of a specific report often require calculations of sub-totals, differences, ratios, averages, etc. from the data. As part of the basic requirements of the system, it is important to ensure that all reporting characteristics have been considered.

Just as there is no one correct approach to using Activity-based Costing information, there is no one system which will provide that information. This situation does not exist because of the complexity and individuality of a good Activity-based Costing system, nor from the need to obtain data from transaction processing applications, customer databases and financial systems. While the requirements of a particular company will obviously be specific to it, it is possible to consider the basic functional modules of cost and profitability reporting systems that will apply almost universally. The features may be modules of a separate cost and profitability system or may represent features of other systems that are accessed to pull together the data required for cost and profitability reporting.

As part of the implementation of an Activity-based Costing system there are also operations and maintenance factors that should be considered. Generically, it is not possible to estimate the cost of these various factors, but in a specific situation, the cost of operating and maintaining a system should be one of the factors weighed in the balance together with the value of the information it produces to the company. Personnel, data processing costs and maintenance costs of the system may or may not be material to the decision to begin the operation of the system but there will be a limit as to the value of activity-based cost and profitability information, that is, simply, there is a point at which you are putting in more than you are getting out.

8 USING ACTIVITY-BASED COSTING FOR STRATEGIC COST MANAGEMENT

INTRODUCTION

Strategic cost management is an activity that is only just becoming popular in the financial sector. As the recession continues to affect Australia, America and, increasingly, Europe, the potential for mergers and takeovers among banks and insurance companies is growing and, hence, the need to focus attention at board level on the vulnerability of the profitability of the current organisation.

The executive team must understand the dynamics of the strategic cost and income profiles within the organisation and ensure that the strategic goals concentrate on improving shareholder value in both the short and longer term. This can only be achieved by also understanding the factors that affect the profitability of the various aspects of the business and the impact of changes on the market's perception of the value of the organisation.

In the following sections is a discussion of the determination of strategic direction and definitions of strategic cost drivers that are appropriate to strategic cost management. Then there is a demonstration of the use of Activity-based Costing in strategic cost management in the case study of North European Bank.

DETERMINING STRATEGIC DIRECTION

The fundamental objective of any organisation is to maximise its value to shareholders, yet, according to a survey in the United States, the great majority of banks lack the tools to achieve this objective. The value of a company to its shareholders can be defined as being the expected future worth of the organisation as estimated by those with an equity stake in the organisation. A typical financial institution will include a variety of business activities, some of which may be lossmaking in a bad economic environment. The management needs to know the impact on this value of each part of its business and how this is likely to change over time.

Strategic planning

Activity-based Costing can be used in strategic planning to focus attention on those factors that determine the expenditure on business activities. It can help assist in the prioritisation of alternative business activities, providing information relating to the cost/benefit to be derived from the particular businesses, geographic markets, products or customer groups and the potential benefit to be derived from future investment in particular strategic directions.

The main use of Activity-based Costing in strategic planning is in the identification of the flexibility within the cost base. This flexibility relates to the ability to utilise costs already incurred to gain competitive advantage and the knowledge of the incremental expenditure necessary to pursue a change in direction. Activity-based Costing can also be used in the development of value chain analysis as a means of breaking down the strategically relevant activities in order to understand the behaviour of costs. The value chain considers the cost/price relationship and ways in which value can be added to differentiate the products or maximise the price which can be realised.

Activities are defined as the types of business executed by the institution, normally analysed by market, either geographic (country or region) or type of customer (retail, high net worth, corporate or international). Cost drivers relate primarily to volumes of activity, service quality and technology.

Resource management

Activity-based Costing can be used to focus attention on those factors that determine the expenditure on key projects or activities. It can help in the cost/benefit analysis of individual projects and hence assist the prioritisation of alternative projects, managing resources to maximise the return on investment in line with the strategic direction of the institution.

It identifies the reasons why costs are incurred and relates these to the activities which take place. It can, therefore, be used to determine when costs should be incurred (such as, when to diversify and move into a new business area). This will enable management to manage costs on the basis of spending (the investment in a new market or business activity) not consumption (the operation of the business). For example, several financial institutions decided to invest in participation in the Sterling Gilts trading when deregulation took place in 1986. There are indications that not all organisations had identified in advance the significant costs associated with the implementation and operation of such a decision.

STRATEGIC COST DRIVERS

The rate of return to shareholders is based on the key factors that drive both cost and revenue for the organisation as a whole. These are generally of four types:

- the competitive position of the organisation
- the volume dynamics within the various business activities
- the cost/quality balance
- the degree to which technology is used to support the effective and efficient operation of the company and to assist it to respond to changes in the market.

Competitive position

The competitive position of the organisation is a function of its market share, product differentiation, market volatility, economic environment and the internal cost/income profiles of the various aspects of the business.

Market share can be measured at a variety of levels. A bank may, for example, have a large share of the retail market, but may specialise in secured lending to certain customer types and have a much smaller market share of depositary and unsecured lending business. Some markets are heavily dominated by a small number of participants. This may be a function of the nature of the activity, which may require heavy investment in order to even enter the market (life assurance, for example, where administrative expenses and claims arise before sufficient premium income has been accumulated) or may be caused by the degree of control exercised by the regulators (the Bank of England currently controls the issuance of banking licences in England, for example, and lays down stringent requirements that must be met before a licence can be obtained).

Market shares are measured and monitored regularly by the financial analysts and the position of the organisation in relation to the competition at corporate, business and product level can be easily identified.

All financial institutions have at least an implicit strategy relating to product development and product differentiation. They will be market makers, reactors or conservative. Market makers are normally the first organisations to initiate a particular new product or line of business. Midland Bank, for example, were the first bank to set up a successful nationwide telephone banking service in the United Kingdom (First Direct). Alternatively, reactors will watch the market makers carefully and decide whether or not to follow with a competitive offering. Conservative organisations will instead watch the market makers *and* reactors carefully but are unlikely to follow until the product or market has reached the maturity stage of its life cycle and all development risks have been eliminated.

Product differentiation may be as simple as repackaging or repricing existing products. Lloyds Bank, for example, were the first bank in the United Kingdom to charge for a credit card, other banks (reactors) following shortly afterwards. The Co-operative Bank is now actively differentiating by offering a credit card without a charge for its use.

Market volatility will also affect a company's competitive position in that a dynamic market will be more changeable and the strengths and weaknesses of the organisation in the market-place will influence its competitive balance. Corporate finance activity and the Lloyd's insurance market are two examples of volatile markets where the position of the organisation is influenced by the level and diversity of customer demand. The degree of specialism within the organisation means that its position in the market is governed, to a large extent, by the degree of customer demand for the specialist services provided. Competitive position will be affected by economic conditions to the extent that some organisations may be less influenced by the changes in interest rates, exchange rates, inflation, political factors and other economic effects than others. Also, those organisations that successfully predict and, hence, benefit from changes in economic conditions are likely to provide the highest value to their shareholders (at least in the short term).

The internal cost/income profiles of the various aspects of a business may influence the competitive position of the organisation, at least indirectly. The impact of several of the environmental conditions mentioned above will be a function of the cost/income profiles within the organisation. The inherent profitability and risk/reward relationships of the various aspects of a business should influence the corporate strategy of the organisation and, hence, its competitive position. It would be an unusual strategy for a company to aim to be the market leader in a business in which it was losing money in the longer term, but it could form part of an overall corporate plan to buy into a market, recognising that this involves making losses in the short term.

Volume dynamics

The volume dynamics within the various business activities must be known and understood by those individuals with responsibility for the enhancement of a company's value to its shareholders. Factors that should be considered include the key step costs, the impact of spare capacity, the impact of changes in product mix and the volatility of the underlying cost base.

Strategic changes in business volumes can have a significant impact on the dynamics of the cost base. The step cost principle assumes that the consequences of increases in volume are known and reflected in strategic decision making. One of the complications encountered in step costs in the financial sector is that incremental costs can be triggered by a range of volume changes and so are rarely linked to one, isolated factor. A new computer, for example, will be required to handle increases in volumes across a range of business activities and any individual increase may only have an incremental impact.

Alternatively, where spare capacity exists, costs are incurred and volumes can be increased at little incremental cost. Many costs in the financial sector are fixed in nature and so bear little relationship to business volumes in other sectors. Spare capacity provides an opportunity to provide an additional contribution to fixed costs and profitability but this must be managed to ensure that it does not cross the boundary and create instead additional fixed costs when the excess capacity has been used.

The product mix may have a significant impact on a company's value to its shareholders in that the balance of profitable and unprofitable products which must be maintained to ensure that the competitive position is retained or enhanced must be monitored carefully to ensure that profitability is maximised within the levels of capacity and cost profiles are attainable within the equity base.

Given the emphasis on fixed costs in the financial sector, cost volatility should not be a problem. Unfortunately, although a large proportion of operating and overhead costs may be fixed (at least in the short term), interest and claims-related costs can be very volatile and therefore require careful management to minimise exposure. There are many sophisticated techniques, such as simulation and duration analysis, that can provide detailed evaluation of the risk and volatility profiles of the interest-rated costs, but these are usually the domain of the treasury function and so are outside the scope of this book.

Cost/quality balance

The cost/quality balance is important in any strategic review and the drivers associated with the provision of all components of financial services can be considered in six segments of the value chain, as shown in Figure 8.1.

Product development
Cost/quality factors in product development relate to the balance between innovation, complexity and the need to maintain profitability in the short and longer term. Innovation in new products tends to involve new systems

Product development	Processing	Distribution	Risk management	Customer service	Marketing and sales
Innovation	Accuracy	Proximity	Quality of analysis	Accuracy	Speed of response
Product tailoring	Speed of response	Speed	Completeness	Speed	Brand names
Complexity	Speed of processing	Convenience		Service level	

Figure 8.1 Segments of the value chain

and procedures to enable staff and customers to understand the product or service and the associated benefits. Alternatively, product tailoring or product differentiation may be achievable quickly and easily in response to competitive action but may be perceived by the customer as less innovative. Innovation is expected in some parts of the industry – capital markets, corporate finance and, to a lesser extent, investment management are all areas where customers may be attracted by innovative developments within the organisation. There may also be a delicate balance that needs to be struck between product complexity and understandability. An example is a retail bank that simplified its range of current accounts, to three types of accounts with differing fee scales. Although market research suggested that the three types most closely matched customer requirements, neither the customers nor, to some extent, the staff understood the accounts in detail and preferred to stay with the traditional product types.

Processing

The key factors that affect the cost and revenue flows of transaction processing relate to the need to balance accuracy of processing with the speed and cost of the operations. The strategic goals of the organisation should include the factors that drive the operational efficiency of the processing of products and services offered and may differentiate the levels of accuracy, response and speed needed for different types of customers or levels of service.

Accuracy of processing should be an important factor in the management of any financial institution. Accuracy can continually be improved by means of the introduction of additional checks and controls, but these will affect both the speed of the operation and the costs associated with the processing of transactions. Technology can be used successfully to improve the efficiency and accuracy of processing but there may be costs connected with the automation of the operations, the training of staff and, possibly, customers in new techniques and procedures.

Speed of response and speed of processing are separate factors that will both affect the cost and quality of operational processing and may be defined differently for different types of customers and products. Speed of response may involve no more than confirming to the customer that his or her instructions have been received and are understood. This may be more important in private banking than in other retail financial services, but could form a means of product differentiation in the competitive market-place. Some customers, however, may be happy with a slower or less efficient response if it costs them less.

Speed of processing will include the completion of the operations necessary to ensure that the instructions received can be carried out effectively. Corporate financial services must generally be processed quickly as the value of large sums of money is dependent on interest rates and exchange rates, which vary over time. Penalty interest may be payable if monies are not made available on a timely basis. There may be an opportunity to differentiate the services provided by providing a cheaper service at a slower rate or by simply balancing response and operational efficiency. Customers may prefer a slower operational efficiency as long as they are kept aware of the progress being made. Some banks, for example, try to ensure that all transactions received are processed within 24 hours. Some customers may be happy to wait a week as long as they know what is happening.

Distribution

One key factor that could impact the cost and revenue of any financial institution is the distribution of the products and services offered. This may be analysed by type of customer, geographic location or type of distribution channel. Any analysis must, however, consider the proximity of the provision of the service (both relationship management and operational support), the speed of delivery and the convenience to the customer.

In general, proximity to the customer is less of an issue in commercial financial services than in retail financial services, because most corporations handle much of their financial business by using telephones, telex and fax machines. Only when original documentation is required (trade finance and final signed contracts) or when an account officer visits a customer will physical location become important.

Proximity and convenience of retail outlets may be important to retail customers, both because of the need to obtain cash from branches of the bank or automated teller machines (ATMs) and the need to obtain application forms or signatures for insurance or loans. When a bank or insurance company reviews its physical locations, it must therefore consider the impact of any closure or relocation on the retention, or otherwise, of its customers, both the actual customers with accounts or policies at that office and those who use the office as a convenient point of access to the organisation, even though their accounts or policies may be based at other offices.

Convenience of opening hours must also be considered. Some banks in Ireland have only recently decided to open branches during lunch-time. Banks in the United Kingdom open some branches on Saturday mornings or stay open later in the evenings (most branches, though, continue to close at 3.00 p.m.). The use of ATMs, the facility in some countries to obtain cash by using credit or debit cards in supermarkets and the emergence of telephone banking and insurance sales has, however, gone some way to reducing the customer's dependence on retail counter services. This does, however, have the negative effect of reducing opportunities to cross-sell other financial services. Branches do form the basis of useful sales outlets, enabling financial institutions to promote their services to a target market at minimal incremental cost.

The location of processing centres may also be an issue to the organisation. Economies of scale may be obtained by concentrating or grouping processing operations in regional or centralised centres. Any physical documents (cheques, debit and credit card vouchers, shipping documents, contracts, etc.) must then be transported to the centres for processing. The cost of distribution and the time factor associated with their physical transportation must be weighed up in the strategic review.

Speed of delivery may be an issue in commercial financial services, when documents must be made available at particular times. However, this is more likely to be an operational issue, as discussed above.

Risk management

Risk management may also form a key component of any strategic review of cost and revenue, both in terms of the quality of the analysis available to enable management to manage all types of risk and the completeness of the information.

Risks vary by type of business and type of customer and the strategy of each business activity should include a statement relating to the level of risk acceptable to the institution.

The cost of products and services will be affected by the risk premium that must be applied to counter the types of risk and the likelihood of the risk emerging. Risk is therefore a key cost driver for any financial institution and is affected by external factors and the corporate strategy.

Customer service

There are also factors that affect the level of service provided to customers which must be considered in the cost/quality balance. Some have already been touched on previously but should be related directly to the quality of customer service as a key to maintaining and improving the value of a company's stock to the shareholders, both in the tangible sense of maximising returns, as well as the intangible value of quality customer care.

Accuracy remains a key factor in customer service in any financial institution. It is important that the organisation is seen to take sufficient care with individual transactions to ensure that values, rates, accounts and value dates are accurate.

Speed of customer service relates both to response times and processing times. In most instances, speed of response may be more important than speed of processing.

Service levels relate to the quality of customer care provided and will vary depending on the type of customer. In general, the quality of care offered to a private banking customer should be higher than that offered to a standard retail banking customer and should bear some relationship to the level of fees and commissions charged. Service levels can be a key factor in differentiating products and services, both within the organisation and from those of competitors.

Marketing and sales

Speed of response to new offerings in the market-place will normally be a strategic decision. All financial institutions have at least an implicit strategy relating to their responses to competitive activity (either new products or changes in prices or rates). They may be market makers, reactors or conservative (see above).

Brand names are becoming more important in the retail financial sector as the degree of competition increases. Many institutions have differentiated their products and services by using different distribution channels and different service levels. BAT has Eagle Star and Allied Dunbar as retail insurance brands. Midland Bank packages its telephone banking as First Direct, thus differentiating it from its branch image. National Westminster maintains Coutts as a separate private banking activity, retaining National Westminster as its core retail business. Product differentiation may be as simple as repackaging, renaming or repricing existing products, but this can be very effective.

Technology

The degree to which technology is used to support the effective and efficient operation of any financial institution and the extent to which technological solutions assist the organisation to respond to changes in the market can have a significant effect on the value placed on the company by the shareholders. The factors that drive the costs associated with the use of technology are generally strategic in nature. Investment in technology has a material impact on the overall cost structure of any organisation.

The strategic cost drivers associated with technology include the extent and suitability of automation, the degree of innovation, the capacity utilisation and the level of integration.

Extent of automation

The extent to which the delivery of products and services can be automated and how suitable existing systems are to deliver the products and services demanded by the customers will have a significant impact on the cost base. The need to replace existing systems (which may have been built on old technology, using out-of-date design and delivering services that are no longer required) can have a material impact on short-term profitability. In the longer term it should *improve* profitability by providing more up-to-date systems that are geared to meeting the needs of the current customer base. It will, however continue to date and will eventually need replacing again.

Innovation

All financial institutions must be innovative to some extent. Retail organisations must ensure that they maintain or improve their market share by offering distinctive products and services. Capital markets, merchant banking and corporate finance operations must continually be innovative in creating products that meet customer needs. This need for innovative products and services must be reflected in the flexibility of the underlying technology to deliver, or at least record, the resulting transactions. This is not easy to achieve in practice. The need to have technology capable of delivering new products efficiently will therefore be a key cost driver.

Capacity

Systems must be capable of handling the peak transaction throughput within pre-defined time frames. Maximum utilisation may occur either during working hours (in dealing rooms, for example) or in the overnight processing runs (when accounting systems are maintained and daily transactions consolidated). This will inevitably mean that systems normally operate below full capacity.

Most financial institutions also require duplicate machines to ensure that business can be maintained if one computer develops a fault or loses power. These parallel machines are normally maintained at separate locations with full duplication of facilities. This inevitably results in significant excess capacity. This capacity can be utilised for any systems that are not time critical and can be halted if the facilities are required for the main banking systems. Many organisations use this capacity for systems development, but some are now offering it to other organisations with full facilities management.

Capacity utilisation is a strategic cost driver in that the step cost principle applies. Any increase in transaction volume will have an impact on capacity utilisation and may, therefore, result in the need to enlarge the systems environment. This may result in significant additional cost.

Integration

Integration of systems can result in more error-free, efficient processing because it reduces the need for the re-keying of data when transferring it from one system to another. Unfortunately, many financial institutions have a variety of systems that have been developed over a period of time which may be difficult to integrate. The organisation, therefore, that has integrated systems may have a strategic advantage. It is important that the organisation has a coherent systems strategy that does not change too frequently, which ensures that any developments can be integrated into existing systems.

CASE STUDY: NORTH EUROPEAN BANK

The North European Bank is an international bank with a variety of financial services that it offers to both retail and corporate customers throughout the world. It is about to undertake a strategic review of its operations with a view to planning its long-term growth and wishes to analyse the profitability of the various activities it undertakes. This should enable the directors of the bank to review the key factors that affect the strategic emphasis on the business activities and the components of the value chain and therefore to identify any areas of financial strength or weakness. Other studies will be undertaken in parallel to review its market position and vulnerability to competition in the markets in which it operates.

Background

The North European Bank is a bank based in the United Kingdom with a UK Banking Licence and operations in retail, corporate and international financial services (its activities are shown in Table 8.1 in the Appendix to this chapter).

North European Bank operates in ten countries: Europe (England, Scotland, Switzerland, Spain, Germany and the Netherlands), the United States of America (New York), Australia (Sydney), Japan (Tokyo) and Hong Kong and has a small offshore office in Jersey. It is organised into three geographic profit centres: the UK head office, Europe (excluding the United Kingdom) and the Rest of the World. The annual financial summary shown to the Group Executive is shown as Table 8.2 in the Appendix to this chapter. There is currently no regular analysis by business or customer type. The types of business by country are shown in Table 8.3 in the Appendix.

The income is easily analysed by business type from the chart of accounts and can therefore be obtained from the trial balance, as shown in Table 8.4 in the Appendix. Cost analysis would be more difficult but is necessary in order to analyse the profitability of the various activities undertaken and identify the key cost drivers that would affect the strategic emphasis on the business activities and the components of the value chain.

Approach

The approach to be undertaken is discussed in Chapter 3, The Activity-based Costing process. Its practical application to North European Bank is shown below.

Review and confirm requirements

The first step in the development of any activity-based cost analysis is to interview key users and identify information requirements, taking account of best market practice and experience. North European Bank wishes to have strategic cost information that will enable it to analyse the profitability of the various activities undertaken and identify the key cost drivers that would affect the strategic emphasis on the areas of business and the components of the value chain.

Define reporting entities

North European Bank has identified its business activities as shown in Table 8.1 in the Appendix. It is now necessary to define in more detail the products and services offered to the customers in each country.

DEFINE PRODUCTS AND TRANSACTIONS

Table 8.3 in the Appendix shows the areas of business by country and the income can be taken from the trial balance, shown in Table 8.4 in the Appendix. The definitions of the individual account lines in the chart of account may define the products or areas of business in sufficient detail to enable these definitions to be used as the basis of cost analysis. Further analysis at transaction level will not be required. The definitions of the income accounts are shown in Table 8.5 in the Appendix. These are the summary accounts used throughout the North European Bank Group. Individual accounts used in each country may differ in line with local practice, but must be capable of summarisation to these levels.

AGREE ACTIVITIES

Activities should be defined at a low enough level to allow the operations within a country to be related to the types of business agreed above and to enable significant differences in cost to be identified. Activities must also be defined for the support functions within the organisation as discussed in Chapter 4, Agreeing activities. The strategic activities to be used within North European Bank are shown in Table 8.6 in the Appendix. As the summary income account definitions relate mainly to customer types, these have been used to define the key business activities to be analysed. In addition to the areas of business, the supporting activities (generally sustaining in nature are also listed. It is expected that these supporting activities will relate primarily to the Group functions based in London, although they may be used to a lesser extent in the three profit centres and individual country centres.

DETERMINE COST DRIVERS

When the activities have been agreed, then the cost drivers can be identified. Where an activity is performed in a country or branch with direct responsibility for business delivery then the drivers invariably are the volume, value or quality of products and services undertaken. There will inevitably be some costs that are incurred for several business areas (joint costs).

Assigning these activities and the associated costs to individual business activities may be difficult.

Retail banking systems, for example, may be used by retail branches, corporate banking offices and private banking. The costs associated with operations, maintenance and development of enhancements may relate to any type of activity. At the strategic level it may only be necessary to identify any material costs that can be separately identifiable and to apply an arbitrary allocation of the costs based on usage. Obviously, given the scale of the retail banking activity, such systems would not be curtailed or eliminated without impacting on the retail banking business strategy.

Those activities defined as sustaining activities may have drivers that bear no relation to direct business-related activity (the drivers for North European Bank are shown in Table 8.7 in the Appendix).

IDENTIFY CUSTOMERS AND CUSTOMER GROUPS
Identification of customers and customer groups is not necessary in a strategic review of this type.

Commence data collection
It is important to begin data collection as soon as the data requirements have been defined. In this way, the data can be accumulated and stored until it is required for analysis and reporting. The data required for this strategic review within North European Bank may be obtained from a variety of sources. These include:

- transaction processing systems
- interviews with country managers
- financial systems
- other analysis (internal and external).

Develop an Activity-based Costing system
The Activity-based Costing system for North European Bank will be very straightforward, but the approach to the development will require the standard steps within the approach described in Chapter 3, The Activity-based Costing process.

DEVELOP REPORT REQUIREMENTS AND CHARACTERISTICS
The reporting requirements for North European Bank are fairly simple. It wishes to have one-off strategic cost information that will enable it to analyse the profitability of the various activities it undertakes and identify the key cost drivers that would affect the strategic emphasis on the business activities and the components of the value chain.

The analysis will be run by a joint team from the Finance Department and the Chief Executive's department and reports will be provided to the Management Executive on paper. Users will not be given access to the analysis and all data will be received and input to the analysis by the team.

The system's characteristics can be derived from these requirements as:

- a stand-alone system using a proprietary analysis package
- producing paper reports as required
- capable of being installed/maintained by financial analysts
- with in-built security to ensure confidentiality of data and reports.

SELECT AND INSTALL SOFTWARE, SET SYSTEMS PARAMETERS

Given the size of the organisation, the volume of data required, the nature of the project and the system's characteristics given above, North European Bank decided to use a standard spreadsheet package.

To ensure that the spreadsheet was designed and built in such a way that it could store and report the data efficiently, a data model was drawn that demonstrated how the base data would be used within the system. This enabled the analysts to develop the spreadsheet in an effective way. Many projects fail or take longer to develop the analysis simply because of lack of forward thinking and advance planning prior to beginning the system's development.

DEVELOP AUTOMATED INTERFACES, INPUT STATIC DATA

North European Bank has decided not to create automated interfaces and must therefore ensure that data is provided in a standard format to allow it to be input directly into the system without needing to be transcribed onto input forms.

When the basic parameters have been set up on the system, it is possible to load the static data. Static data includes the standard linkages between activities and cost drivers and the relationships between countries and business activities to ensure consistent reporting and summarisation. It also defines the report layouts and reporting hierarchies. For North European Bank, identification of the linkages at business activity and country level will be relatively easy, but the links between the support functions of Management, Personnel, Finance and Systems will be more difficult.

LOAD DATA AND TEST REPORTING CAPABILITY

Once the static data has been loaded and verified, the variable data can be input and the first reports produced.

Determine costs and revenues

North European Bank has identified the time taken on the activities performed within the Bank by interviewing individual country managers and reviewing with them the statistical analysis that has been summarised. The analysis included:

- number of accounts and customers, by type of customer
- income and balances by type of business activity
- number and grade of staff.

CALCULATE COSTS

The cost of the activities identified as a percentage of departmental time can be calculated immediately by taking the management accounts and using the departmental cost as a basis for the calculation (the resulting cost analysis is shown in Table 8.8 in the Appendix).

Funding costs are driven by the average debit and credit balances utilised by the business activities and the cost of obtaining or utilising the necessary funds. The rate applied to funds provided (cost of funds) or offered (earning credits) will be affected by the asset mix of the balance sheet and the funding policy of the organisation.

ESTIMATE REVENUES

North European Bank, as an international bank with a strong retail banking base, has access to a large base of customer deposits and can therefore match its book with relative ease. Individual business activities are treated separately and the Treasury function assigns rates to areas of the business as business is accepted. The income figures shown in the trial balance (Table 8.4 in the Appendix) are net of funding costs.

Review results and prioritise recommendations

As with any Activity-based Costing exercise, producing the approach is only half the battle, using the results in practice is more important.

PRODUCE OUTPUT

The report for North European Bank is shown in Table 8.8 in the Appendix. The report shows the costs analysed into direct costs (staff, premises, and systems-related) and the provisions (loan loss, insurance claims, sovereign debt and other loss provisions). The profitability report, shown in Table 8.9 in the Appendix, presents the income received, direct costs, provisions and profit before taxation.

REVIEW OPTIONS

The reports in Tables 8.8 and 8.9 in the Appendix demonstrate the profitability of the various business activities performed by North European Bank. They analyse the income, cost and provisions by business activity for each region of the world. This type of analysis can be used to focus attention on those activities that are highly profitable and that could perhaps be extended and those activities which are unprofitable and could be reduced.

The insurance activity, for example, seems highly profitable in a very competitive market. This confirms the strategy agreed five years ago, to invest in penetrating the retail insurance market in the United Kingdom and Spain. The investment in staff and marketing has been successful and the executive should now consider whether this performance could be repeated in other countries and how the positions in the existing markets can be consolidated.

Alternatively, international banking appears relatively unprofitable and the executive should consider whether this activity is necessary to provide a base from which to offer other services or how the profitability could be improved by reviewing the drivers underlying the costs. As shown in Table 8.7 in the Appendix, the strategic cost drivers that affect international banking activity include processing speed, distribution, risk management and customer service. Processing speed is affected by the quality of the operating staff and the systems used to deliver the products and services to international customers. The bank is unlikely to invest in systems developments for international banking, this activity is currently supporting using the retail and corporate banking systems and this is unlikely to change. The bank could consider the level of customer service provided. North European Bank should compare its service levels to those offered by its competitors and determine if service levels could be reduced to reduce cost or if, by improving the level of customer service, it could increase its prices and/or customer numbers. This would permit better use of resources and improved profitability.

RECOMMEND ACTION AND AGREE IMPLEMENTATION PLANS
It is important for North European Bank, then, to develop recommendations from the various options identified above, prioritise them, and agree plans for their implementation.

SUMMARY

The executive team must understand the dynamics of the strategic cost and income profiles within the organisation and ensure that the strategic goals concentrate on improving its value for the shareholders in both the short and longer term. This can only be achieved if corporate goals and strategic plans are based on an understanding of the factors that affect the profitability of the various areas of the business and the impact of changes on the market's perception of the value of the organisation.

Then the strategic cost drivers need to be considered in the development or review of the strategy and Activity-based Costing can then be used to assist in the review.

APPENDIX: NORTH EUROPEAN BANK

Branch networks and retail delivery	Banking operations and IT	Management structures/central functions	Corporate and institutional banking	Private banking and investment management
Branch networks ATMs Card services Insurance Leasing	Banking operations IT	Executive management Finance Personnel Other central functions	Treasury and capital markets Corporate banking Correspondent banking International banking services Developing countries Corporate finance Venture capital	Private banking Investment management Global custody Offshore trust business

Table 8.1 North European Bank – analysis of business activities

	United Kingdom	Europe	Rest of World	Total
Net interest income	1892	296	73	2261
FX income	257	49	113	419
Fees and commissions	1485	453	70	2008
Other income	119	89	10	218
Total income	3752	887	266	4905
Personnel costs	(1242)	(242)	(72)	(1556)
Premises costs	(180)	(68)	(47)	(295)
Systems costs	(338)	(16)	(5)	(358)
Other costs	(172)	(23)	(7)	(203)
Total costs	(1932)	(349)	(131)	(2412)
Profit before provisions	1820	538	134	2493
Provisions	(1426)	(224)	(55)	(1705)
Pretax profit	394	315	79	788
Taxation				(189)
Net profit				599

Table 8.2 North European Bank – profit statement 199X

Areas of business	England	Scotland	Jersey	Switzerland	Spain	Germany	Netherlands	USA	Australia	Hong Kong
Branch network	▨	▨	▨							
ATMs	▨									
Cards	▨	▨								
Insurance	▨				▨					
Leasing	▨				▨					
Treasury and capital markets	▨			▨		▨		▨	▨	▨
Corporate banking	▨			▨	▨	▨	▨			
Correspondent banking	▨							▨	▨	▨
International banking	▨				▨					▨
Developing countries	▨									
Corporate finance	▨									
Venture capital	▨									
Private banking	▨			▨	▨					
Investment management	▨									
Global custody				▨						
Offshore trust			▨							

Table 8.3 North European Bank – country analysis

Business activity	Country	Income
Branch network	England	1668
Branch network	Scotland	480
Branch network	Jersey	12
Cards	England	155
Cards	Scotland	45
Insurance	England	194
Insurance	Scotland	154
Insurance	Spain	154
Leasing	England	120
Leasing	Scotland	72
Leasing	Spain	108
Treasury and capital markets	England	19
Treasury and capital markets	Switzerland	7
Treasury and capital markets	Germany	12
Treasury and capital markets	USA	46
Treasury and capital markets	Australia	19
Treasury and capital markets	Hong Kong	32
Corporate banking	England	119
Corporate banking	Scotland	24
Corporate banking	Switzerland	68
Corporate banking	Spain	40
Corporate banking	Germany	56
Corporate banking	Netherlands	32
Corporate banking	Hong Kong	112
Correspondent banking	England	44
Correspondent banking	USA	12
Correspondent banking	Australia	12
Correspondent banking	Hong Kong	18
International banking	England	11
International banking	Switzerland	16
International banking	Spain	4
International banking	Germany	9
International banking	USA	5
International banking	Australia	2
International banking	Hong Kong	3
Developing countries	England	280
Corporate finance	England	120
Venture capital	England	135
Private banking	Jersey	22
Private banking	Switzerland	238
Private banking	Spain	130
Investment management	England	45
Global custody	England	17
Global custody	Jersey	10
Global custody	Switzerland	13
Offshore trust	Jersey	9
Offshore trust	Hong Kong	6
Total		4907

Table 8.4 North European Bank – excerpt from trial balance year ended 199X

Areas of business	Interest income	Foreign exchange	Fees and commissions	Other income
Branch networks	Interest income and interest expense relating to retail customer loans and deposits (including current accounts).	Foreign exchange income relating to exchange of currency and purchase/sale of travellers' cheques in branches.	Fees and commissions received for services offered through branches and other retail account related transactions.	Sundry other income received through branches.
Card services		Foreign exchange income relating to currency use of credit and debit cards.	Fees and commissions payable by merchants and card holders for use of credit and debit card services.	
Insurance services	Interest income received on the insurance reserves.		Premiums paid in relation to insurance policies sold through branches brokers and other agents.	
Leasing				Income received on leases to retail customers.
Treasury	Interest income received through management of assets liabilities and cash on behalf of the Bank.	Foreign exchange income received through currency management of the balance sheet.	Fees and commissions paid and payable in relation to management of the balance sheet.	Any other income received in relation to management of the balance sheet.
Capital markets	Interest margins received as a result of capital markets activity.	Foreign exchange income received as a result of capital markets activity.	Fees and commissions received as a result of capital markets activity.	

Table 8.5 North European Bank – chart of accounts income definitions

Areas of business	Interest income	Foreign exchange	Fees and commissions	Other income
Corporate banking	Interest income and interest expense relating to corporate and commercial customer loans and deposits (including current accounts).	Foreign exchange income relating to exchange of currency in corporate banking centres and on behalf of corporate account holders.	Fees and commissions received for services offered through corporate banking centres and other commercial account-related transactions including trade finance.	Sundry other income received through corporate banking centres.
Correspond-ent banking	Interest income and interest expense relating to balances held on behalf of correspondent banks.	Foreign exchange income relating to exchange transactions performed on behalf of correspondent banks.	Fees and commissions received for services performed on behalf of correspondent banks.	Sundry other income received from correspondent banks.
International banking	Interest income and interest expense relating to international customer loans and deposits.	Foreign exchange income relating to exchange of currency on behalf of international account holders.	Fees and commissions received for services offered to international customers including trade finance.	Sundry other income received from international customers.
Corporate finance			Fees and commissions received in relation to corporate finance and merchant banking advisory services.	
Developing countries	Interest income and interest expense relating to transactions undertaken with/ in developing countries.	Foreign exchange income relating to exchange of currency on behalf of developing countries.	Fees and commissions received for services offered to developing countries including trade finance.	Sundry other income received from developing countries.

Table 8.5   Contd.

Areas of business	Interest income	Foreign exchange	Fees and commissions	Other income
Venture capital	Net interest income associated with long-term debentures issued to venture capitalists.		Fees and commissions received relating to venture capital transactions.	Dividends and profits on sales relating to investments in ventures.
Private banking	Interest income and interest expense relating to corporate and commercial customer loans and deposits, including current accounts.	Foreign exchange income relating to exchange of currency in corporate banking centres and on behalf of corporate account holders.	Fees and commissions received for services offered through corporate banking centres and other commercial account-related transactions.	Sundry other income received through corporate banking centres.
Investment management		Foreign exchange income relating to conversion of investment balances between currencies.	Fees and commissions received for investment management and related advisory services.	
Global custody			Fees and commissions received for custodian services.	
Offshore trust			Fees and commissions received in relation to offshore trust management.	

Table 8.5 Contd.

Strategic activities
Branch banking
ATMs
Card services
Insurance
Leasing
Treasury
Capital markets
Corporate banking
Correspondent banking
International banking
Developing countries
Corporate finance
Venture capital
Private banking
Investment management
Global custody
Offshore trust
Banking operations
IT
Executive
Finance
Personnel
Premises
Regional management
Country management

*Table 8.6 North European
Bank – strategic activity list*

Services	Product development	Processing speed	Distribution	Risk management	Customer service	Marketing and sales
Branch banking	▓		▓			
ATMs			▓			
Card services				▓		
Insurance	▓			▓	▓	
Leasing			▓	▓		
Treasury		▓		▓		
Capital markets	▓			▓		▓
Corporate banking		▓		▓	▓	
Correspondent banking		▓				
International banking		▓		▓		
Developing countries				▓		
Corporate finance	▓				▓	
Venture capital	▓				▓	
Private banking			▓		▓	
Investment management	▓				▓	
Global custody		▓			▓	
Offshore trust	▓				▓	
Banking operations	▓			▓		
IT	▓			▓		
Executive	▓				▓	
Finance				▓		
Personnel			▓		▓	
Premises			▓			
Regional management						
Country management			▓			

Table 8.7 North European Bank – strategic cost drivers

Services	Direct costs			Provisions		
	UK	Europe	World	UK	Europe	World
Branch network	845	0	0	525	0	0
ATMs	50	0	0	5	0	0
Cards	18	0	0	70	0	0
Insurance	42	18	0	51	39	0
Leasing	83	47	0	68	72	0
Treasury	2	0	0	0	0	0
Capital markets	2	4	15	0	0	0
Corporate banking	57	61	18	31	96	53
Correspondent banking	16	0	14	0	0	0
International banking	25	21	14	4	4	2
Developing countries	35	0	0	630	0	0
Corporate finance	45	0	0	0	0	0
Venture capital	30	0	0	30	0	0
Private banking	4	61	0	12	13	0
Investment management	12	0	0	0	0	0
Global custody	5	2	0	0	0	0
Offshore trust	5	0	3	0	0	0
Banking operations	289	36	7	0	0	0
IT	146	16	5	0	0	0
Executive	12	0	0	0	0	0
Finance	21	3	3	0	0	0
Personnel	11	2	1	0	0	0
Premises	180	68	47	0	0	0
Regional management	0	0	0	0	0	0
Country management	0	10	4	0	0	0
Total	1932	349	131	1426	224	55

Table 8.8 North European Bank – strategic cost analysis

Services	UK				Europe				World			
	Income	Cost	Provision	Pretax Profit	Income	Cost	Provision	Pretax Profit	Income	Cost	Provision	Pretax Profit
Branch network	2160	(845)	(525)	790	0	0	0	0	0	0	0	0
ATMs	0	(50)	(5)	(55)	0	0	0	0	0	0	0	0
Cards	200	(18)	(70)	112	0	0	0	0	0	0	0	0
Insurance	346	(42)	(51)	254	154	(18)	(39)	96	0	0	0	0
Leasing	192	(83)	(68)	41	108	(47)	(72)	(11)	0	0	0	0
Treasury	3	(2)	0	1	0	0	0	0	0	0	0	0
Capital markets	19	(4)	0	15	19	(4)	0	15	97	(15)	0	82
Corporate banking	143	(57)	(31)	56	195	(61)	(96)	38	112	(18)	(53)	41
Correspondent banking	44	(16)	0	28	0	0	0	0	41	(14)	0	27
International banking	11	(25)	(4)	(18)	29	(21)	(4)	4	10	(14)	(2)	(6)
Developing countries	280	(35)	(630)	(385)	0	0	0	0	0	0	0	0
Corporate finance	120	(45)	0	75	0	0	0	0	0	0	0	0
Venture capital	135	(30)	(30)	75	0	0	0	0	0	0	0	0
Private banking	22	(4)	(12)	6	368	(61)	(13)	294	0	0	0	0
Investment management	45	(12)	0	33	0	0	0	0	0	0	0	0
Global custody	27	(5)	0	22	13	(2)	0	11	0	0	0	0
Offshore trust	9	(5)	0	4	0	0	0	0	6	(3)	0	3
Banking operations	0	(289)	0	(289)	0	(36)	0	(36)	0	(7)	0	(7)
IT	0	(146)	0	(117)	0	(16)	0	(9)	0	(5)	0	(40)
Executive	0	(12)	0	(12)	0	0	0	0	0	0	0	0
Finance	0	(21)	0	(21)	0	(3)	0	(3)	0	(3)	0	(3)
Personnel	0	(11)	0	(11)	0	(2)	0	(2)	0	(1)	0	(1)
Premises	0	(180)	0	(180)	0	(68)	0	(68)	0	(47)	0	(47)
Regional management	0	0	0	0	0	(4)	0	(4)	0	(1)	0	(1)
Country management	0	0	0	0	0	(6)	0	(6)	0	(3)	0	(3)
Total	3752	(1932)	(1426)	423	887	(349)	(224)	321	266	(131)	(55)	44

Table 8.9 North European Bank – strategic profitability analysis

9 USING ACTIVITY-BASED COSTING FOR PRODUCT COSTING

INTRODUCTION

Product costing is the commonest use of Activity-based Costing and often forms the basis for product pricing and product profitability. This is of particular importance in the financial sector where the increasingly competitive environment and the degree of product differentiation necessary to maintain or improve market share requires effective information relating to the costs of developing and providing products and services.

Increasingly, competition is coming from other financial institutions throughout the world and from other types of organisations expanding out of traditional marketing into financial services. New entrants may be focusing on gaining market share and, therefore, offering products and services at lower prices. They are likely to have new systems and procedures that provide effective and efficient processing. Customers are becoming increasingly aware of the differentiation in products and levels of service offered by the financial institutions. Institutions must therefore be aware of the impact on costs and quality of service of the need to meet customer requirements at prices that the market will bear.

Product costing and product profitability measurement uses operational and financial information summarised into a form that aids the decision-making process. Product cost and profitability information can be used to analyse and monitor costs, revenues and balances relating to defined products and services throughout the organisation. The activities in each department that are performed to support particular products or services and measures can be identified and their costs associated with each activity. The direct interest income, fee income, funding costs and operating costs then form the basis of a product contribution towards support costs and provide information that can support product pricing and marketing strategies.

Product costing can be based on Activity-based Costing and allows information to be made available by department, product and cost driver. Reporting can be achieved at the lowest level, by the identification and monitoring of costs that are within the control of the individual manager. It is, however, necessary to be able to attribute the costs associated with individual activities to products, product groups or operations necessary to sustain the basic fabric of the business. This creates a multidimensional reporting system that ensures that all costs can be analysed by organisational unit (cost centre or profit centre), activity or product, as shown in Figure 9.1.

PRODUCT PROFITABILITY

The changes in the financial services sector in the 1980s have had a significant effect on profitability, forcing financial institutions to change their focus. Reduced interest rate spreads and balances and the increased risk of loss on lending have raised the importance of non-interest revenues, while competitive pressures have made price or volume increases more difficult to achieve. Managers must take responsibility for the profitability of products or groups of products and must take control of the interest- and non-interest- related cost and income flows. Activity-based Costing will assist in the identification of non-interest-related costs, but will only support analysis of income and interest costs if products and the volume of activity are defined.

One of the most fundamental issues to be resolved is the identification and tracking of income by product. The types of revenue are discussed in detail in Chapter 6, Calculating costs. There will be wide variances in the capabilities of individual financial institutions to extract detailed income information from their transaction processing systems. If the amount and quality of information at the product level is limited, it may prove too expensive to enhance existing systems and, therefore, other options for tracking income will need to be identified.

In practice, most financial institutions will be able to track fees and interest that are debited or credited to customer accounts as they can be

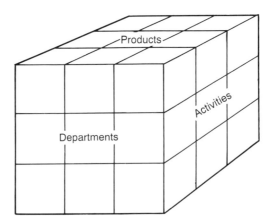

Figure 9.1 Multidimensional reporting

linked to products via the account number. However, income collected by means of cheque or cash (where an account number and hence a product cannot be clearly identified) will require either a change in procedures or the implementation of manual tracking processes. In many cases it will not prove cost-effective to try to track this income by product as it usually represents no more than 1 per cent of total income. This income should therefore be recorded as a pool item, say against a dummy product. The dummy product entries are essential in order to achieve a full reconciliation of total income to the total income figures in other profitability systems.

KEY ISSUES

The development of product costs may not always be as simple as it sounds. Operating expenses are not usually associated with products in the financial accounting ledgers unless they relate to a department that is fully dedicated to one product or service. Definitions of products and services are frequently not established and there may also be many products for which no single manager has ultimate responsibility. The identification of interest cost by product may be difficult because of the need to identify and analyse the cost of funds utilised over a period of time and the availability of data relating to average balances and rates by product. Claims can normally be identified by product or policy type, but may relate to products undertaken in previous accounting periods.

Associating operating expenses with products

Operating expenses may not be associated with products in the financial accounting ledgers unless they relate to a department that is fully dedicated to one product or service. This demonstrates the need for Activity-based Costing. By analysing the activities performed within the department, the individual activities can be aligned to products more easily than can whole departments. Where an activity is performed to support more than one product, then the cost can be included in the total product cost of all products that use that particular activity in ratio to the usage.

Definitions of products and services

Definitions of products and services are frequently not established. One of the most difficult questions for any financial institution to answer is what products do they sell. Each functional area of the organisation is likely to have a different perspective on this issue. For example, the sales force are likely to argue that the current account and money transmission services are one product whereas the operational staff are likely to view the current account and transmission business in terms of a number of different products requiring individual processing treatment. For reporting purposes, as we have seen, it is important to agree on product definitions that can be supported by the tracking of clearly identifiable income and costs but which also provide adequate sales and marketing information to the end users.

Another associated issue is the need to construct a product coding convention that supports the grouping of individual products into product 'families' (for example, lending, deposits, investments and advisory services) in order to satisfy product grouping reporting requirements.

Identification of interest cost by product

The identification of interest cost by product may be difficult because of the need to identify and analyse the cost of funds utilised over a period of time and the availability of data relating to average balances and rates by product. For asset-type products, such as overdrafts and loans, the financial institutions will need to calculate the cost of funding products and then to set this off against the interest paid. In essence, the objective is to calculate the *net* interest income position for each product. The net interest income figure, plus associated fees, represents the gross profit before deduction of product delivery and maintenance costs.

Similarly, for liability-type products, such as deposits and high-interest accounts, the financial institutions will need to calculate the income to be derived from use of each type of deposit. In this way, the net interest income position for each deposit product can be quantified.

Insurance-related products are generally supported by the investment fund, but in a bad cycle it is possible that the value of claims paid may exceed the reserves available for a particular policy type. In these circumstances, it would also be necessary to estimate the cost of funding the excess and to include this cost in the product cost calculation. In general, insurance funds must be allocated to products to match interest and investment income to the specific policy types in order to estimate product profitability.

Facilitating these calculations will require the construction of periodic average balances (monthly or quarterly depending on individual reporting requirements) for each asset- and liability-based product, together with an agreement on what funds transfer pricing rates should be used for calculating both the cost and use of funds for each product. The treasury staff of the organisation should be consulted regarding this latter decision.

Specific and general bad debt provisions

The majority of banks raise specific provisions at the individual customer level *without* allocating provision coverage against individual products. However, to analyse product profitability effectively, it is necessary to review profitability at three levels: gross profit, net profit after deduction of operating costs and net profit after deduction of operating costs and specific bad debt provisions. It may therefore be necessary to modify provisioning procedures to ensure that specific provisions are established at the product as well as customer level. An associated issue is whether it is appropriate to designate general provisions to individual products (perhaps in relation to risk/asset weighting).

Claims

Claims can normally be identified by product or policy type, but may relate to products undertaken in previous accounting periods. As profit margins are squeezed, actuaries begin to examine the underwriting assumptions on which their calculations are based. Many insurers are now facing problems because they have not conducted their business on a sufficiently con-servative basis and so are having difficulty meeting continuing admini-strative costs and claims received.

Statistically speaking, the storm that swept across Europe in October 1987 should only occur once every 300 years. Yet, in February 1990 a storm of similar force occurred, causing severe property damage. This is just one example of the increasing incidence of catastrophes that impact directly on the underwriting results of insurers and also increase the cost of buying reinsurance protection.

Increased technological developments in medicine also increase the inci-dence of claims on life assurance and health insurance as incidents can be traced back to insured risks (such as asbestosis). This tends to be most common in the USA. Policies that may generate claims relating to activities undertaken in past policy periods creating 'long tail exposure' give rise to further uncertainty on profit margins, such as employer's liability claims, relating to health hazards in the working environment, which may not be identified until years after the period of employment.

THE RELEVANCE OF PRODUCT COSTING

Product costing can relate to new product development or to the costing of the existing product range. Using Activity-based Costing as the basis of product costing can be done in all types of financial institutions, although the importance of detailed analysis of operational costs by product may be less relevant to those organisations where many costs are not related to activities but to interest cost or reinsurance cost. This former type of activity is more common in certain types of financial institutions, as shown below.

Retail banking and building societies

The large volume of relatively small analogous transactions processed in the retail market is an ideal environment in which to make effective use of product costing. The pricing of products tends to be market-led and the importance of so identifying loss leaders and unprofitable products can be a key to maintaining a competitive advantage.

Corporate and wholesale banking

Most corporate and wholesale banks offer a range of comparable products and services from each office. Product costing can therefore be performed either by office or by calculating average costs across a group of offices.

Products tend to be common and not tailored to meet individual customer needs, and hence, product cost analysis is important in order to focus marketing effort and aid the development of customer profitability analysis.

Merchant banking

Merchant banks offer tailored products for individual customers and are unlikely, therefore, to calculate standard product costs. They may, however, require some form of Activity-based Costing to assist in the pricing of individual services. In this environment, it becomes necessary to calculate component costs and to link cost drivers to individual services.

Private banking

The services offered by private banks are generally tailored retail banking products but may be extended to provide more specialist services, such as taxation and investment advice. They may calculate product costs for all standard products and provide a time-based unit charge for advisory services.

Capital markets

Capital markets organisations generally offer tailored deals for each large corporate client. The major costs associated with these types of products relate to the time value of money and the related interest and exchange rate risks. The operational costs associated with the delivery of these services are normally a small part of the overall cost equation. It may still be important, however, to manage the cost base, but not in relation to product costing.

Life assurance

Life assurance product costs constitute the actuarial value of the expected claim, the cost of administration and a projected profit contribution. The major component is the value of the expected claim and, hence, the importance of product costing may be brought into question. The margins on this type of product, however, are such that it may be important to understand the make-up and timing of the administration costs to ensure that the profitability of the portfolio reported can be justified.

A high proportion of the administration costs are incurred at the application and acceptance stage of the policy and at its maturity, claim or termination. The maintenance costs of receipt of instalment payments and issuance of statements are minor in comparison.

Product longevity also creates pressures on profitability, particularly on long tail business, where products sold in the past must continue to be administered and managed even when no longer sold. Insurance products tend to have a shorter 'shelf-life' than most financial services products, but product changes in long-term business have a higher cost impact than in short-term insurance. Existing policies must continue to be administered and systems support provided until their maturity. Any new product cannot, therefore, simply replace existing products, but will create the need for additional administrative systems support.

General insurance

General insurance products tend to be short-term products where costs are incurred at inception and on claim. Product analysis has traditionally been limited to calculating premiums less underwriting profit and has concentrated on premium and claims management. It has often included reinsurance analysis but, generally, has placed less emphasis on allocation of support and indirect costs, for costing and pricing purposes. The costs are left to the individual administration managers to control. The differentiation between costs of new and renewed policies can be significant. Product costing is important in this market as a means of monitoring the value of claims paid and ensuring that the premium rates remain sufficient to provide a profit contribution.

Reinsurance

Reinsurance activity relates to the sharing of risks associated with various types of insurance cover. The costs, therefore, relate to the risk of claim and the administrative costs of managing the portfolio. The definition of 'products' in this type of business can be difficult as the cover normally relates to either a batch of retail policies or a large individual policy. Product costing may be irrelevant as each transaction will be different. It may be more appropriate to identify the generic processing costs and apply this to each transaction and/or customer as appropriate.

Investment management

The importance of product costing in investment management depends on the type of clients and the service provided. Those investment management organisations, which focus on the large pension funds and investment trusts, will normally analyse the costs of the components of the services provided and estimate the costs of managing a fund by accumulating the components applicable to the particular characteristics of the portfolio and level of service required.

Those organisations that provide retail pension funds and unit trust services are more likely to calculate a composite product cost and use this to calculate the level of management fee that should be charged. In practice, however, the percentage management fee is generally defined by the market and the decision to be made may relate to the need to participate.

PRODUCT COSTING IN PRACTICE

It is very important to be clear about the use to which the product costs will be put as this may have a significant impact on the complexity of the exercise and the frequency, style and content of the reporting required. Activities must be defined at a level that enables costs to be attributed and which allows activity costs to be aligned to products or product groups or, alternatively, identified as part of the structure required to sustain the overall operation of the organisation. Costs of funds and the related earnings credits are prime cost components of all depositary and lending products. These costs usually vary over time and may have a significant impact on the price and profitability of the product base, so the development of funds transfer pricing can be an exercise in its own right. Where full absorption costing is required, the indirect costs must also be allocated to products. This can be a complex issue as these costs could have a significant impact on the overall product costs and hence on the pricing and profitability of the individual products. There are many grey areas in cost allocation. These relate mainly to the definition of direct and indirect costs. Activity-based Costing does assist in this area, as it attempts, by means of cost drivers, to align costs to products or product groups. Only those costs that exist to sustain the basic fabric of the business should remain to be allocated as part of fully absorbed product costs.

When the technical exercise has been completed and the product costs produced, the real work must start. It is very important that the information produced is used effectively. For new product development, direct costs provide an indication of the marginal costs of undertaking additional products or services. For product pricing and prioritisation of marketing and sales initiatives, both direct cost and total costs should be shown. In this way management can ensure that the prices at least contribute to indirect costs in order to ensure overall profitability and the product initiatives can be concentrated on the products that are profitable after indirect cost allocation.

CASE STUDY: PARKER BANK

Parker Bank provides an opportunity to highlight some of the problems encountered in the data collection and analysis of information for product costing in a small bank servicing retail and small corporate customers. It provides an example of a practical approach to the solution of some issues countered, such as the use of productivity information in activity analysis, the identification and allocation of systems and other central costs and the presentation and use of product cost information.

Background

Parker Bank is a small financial institution that has a head office and centralised processing environment handling transaction processing for ten branches. Transaction types include trade finance, money transfer, foreign exchange, lending, deposit taking and current accounts. The organisation concentrates on servicing retail and small corporate customers.

The management accounts for the current period are shown in Table 9.1 in the Appendix to this chapter and Table 9.2, also in the Appendix, shows the analysis of departmental costs in the central processing unit. The bank has a small production support unit within the management group that is responsible for production control and productivity improvement. It has now decided to develop product cost information based on an Activity-based Costing analysis.

Approach

The approach to be undertaken is as discussed in Chapter 3, The Activity-based Costing process. Its practical application to Parker Bank is shown below:

Review and confirm requirements

The first step in the development of product costs is to interview key users and identify their information requirements, taking account of best market practice and experience. Parker Bank wishes to have product cost information that will enable it to find those products and services that are profitable and should be accentuated and those that are unprofitable. It also wishes to differentiate the products and services that *must* be provided but which contribute to the profitability of the bank from those that do not make a contribution and so can be curtailed.

Define reporting entities

Parker Bank has identified its product types as being documentary services, payment transmission services, foreign exchange, safe custody, lending, deposit taking and current accounts.

DEFINE PRODUCTS AND TRANSACTIONS

It is now necessary to define the detailed products and services it offers its customers. The easiest way to determine the products and services provided is to consider the tariff or price list that is used in the branches. The standard tariff for Parker Bank is shown in Table 9.3 in the Appendix. This differentiates the products and services performed for personal customers from those performed for commercial customers and provides a basic list of the full range of products offered by the bank. It also identifies some products that are offered for which no standard price is quoted and those for which a minimum charge is quoted.

It may be necessary to define some products and services at a lower level than that quoted in the standard tariff as the cost profile may vary significantly within some of the products. Current accounts, for example, comprise account opening, issuance of cheque book, issuance of cheque card and may then include any number of payment and withdrawals within the branches, payments by cheque in other organisations, balance notifications, ATM usage, statement requests, standing orders, direct debits and so on. For any individual current account, therefore, the *costs* may vary significantly, even though the *revenue* may not.

AGREE ACTIVITIES

Activities should be defined at a low enough level to allow the operations within a department to be related to the various products and services agreed above and to enable significant differences in cost to be identified. In several circumstances, the activities necessary for product costing may be a standard product or service where that service is performed wholly within one department. Activities must also be defined for the support functions within the organisation, as discussed in Chapter 4, Agreeing activities (the activities to be used within Parker Bank are shown in Table 9.4 in the Appendix).

DETERMINE COST DRIVERS

When the products and activities have been agreed, then the cost drivers can be identified. Where an activity is performed in a branch or department with direct responsibility for product delivery, then the cost drivers invariably are the volume, value or quality of products and services undertaken. There will inevitably be some costs that are incurred for several products (joint costs). Assigning these activities and the associated costs to individual products, or even product groups, may be difficult. Counter staff, for example, perform activities relating to deposits, loans and current accounts and the costs of cash deposits, withdrawals, standing orders and statements could relate to any type of product. It is important, therefore, that the account maintenance system can identify the type of account to which the deposit or withdrawal relates and the source of the transaction (branch, ATM or another bank).

Those activities defined as sustaining activities may have cost drivers that bear no relation to direct, product-related activity (the cost drivers for Parker Bank are shown in Table 9.4 in the Appendix).

Cost drivers have been assigned to each activity. Some of the activities, such as training and counselling, can be linked to products on the basis of the percentage of overall staff time spent on the activities. Others, such as general management, must be allocated on an arbitrary basis. More specific activities, such as systems, credit management and marketing, can be apportioned on the basis of usage, as discussed in Chapter 5, Determining cost drivers.

IDENTIFY CUSTOMERS AND CUSTOMER GROUPS
Identification of customers and customer groups is not necessary in an analysis of product costs.

Commence data collection

It is important to begin data collection as soon as the data requirements have been defined. In this way, the data can be accumulated and stored until it is required for analysis and reporting. The data required within Parker Bank may be obtained from a variety of sources, including:

- loan processing system
- foreign exchange system
- documentary services system
- account administration system
- manual counts.

The source of each cost driver is shown in Table 9.6 in the Appendix.

Develop an Activity-based Costing system

The system for Parker Bank will be based on the reporting characteristics and functional requirements as described below.

DEVELOP REPORTING REQUIREMENTS AND SYSTEM CHARACTERISTICS
The reporting requirements for Parker Bank are very straightforward. It wishes to have product cost information that will enable it to determine

those products and services that are profitable, those that make a contribution and those that are unprofitable. It wishes to have this information in the form of standard reports and rankings and to be able to review the various components of cost that make up the product costs.

The bank also wishes to review the profitability of each product and will, therefore, need to consider not just the product cost, but also the associated income areas. It wishes to have this information periodically (at least once each year) with the facility to amend and rerun the reporting as necessary.

The system will be run by a joint team from the Finance Department and the Production Support Section and reports will be provided on paper. Users will not be given access to the system and all data feeds will be manual initially.

The system's characteristics can be derived from these requirements as:

- a stand-alone system
- producing paper reports including
  - profitability statement by product and product group
  - profitability ranking by product and product group
  - cost ranking by product and product group
- capable of calculating activity costs based on times and percentages
- capable of apportioning support and sustaining costs to products
- capable of reporting at contribution and fully absorbed cost levels
- capable of handling a minimum of 99 products, 200 activities, 20 departments and 20 cost types
- capable of being installed/maintained by financial and production analysts.

SELECT AND INSTALL SOFTWARE, SET SYSTEMS PARAMETERS

Given the size of the organisation, the volume of data required, the frequency of reporting and the system's characteristics, shown above, Parker Bank decided to use a standard spreadsheet package to develop their reporting system in-house.

To ensure that the spreadsheet is designed and built in such a way that it can store and report the data efficiently, a data model is drawn that shows how the base data is used within the system. This enables the data to be defined in systems terms and the spreadsheet to be built in the most efficient manner.

DEVELOP AUTOMATED INTERFACES, INPUT STATIC DATA

Parker Bank has decided not to create automated interfaces and must therefore ensure that data is provided in a standard format to allow it to be input directly to the system without needing to be transcribed onto input forms.

LOAD DATA AND TEST REPORTING CAPABILITY

When the basic parameters have been set up on the system, it is possible to load the static data (static data includes the standard linkages between activities, products and cost drivers and relates the regular variable data to the base data to ensure consistent reporting and summarisation and defines the report layouts and reporting hierarchies).

The data will only be finalised when data collection has started and costs have been calculated, so that definitions can be finalised based on data availability. For Parker Bank, this will involve the agreement of the activity/product linkages for operating departments, branches and support departments in order for product costs to be calculated at both the contribution and fully absorbed cost levels. Identification of the linkages at branch and operating department level will be relatively easy, but the links between the support functions in Management, Personnel, Finance and Systems will be more difficult.

Once the static data has been loaded and verified and the cost and revenue calculations described below have been agreed and input, the first period of variable data can be input and the first reports produced. The product cost reports for Parker Bank are shown in Table 9.11 in the Appendix. The reports show the costs broken down into direct costs (staff-, premises-, marketing- and systems-related) and the supporting costs (management, personnel, finance and other costs). The profitability reports shown in Table 9.12 in the Appendix present the income received, direct costs, contribution to supporting costs, supporting cost and net profitability before bad debt provisions and taxation.

Determine costs and revenues

As Parker Bank requires product cost and profitability reports, they will need to gather costs and revenues, although revenues will consist of standard tariffs and will take no notice of any discounts or waivers offered.

CALCULATE COSTS

Parker Bank has identified the time taken on the activities performed within the Bank in two ways:

- by using work measurement to estimate the minutes taken to perform an activity
- by estimating the percentage of time spent within a department on the activity.

The cost of the activities, identified as a percentage of departmental time can be calculated immediately by taking the management accounts and using the departmental cost as a basis of the calculation.

The costs of the activities for which minute values have been identified can be calculated in two ways – either by estimating the value of a minute in the relevant department by taking the cost of the department divided by the total available staff time and thus calculating the value of the time taken to perform the activity or by taking the normal volume of activity within the department and calculating the number of productive minutes within the department before estimating the value of a minute on which to base the cost of each activity (the advantages and disadvantages of each method are discussed in more detail in Chapter 6, Calculating costs).

In this example, the latter method has been used and the costs estimated by calculating the cost of each productive minute within the relevant departments, as shown in Table 9.7 in the Appendix. Activities within the support functions have been defined as shown in Table 9.4, also in the Appendix.

Many systems-related costs vary with the diversity of products offered, not with the volume of transactions. The system must have sufficient available capacity, however, to cope with the maximum number of deals that *could* be performed. It will not be sufficient to apportion the activities within the systems department to the products because many of the costs incurred are not related to activities but to other types of cost. The detailed expense report for the systems department in Parker Bank is shown in Table 9.8 in the Appendix. This enables the costs to be analysed by number of application systems, the management of storage, communications and networks and transaction volumes as shown in Table 9.9 in the Appendix.

There are still costs within the Systems Department that may be classified as sustaining costs and will be apportioned on an arbitrary basis, as shown in Table 9.10 in the Appendix.

Marketing costs within Parker Bank may be identified at two levels: corporate marketing and product marketing. Corporate marketing may be treated as a sustaining cost and will be apportioned on an arbitrary basis, as shown in Table 9.10 in the Appendix, while product marketing may be apportioned to product groups on the basis of actual expenditure and then to individual products as a percentage of revenue generated.

Funding costs are driven by the average debit and credit balances utilised by individual products and the cost of obtaining or utilising the necessary funds. Debit and credit products will, therefore, be treated differently in product costing. Credit products, such as loans, overdrafts and guarantees must be funded either from debit products, i.e. deposits, or by borrowing in the inter-bank market. The rate applied to funds provided (cost of funds) or offered (earning credits) will be affected by the asset mix of the balance sheet and the funding policy of the organisation.

Parker Bank, as a small consumer bank, has access to a large base of customer deposits and can therefore match its book with relative ease. The bank aims to control risk by means of a pricing policy and, therefore, use a mid-point funding rate for funds transfer pricing.

The cost drivers shown in Table 9.4 in the Appendix only relate to costs driven by activities and therefore exclude the marketing budgets, premises costs, capital expenditure and the related depreciation and other systems costs. Cost drivers can also be assigned to these cost types, as shown in Table 9.5 in the Appendix.

ESTIMATE REVENUES
As product tariffs are stated in the tariff list, no further analysis is necessary.

Review results and prioritise recommendations

The reports in Tables 9.11 and 9.12 in the Appendix show the cost and profitability reports produced by the system.

PRODUCE OUTPUT
The unit cost reports need to be compared with the standard tariffs to identify any products that do not contribute to sustaining costs and any that generate supra-profits. This analysis is shown in Table 9.13 in the Appendix. As can be seen from the report, most of the products are profitable, even those that are not totally profitable do contribute to sustaining costs. The current accounts and lending facilities need further analysis because the products for which standard tariffs are identified are not those for which costs can be estimated. The activities for which costs can be estimated must be accumulated in relation to the needs of the customer.

For any current account, the costs of the following services can be combined in relation to usage over one year as shown below:

- open account × 1
- set up direct debit × 3
- set up standing order × 4
- issue cheque books × 2
- issue cheque card × 1
- issue statements × 12
- monitor activities × 12
- close account × 1

The mix of activities will vary with the customer or type of customer.

REVIEW OPTIONS, RECOMMEND ACTION AND AGREE IMPLEMENTATION PLANS
It is important for Parker Bank to review the reports in detail, identify and recommend actions. The actions can then be presented to the users prioritised and plans agreed for their implementation.

SUMMARY

Product costing is the commonest use of Activity-based Costing and often forms the basis for product pricing and product profitability. This is of particular importance in the financial sector, where the increasing competition from other financial institutions throughout the world and from other types of organisations expanding out of traditional marketing into financial services is squeezing profit margins. Customers are becoming increasingly aware of the differentiation in products and levels of service offered by the various financial institutions. They must therefore be aware of the impact on costs and quality of service of the need to meet customer requirements at prices that the market will bear.

Product cost and profitability information indicates and monitors costs, revenues and balances relating to defined products and services throughout the organisation. It pinpoints the activities in each department that are performed to support particular products or services and measures the costs associated with each activity. The direct interest income, fee income, funding costs and operating costs then form the basis of a product contribution towards support costs and provide information to support product pricing and marketing strategies.

Reduced interest rate spreads and balances and the increased risk of loss on lending have increased the importance of non-interest revenues, while competitive pressures have made price or volume increases more difficult to achieve. Activity-based Costing will assist in the identification of non-interest related costs but will only support analysis of income and interest costs when products have been defined and the volume of activity is known.

The development of product costs may not always be as simple as it sounds. Operating expenses are not usually associated with products in the financial accounting ledgers unless they relate to a department that is fully dedicated to one product or service. Definitions of products and services are frequently not established and there may also be many products for which no single manager has ultimate responsibility. The identification of interest cost by product may also be difficult because of the need to identify and analyse the cost of funds utilised over a period of time and have available data relating to average balances and rates by product. Claims can normally be identified by product or policy type, but may relate to products undertaken in previous accounting periods.

In summary, Activity-based Costing will support the development of product profitability information, but may require information to be gathered from a variety of sources and will need to be supplemented with income data that is collated by product.

APPENDIX: PARKER BANK

£000s	Current month			Year to date			Full-year budget
	Actual	Budget	Variance	Actual	Budget	Variance	
Interest income	5177	5000	177	47 108	45 000	2108	60 000
Interest expense	(3434)	(3300)	(134)	(30 561)	(29 700)	(861)	(39 600)
Net interest income	1743	1700	43	16 546	15 300	1246	20 400
Arrangement fees	54	75	(21)	493	675	(182)	900
Commissions	640	600	40	5826	5400	426	7200
Total revenue	2437	2375	62	22 865	21 375	1490	28 500
Staff costs	(739)	(700)	(39)	(6722)	(6300)	(422)	(8400)
Premises costs	(206)	(200)	(6)	(1875)	(1800)	(75)	(2400)
Equipment costs	(464)	(400)	(64)	(4219)	(3600)	(619)	(4800)
Other costs	(115)	(150)	(35)	(1046)	(1350)	304	(1800)
Total costs	(1523)	(1450)	(73)	(13 862)	(13 050)	(812)	(17 400)
Contribution	914	925	(11)	9003	8325	678	11 100
Bad debt provision	(693)	(600)	(93)	(6270)	(5400)	(870)	(7200)
Profit before tax	221	325	(104)	2733	2925	(192)	3900

Table 9.1 Parker Bank – management accounts

Departmental cost report	Current month			Year to date			Full-year budget
	Actual	Budget	Variance	Actual	Budget	Variance	
Branches	(74)	(100)	26	(657)	(900)	243	(1200)
Documentary services	267	250	17	2455	2250	205	3000
Foreign exchange	96	100	(4)	931	900	31	1200
Payment transmission	90	100	(10)	946	900	46	1200
Loan services	1064	1150	(86)	9845	10 350	(505)	13 800
Contribution to fixed costs	1443	1500	(57)	13 520	13 500	20	18 000
Premises	(206)	(200)	(6)	(1854)	(1800)	(54)	(2400)
Systems	(695)	(660)	(35)	(6050)	(5940)	(110)	(7920)
Finance	(54)	(50)	(4)	(488)	(450)	(38)	(600)
Personnel	(36)	(35)	(1)	(326)	(315)	(11)	(420)
Management	(230)	(230)	0	(2069)	(2070)	1	(2760)
Profit before tax	221	325	(104)	2733	2925	(192)	3900

Table 9.2 Parker Bank – analysis of departmental costs (£ millions)

Products and services	Standard Tariff	
Bills		
Inward documentary/clean collections	£20 minimum charge	£1 per £1000
Payment of collections	£20 minimum charge	£1 per £1000
Discount of bills	£20 standard charge	
Sterling advance against bill/cheque purchased	£25 minimum charge	£1 per £1000
Sterling advance repaid	£20 standard charge	
Negotiation of exchange	£25 minimum charge	£2 per £1000
Currency loan against bill	£25 minimum charge	£2 per £1000
Outward documentary/clean collection	£20 minimum charge	£1 per £1000
Collection proceeds paid away	£20 standard charge	
Credits – inwards		
Confirmation of letter of credit	£40 minimum charge	£2 per £1000
Advising letter of credit without confirmation	£25 standard charge	
Amendment to letter of credit	£40 minimum charge	£2 per £1000
Pay/check documentation presented under leter of credit	£60 minimum charge	£2 per £1000
Payment of bills at maturity drawn on opening bank	£60 minimum charge	£2 per £1000
Credit bills negotiated (advances under acceptances)	Charge on application	
Clean reimbursements	£25 minimum charge	£1 per £1000
Credits – outwards		
Opening/issuing letter of credit	£40 minimum charge	£2 per £1000
Amendment to letter of credit	Charge on application	
Check documentation presented under letter of credit	£40 minimum charge	£2 per £1000
Despatch documentation presented under letter of credit	£25 standard charge	
Accept draft in respect of documents presented	£40 minimum charge	£2 per £1000
Payment of documents presented under letter of credit	£40 minimum charge	£2 per £1000
Commercial lending		
Fixed-rate sterling loan	Charge on application	
Fixed-rate currency loan	Charge on application	
Floating-rate sterling loan	Charge on application	
Fixed-rate currency loan	Charge on application	
Overdraft facility	Charge on application	
Foreign exchange		
Telegraphic transfer	£10 minimum charge	
Inward remittance	£15 minimum charge	
Mail transfer	£15 standard charge	
Journal entries (intercurrency account transfer)	£10 minimum charge	
Journal entries (single currency account transfer)	No charge	
Issue of sterling/dollar bankers' payments/ cheques	£15 minimum charge	
Forward foreign exchange deal	£10 minimum charge	

Table 9.3   Parker Bank – standard tariffs

Products and services	Standard Tariff	
Sterling transfers		
Effect payment by bankers' payment/cheque	£15 standard charge	
Effect payment by CHAPS	£15 standard charge	
Receive payment by CHAPS	£5 standard charge	
In-house funds transfer	No charge	
Receipt of payments over £10 000	£10 standard charge	
Effect cover payment, etc. by bankers' payment/ cheque	£15 standard charge	
Telegraphic transfer	£10 minimum charge	
Mail transfer	£15 standard charge	
Issue of draft	£15 minimum charge	
Effect payment by BACS	£15 standard charge	
Corporate banking		
Commercial current account	£10 standard charge	
Commercial fixed-interest account	£10 standard charge	
21-day notice account	£10 standard charge	
Safe custody		
Issue of standard corporate cheque books	£5 standard charge	
Issue of special corporate cheque books	£10 standard charge	
Lodgement of safe custody items	£10 standard charge	
Withdrawal of safe custody items	£10 standard charge	
Temporary withdrawal of safe custody items	£5 standard charge	
Provision of lists of securities held	£10 minimum charge	£1 per item
Provision of valuations of holdings	£20 minimum charge	£5 per item
Registration of death/probates, etc.	£20 minimum charge	£5 per item
Auditors' certificates	£30 minimum charge	£5 per item
Rental charge – per month	£3 minimum charge	£3 per item
Counter services		
Issue of personal cheque books	£2 minimum charge	
Issue of cheque cards	£2 minimum charge	
Personal – sterling pay in	30p minimum charge	
Cash dispenser	20p minimum charge	
Sterling withdrawal	£1 minimum charge	
Currency pay in	£5 minimum charge	£5 per £100
Currency withdrawal	£5 minimum charge	£5 per £100
Commercial – sterling pay in	£1 minimum charge	
Sterling withdrawal	£2 minimum charge	
Currency pay in	£5 minimum charge	£10 per £1000
Currency withdrawal	£5 minimum charge	£10 per £1000
Personal foreign exchange		
Travellers' cheques purchased	£3 minimum charge	£5 per £100
Travellers' cheques sold	£2 minimum charge	£5 per £100

Table 9.3 Contd.

Products and services	Standard Tariff	
Current/deposit accounts		
Personal current accounts	Charge on application	
Personal high-interest current accounts	No charge	
Personal deposit accounts	No charge	
Personal 21-day notice account	No charge	
Personal lending		
Fixed-rate mortgage	Charge on application	
Floating-rate mortgage	Charge on application	
Personal loan – secured	Charge on application	
Personal loan – unsecured	Charge on application	
Authorised overdraft	Charge on application	
Unauthorised overdraft	£10 minimum charge	£2 per £100

Table 9.3 Contd.

Activities	Cost driver
Documentary services department	
Documentary/clean collections	Number of inward collections
Payment of collections	Number of inward collections paid
Discount of bills	Number of bills discounted
Sterling advance against bill/cheque purchased	Number of advances made
Sterling advance repaid	Number of advances repaid
Negotiation of exchange	Number of negotiations
Negotiation repayments	Number of negotiations repaid
Currency loan against bill	Number of currency loans made
Outward documentary/clean collection	Number of outward collections
Collection proceeds paid away	Number of outward collections paid
Confirmation of letter of credit	Number of letters of credit confirmed
Advising letter of credit without confirmation	Number of letters of credit advised
Amendment to inward letter of credit	Number of inward letters of credit amended
Pay/check documentation presented under letter of credit	Number of letters of credit paid
Payment of bills at maturity drawn on opening bank	Number of bills paid
Credit bills negotiated (advances under acceptances)	Number of bills negotiated
Clean reimbursements	Number of clean reimbursements
Opening/issuing letter of credit	Number of letters of credit opened/issued
Amendment to outward letter of credit	Number of outward letters of credit amended
Check documentation presented under letter of credit	Volume of documents checked
Despatch documentation presented under letter of credit	Volume of documents dispatched
Accept draft in respect of documents presented	Number of drafts accepted
Payment of documents presented under letter of credit	Number of payments made

Table 9.4 Parker Bank – list of activities and cost drivers

Activities	Cost driver
Foreign exchange department	
Travellers' cheques purchased	Number of cheques purchased
Travellers' cheques sold	Number of cheques sold
Telegraphic transfer	Number of telegraphic transfers made
Inward remittance	Number of remittances received
Mail transfer	Number of mail transfers made
Journal entries (intercurrency account transfer)	Number of intercurrency account transfers made
Journal entries (single-currency account transfer)	Number of single-currency account transfers made
Issue of sterling/dollar bankers' payments/cheques	Number of bankers' payments/cheques issued
Set up forward deal	Number of forward foreign exchange deals
Set up spot deal	Number of spot foreign exchange deals
Payment services department	
Effect payment by bankers' payment/cheque	Number of payments by bankers' payment/cheque
Effect payment by CHAPS	Number of CHAPS payments made
Receive payment by CHAPS	Number of CHAPS payments received
In-house funds transfer	Number of single-currency account transfers made
Receipt of payments over £10 000	Number of £10 000+ payments received
Effect cover payment,etc. by bankers' payment/cheque	Number of cover payments made by bankers' payment/cheque
Telegraphic transfer	Number of telegraphic transfers made
Mail transfer	Number of mail transfers made
Issue of draft	Number of drafts issued
Effect payment by BACS	Number of BACS payments received
Loan services department	
Open account	Number of loan accounts opened
Set up direct debit	Number of direct debits initiated
Input loan application	Number of applications made
Obtain credit authorisation	Number of applications made
Obtain/verify security	Volume of security requested
Review facility	Number of loan accounts held
Monitor repayments	Number of loan accounts held
Debit account for loan fees	Number of applications accepted
Close account	Number of loan accounts closed
Custodian services (branches)	
Issue of special corporate cheque books	Number of special corporate cheque books issued
Lodgement of safe custody items	Number of items lodged
Withdrawal of safe custody items	Number of items withdrawn
Temporary withdrawal of safe custody items	Number of temporary withdrawals
Provision of lists of securities held	Number of lists requested
Provision of valuations of holdings	Number of valuations requested
Registration of death/probates etc.	Number of registrations made
Auditors certificates	Number of certificates issued
Rental charge – per month	Number of items held

Table 9.4 Contd.

Activities	Cost driver
Counter services	
Issue of personal cheque books	Number of personal cheque books issued
Issue of cheque cards	Number of cards issued
Interview customer	Number of interviews held
Personal – sterling pay in	Number of personal sterling deposits made
Personal – cash dispenser	Number of ATM transactions made
Personal – sterling withdrawal	Number of personal sterling withdrawals
Personal – currency pay in	Number of personal currency deposits
Personal – currency withdrawal	Number of personal currency withdrawals
Commercial – sterling pay in	Number of commercial sterling deposits made
Commercial – sterling withdrawal	Number of commercial sterling withdrawals
Commercial – currency pay in	Number of commercial FX deposits
Commercial – currency withdrawal	Number of commercial FX withdrawals
Management	
General management	Quality of management team
Membership of external committees	Number of external committees attended
Strategic planning	Level of detail required/market volatility
Contingency planning	Level of detail required/degree of organisational change
Marketing	Level of marketing activity
Public relations	Level of PR activity
Product development	Frequency of new product development
Relationship management	Number of key commercial accounts
Legal	Complexity of legal environment
Security	Number of branches
Organisation and Methods	Number of branches
Personnel	
Recruitment	Number of applications/recruitments
Training	Number of staff
Industrial relations	Number of staff
Appraisals/counselling	Number of staff
Payroll	Number of staff
Pensions management	Number of staff
Employee relations	Number of staff
Finance	
Accounts payable	Number of invoices paid
Bank reconciliations	Number of payments made/received
Financial accounting	Number of accounts payable/general ledger transactions/cost centres
Statutory and regulatory reporting	Regulatory requirements
Consolidations	Number of units to consolidate
Tax management	Complexity of tax environment
Property management	Number of properties occupied
Management reporting	Level of detail required/degree of automation
Budgeting and forecasting	Level of detail required/degree of automation
Capital appraisals	Number of projects appraised
Internal audit	Level of control necessary
Credit management	Number of loan accounts/applications
Cash management	Number of correspondent banking relationships maintained
Asset and liability management	Complexity of balance sheet structure

Table 9.4 Contd.

Activities	Cost driver
Systems	
Systems planning	Level of detail required/degree of organisational change
General management	Quality of management
Contingency planning	Level of detail required/degree of organisational change
Capacity planning	Number of hardware platforms/systems applications maintained
Computer operations	Number of transactions/level of service
Systems maintenance	Number of systems applications maintained
Systems development	Volume of development
Communications management	Number/complexity of communication channels
Storage management	Amount of storage required
PC support	Number of PCs supported
Network support	Size and complexity of the network

Table 9.4 Contd.

Non-activity costs	Cost drivers
Marketing expenditure	Number of campaigns/brands
Premises costs – maintenance	Number/age of offices/branches
Premises costs – depreciation	Value of premises owned
Premises costs – rental	Cost of leased premises occupied
Systems costs – maintenance	Number/age/complexity of systems
Systems costs – depreciation	Value of equipment purchased
Systems costs – rental	Cost of leased equipment

Table 9.5 Parker Bank – non-activity costs and their cost drivers

Cost drivers	Source of information
Number of inward collections	Documentary services system
Number of inward collections paid	Documentary services system
Number of bills discounted	Documentary services system
Number of advances made	Documentary services system
Number of advances repaid	Documentary services system
Number of negotiations	Documentary services system
Number of negotiations repaid	Documentary services system
Number of currency loans made	Loans system
Number of outward collections	Documentary services system
Number of outward collections paid	Documentary services system
Number of letters of credit confirmed	Documentary services system
Number of letters of credit advised	Documentary services system
Number of inward letters of credit amended	Documentary services system
Number of letters of credit paid	Documentary services system
Number of bills paid	Documentary services system
Number of bills negotiated	Documentary services system
Number of clean reimbursements	Documentary services system
Number of letters of credit opened/issued	Documentary services system
Number of outward letters of credit amended	Documentary services system
Volume of documents checked	Documentary services system
Volume of documents dispatched	Documentary services system
Number of drafts accepted	Documentary services system
Number of payments made	Documentary services system
Number of cheques purchased	Payments system
Number of cheques sold	Payments system
Number of telegraphic transfers made	Payments system
Number of remittances received	Payments system
Number of mail transfers made	Payments system
Number of intercurrency account transfers made	Payments system
Number of single-currency account transfers made	Payments system
Number of bankers' payments/cheques issued	Payments system
Number of forward foreign exchange deals	Foreign exchange system
Number of spot foreign exchange deals	Foreign exchange system
Number of payments by bankers' payment/cheque	Payments system
Number of CHAPS payments made	Payments system
Number of CHAPS payments received	Payments system
Number of £10 000 + payments received	Payments system
Number of cover payments made by bankers' payment/ cheque	Payments system
Number of drafts issued	Payments system
Number of BACS payments received	Payments system
Number of accounts opened	Account maintenance system
Number of statements issued	Account maintenance system
Number of accounts held	Account maintenance system
Number of standing orders initiated	Account maintenance system
Number of direct debits initiated	Account maintenance system
Number of accounts closed	Account maintenance system
Number of standard corporate cheque books issued	Manual count
Number of special corporate cheque books issued	Manual count
Number of items lodged	Manual count

Table 9.6 Parker Bank – sources of information

Cost drivers	Source of information
Number of items withdrawn	Manual count
Number of temporary withrawals	Manual count
Number of lists requested	Manual count
Number of valuations requested	Manual count
Number of registrations made	Manual count
Number of certificates issued	Manual count
Number of items held	Manual count
Number of personal cheque books issued	Manual count
Number of cards issued	Invoiced from supplier
Number of interviews held	Manual count
Number of personal sterling deposits made	Payments system
Number of ATM transactions made	Payments system
Number of personal sterling withdrawals	Payments system
Number of personal currency deposits	Payments system
Number of personal currency withdrawals	Payments system
Number of commercial sterling deposits made	Payments system
Number of commercial sterling withdrawals	Payments system
Number of commercial currency deposits	Payments system
Number of commercial currency withdrawals	Payments system
Number of loan accounts opened	Loan system
Number of direct debits initiated	Account maintenance system
Number of applications made	Loan system
Volume of security requested	Manual count
Number of loan accounts held	Loan system
Number of applications accepted	Loan system
Number of loan accounts closed	Loan system
Quality of management team	Management audit
Number of external committees attended	Manual records
Level of detail required in strategic plans	Manual records
Market volatility	External statistics
Level of detail required in contingency plans	Manual records
Degree of organisational change	Manual count
Level of marketing activity	Manual count
Level of PR activity	Manual count
Frequency of new product development	Manual count
Number of key commercial accounts	Manual count
Complexity of legal environment	Manual records
Number of branches	Manual count
Number of applications/recruitments	Manual count
Number of staff	Payroll system
Number of invoices paid	Accounts payable system
Number of payments made/received	General ledger
Number of accounts payable/general ledger transactions	System management system
Number of cost centres	General ledger
Regulatory requirements	Manual records
Number of units to consolidate	General ledger
Complexity of tax environment	Manual records
Number of properties occupied	Manual records
Level of detail in management reporting	Manual records
Degree of automation in management reporting	Manual records

Table 9.6 Contd.

Cost drivers	Source of information
Level of detail in budgeting and forecasting	Manual records
Degree of automation in budgeting and forecasting	Manual records
Number of projects appraised	Manual records
Level of control required by internal audit	Manual records
Number of loan accounts/applications	Loans system
Number of correspondent banking relationships maintained	General Ledger
Complexity of balance sheet	Manual records
Number of hardware platforms	Manual records
Number of systems applications maintained	Systems management system
Number of transactions and level of service	Systems management system
Number of systems applications maintained	Systems management system
Volume of development	Manual records
Number of communication channels	Manual records
Complexity of communication channels	Manual records
Amount of storage required	Systems management system
Number of PCs supported	Manual records
Size and complexity of the network	Manual records

Table 9.6 Contd.

Activity list	Unit time (mins)	Total volume	Total time (mins)	Unit cost (£s)
Documentary services				
Documentary/clean collections	2.9185	1334	3893	2.33
Payment of collections	3.5765	1313	4696	2.86
Discount of bills	13.2137	35	462	10.55
Sterling advance against bill/cheque purchased	6.1609	15	92	4.92
Sterling advance repaid	2.6709	31	83	2.13
Negotiation of exchange	5.8491	35	205	4.67
Negotiation repayments	0.7270	30	22	0.58
Currency loan against bill	7.2298	136	983	5.77
Outward documentary/clean collection	4.6192	386	1783	3.69
Collection proceeds paid away	2.0318	412	837	1.62
Confirmation of letter of credit	5.3647	226	1212	4.28
Advising letter of credit without confirmation	4.8026	443	2128	3.83
Amendment to letter of credit	3.0765	550	1692	2.46
Pay/check documentation presented under letter of credit	16.9044	483	8165	13.50
Payment of bills at maturity drawn on opening bank	14.4868	120	1738	11.57
Credit bills negotiated (advances under acceptances)	20.4214	21	429	16.30
Clean reimbursements	4.2817	430	1841	3.42
Opening/issuing letter of credit	8.6837	463	4021	6.93
Amendment to letter of credit	4.5054	0	0	3.60
Check documentation presented under letter of credit	6.9438	368	2555	5.54
Despatch documentation presented under letter of credit	1.6834	564	949	1.34
Accept draft in respect of documents presented	4.8290	426	2057	3.86
Payment of documents presented under letter of credit	7.5047	675	5066	5.99
Foreign exchange				
Travellers' cheques purchased	2.9890	769	2299	2.95
Travellers cheques sold	3.9588	934	3697	3.91
Telegraphic transfer	3.5470	1891	6707	3.50
Inward remittance	2.3950	1246	2984	2.37
Mail transfer	2.3370	755	1764	2.31
Journal entries (intercurrency account transfer)	1.4800	1899	2811	1.46
Journal entries (single-currency account transfer)	1.4800	390	577	1.46
Issue of sterling/dollar bankers' payments/cheques	3.1670	1062	3363	3.13
Set up forward deal	5.2050	214	1114	5.14
Set up spot deal	3.4700	5791	20095	3.43

Table 9.7 Parker Bank – activity costs

Activity list	Unit time (mins)	Total volume	Total time (mins)	Unit cost (£s)
Payment transmission services				
Effect payment by bankers' payment/cheque	0.7284	4041	2944	0.35
Effect payment by CHAPS	0.5593	6297	3522	0.27
Receive payment by CHAPS	0.5503	5426	2986	0.27
In-house funds transfer	0.5450	30446	16594	0.26
Receipt of payments over £10 000	0.6125	1372	840	0.30
Effect cover payment, etc.	1.8584	370	688	0.90
Telegraphic transfer	2.4056	779	1874	1.17
Mail transfer	2.2435	0	0	1.09
Issue of draft	1.6887	65	110	0.82
Effect payment by BACS	0.4560	63 504	28 955	0.22
Account administration				
Commercial current account		11 210	0	0.00
Commercial fixed-interest account		8052	0	0.00
21-day notice account		1422	0	0.00
Personal current accounts		46 521	0	0.00
Personal high-interest current accounts		8279	0	0.00
Personal deposit accounts		5049	0	0.00
Personal 21-day notice account		442	0	0.00
Open account	1.1240	2429	2730	0.54
Issue statement	1.3670	40 487	55 346	0.66
Monitor activity	0.5870	80 975	47 532	0.28
Set up standing order	1.6887	2192	3702	0.81
Set up direct debit	1.6887	1644	2776	0.81
Close account	1.9728	437	863	0.95
Safe custody				
Issue of standard corporate cheque books	2.5984	135	351	1.94
Issue of special corporate cheque books	3.5078	9	32	2.62
Lodgement of safe custody items	3.3140	1190	3944	2.47
Withdrawal of safe custody items	3.9452	1099	4336	2.94
Temporary withdrawal of safe custody items	5.1288	100	513	3.82
Provision of lists of securities held	1.7263	22	38	1.29
Provision of valuations of holdings	7.6536	1	8	5.71
Registration of death/probates etc.	6.2873	14	88	4.69
Auditors' certificates	8.8636	123	1090	6.61
Rental charge – per month	0.0000	5479	0	0.00
Counter services				
Issue of personal cheque books	3.1181	19 089	59 521	1.68
Issue of cheque cards	2.4945	4194	10 462	1.35
Interview customer	15.0000	2118	31 770	8.10
Personal – sterling pay in	0.7328	13 956	10 227	0.40
Cash dispenser	0.0192	29 848	574	0.01
Sterling withdrawal	1.1725	15 230	17 857	0.63
Currency pay in	1.4656	1568	2298	0.79
Currency withdrawal	2.3450	3991	9359	1.27
Commercial – sterling pay in	1.7587	9234	16 240	0.95
Sterling withdrawal	2.8140	2144	6032	1.52
Currency pay in	3.5175	192	675	1.90
Currency withdrawal	5.6280	426	2398	3.04

Table 9.7 Contd.

Activity list	Unit time (mins)	Total volume	Total time (mins)	Unit cost (£s)
Loan services				
Fixed-rate mortgage		728	0	0.00
Floating-rate mortgage		963	0	0.00
Personal loan – secured		672	0	0.00
Personal loan – unsecured		395	0	0.00
Authorised overdraft		829	0	0.00
Unauthorised overdraft		516	0	0.00
Fixed-rate sterling commercial loan		1027	0	0.00
Fixed-rate currency commercial loan		102	0	0.00
Floating-rate sterling commercial loan		4987	0	0.00
Floating-rate currency commercial loan		192	0	0.00
Commercial overdraft facility		6923	0	0.00
Open account	1.1240	75	84	0.91
Set up direct debit	1.6887	75	127	1.37
Input loan application	1.9784	75	148	1.60
Obtain credit authorisation	15.9286	75	1195	12.91
Obtain/verify security	7.2831	68	495	5.90
Review facility	10.9284	3856	42134	8.86
Monitor repayments	0.5293	9066	4799	0.43
Debit account for loan fees	2.3820	75	179	1.93

Activity list	% of department time	Total man years	unit cost (£s)
Management		57.00	
General management	10.59	6.00	16 420
Membership of external committees	1.77	1.00	2737
Strategic planning	3.53	2.00	5473
Contingency planning	1.77	1.00	2737
Marketing	5.30	3.00	83 210
Public relations	3.53	2.00	5473
Product development	1.77	1.00	2737
Relationship management	17.66	10.00	27 366
Legal	3.53	2.00	5473
Security	42.38	24.00	65 678
Organisation and Methods	8.83	5.00	13 683
Personnel		8.00	
Recruitment	6.25	0.50	2261
Training	25.00	2.00	9043
Industrial relations	12.50	1.00	4521
Appraisals/counselling	12.50	1.00	4521
Payroll	25.00	2.00	9043
Pensions management	6.25	0.50	2261
Employee relations	12.50	1.00	4521

Table 9.7 Contd.

Activity list	% of department time	Total man years	unit cost (£s)
Finance		12.00	
Accounts payable	4.00	0.48	2170
Bank reconciliations	4.00	0.48	2170
Financial accounting	15.00	1.80	8139
Statutory and regulatory reporting	7.50	0.90	4069
Consolidations	4.00	0.48	2170
Tax management	2.00	0.24	1085
Property management	5.00	0.60	2713
Management reporting	10.50	1.26	5697
Budgeting and forecasting	6.25	0.75	3391
Capital appraisals	2.00	0.24	1085
Internal audit	18.75	2.25	10 173
Credit management	10.00	1.20	5426
Cash management	5.00	0.60	2713
Asset and liability management	6.00	0.72	3255

Table 9.7 Contd.

Systems	Staff cost	Premises cost	Equipment cost	Systems cost	Other cost	Total costs
Computer operations	54	5	102	50	6	262
Systems maintenance	12	2	12	16	3	66
Storage management	14	8	108	33	1	140
Communications management	15	3	36	18	4	57
Network management	19	4	30	25	2	43
Support functions	76	14	12	6	8	127
Total systems costs	188	36	301	147	24	695

Table 9.8 Parker Bank – expense report for the Systems Department

Application Systems	Computer operations	Systems maintenance	Storage management	Communications management	Network management	Support functions	Total costs
Documentary services system	25	6	13	5	4		53
Foreign exchange system	20	5	11	4	3		44
Payments system	43	11	23	9	7		93
Loan system	29	7	15	6	5		62
Account maintenance system	63	16	34	14	10		138
General ledger	14	4	8	3	2		31
Accounts payable	6	2	3	0	0		11
Systems Development	61	15	33	0	0	60	170
Sub-total	262	66	140	42	32	60	603
Other costs				15	11	67	93
Total							695

Table 9.9 Parker Bank – analysis of systems costs

Sustaining activities	% time spent	Man years
Management		57.00
General management	10.59	6.00
Membership of external committees	1.77	1.00
Strategic planning	3.53	2.00
Contingency planning	1.77	1.00
Marketing	5.30	3.00
Public relations	3.53	2.00
Product development	1.77	1.00
Relationship management	17.66	10.00
Legal	3.53	2.00
Security	42.38	24.00
Organisation and Methods	8.83	5.00
Personnel		8.00
Recruitment	6.25	0.50
Training	25.00	2.00
Industrial relations	12.50	1.00
Appraisals/counselling	12.50	1.00
Payroll	25.00	2.00
Pensions management	6.25	0.50
Employee relations	12.50	1.00
Finance		12.00
Accounts payable	4.00	0.48
Bank reconciliations	4.00	0.48
Financial accounting	15.00	1.80
Statutory and regulatory reporting	7.50	0.90
Consolidations	4.00	0.48
Tax management	2.00	0.24
Property management	5.00	0.60
Management reporting	10.50	1.26
Budgeting and forecasting	6.25	0.75
Capital appraisals	2.00	0.24
Internal audit	18.75	2.25
Credit management	10.00	1.20
Cash management	5.00	0.60
Asset and liability management	6.00	0.72

Table 9.10 Parker Bank – sustaining costs

Products	Direct unit cost	Premises	Systems	Personnel	Other	Total unit cost
Documentary services						
Documentary/clean collections	2.33	0.88	4.23	0.23	2.59	10.25
Payment of collections	2.86	1.08	4.23	0.28	3.17	11.61
Discount of bills	10.55	3.97	4.23	1.03	11.73	31.51
Sterling advance against bill/cheque purchased	4.92	1.85	9.84	0.48	5.47	22.56
Sterling advance repaid	2.13	0.80	4.23	0.21	2.37	9.74
Negotiation of exchange	4.67	1.76	2.14	0.46	5.19	14.21
Negotiation of repayments	0.58	0.22	4.23	0.06	0.65	5.73
Currency loan against bill	5.77	2.17	8.16	0.56	6.42	23.08
Outward documentary/clean collection	3.69	1.39	4.23	0.36	4.10	13.76
Collection proceeds paid away	1.62	0.61	4.23	0.16	1.80	8.42
Confirmation of letter of credit	4.28	1.61	2.14	0.42	4.76	13.21
Advising letter of credit without confirmation	3.83	1.44	2.14	0.37	4.26	12.05
Amendment to letter of credit	2.46	0.93	2.14	0.24	2.73	8.49
Pay/check documentation presented under letter of credit	13.50	5.08	4.23	1.32	15.00	39.12
Payment of bills at maturity drawn on opening bank	11.57	4.36	4.23	1.13	12.86	34.13
Credit bills negotiated (advances under acceptances)	16.30	6.14	2.14	1.59	18.12	44.30
Clean reimbursements	3.42	1.29	4.23	0.33	3.80	13.07
Opening/issuing letter of credit	6.93	2.61	2.14	0.68	7.71	20.07
Amendment to letter of credit	3.60	1.36	2.14	0.35	4.00	11.44
Check documentation presented under letter of credit	5.54	2.09	2.14	0.54	6.16	16.47
Despatch documentation presented under letter of credit	1.34	0.51	2.14	0.13	1.49	5.61
Accept draft in respect of documents presented	3.86	1.45	4.23	0.38	4.29	14.20
Payment of documents presented under letter of credit	5.99	2.26	4.23	0.58	6.66	19.72

Table 9.11 Parker Bank – product costs report

Products	Direct unit cost	Premises	Systems	Personnel	Other	Total unit cost
Foreign exchange						
Travellers' cheques purchased	2.95	1.11	4.63	0.29	3.28	12.26
Travellers' cheques sold	3.91	1.47	4.63	0.38	4.35	14.74
Telegraphic transfer	3.50	1.32	4.63	0.34	3.89	13.69
Inward remittance	2.37	0.89	4.63	0.23	2.63	10.75
Mail transfer	2.31	0.87	4.63	0.23	2.57	10.60
Journal entries (intercurrency account transfer)	1.46	0.55	6.40	0.14	1.62	10.18
Journal entries (single-currency account transfer)	1.46	0.55	3.85	0.14	1.62	7.63
Issue of sterling/dollar bankers' payments/cheques	3.13	1.18	4.63	0.31	3.48	12.72
Set up forward deal	5.14	1.94	2.54	0.50	5.71	15.83
Set up spot deal	3.43	1.29	2.54	0.33	3.81	11.40
Payment transmission services						
Effect payment by bankers' payment/cheque	0.35	0.13	2.09	0.03	0.39	3.00
Effect payment by CHAPS	0.27	0.10	2.09	0.03	0.30	2.79
Receive payment by CHAPS	0.27	0.10	2.09	0.03	0.30	2.78
In-house funds transfer	0.26	0.10	3.85	0.03	0.29	4.54
Receipt of payments over £10 000	0.30	0.11	2.09	0.03	0.33	2.86
Effect cover payment, etc. by bankers' payment cheque	0.90	0.34	2.09	0.09	1.00	4.42
Telegraphic transfer	1.17	0.44	2.09	0.11	1.30	5.11
Mail transfer	1.09	0.41	2.09	0.11	1.21	4.91
Issue of draft	0.82	0.31	2.09	0.08	0.91	4.21
Effect payment by BACS	0.22	0.08	2.09	0.02	0.25	2.66

Table 9.11 Contd.

Products	Direct unit cost	Premises	Systems	Personnel	Other	Total unit cost
Account administration						
Commercial current account	0.00	0.00	1.77	0.00	0.00	1.77
Commercial fixed-interest account	0.00	0.00	1.77	0.00	0.00	1.77
21-Day notice account	0.00	0.00	1.77	0.00	0.00	1.77
Personal current accounts	0.00	0.00	1.77	0.00	0.00	1.77
Personal high-interest current accounts	0.00	0.00	1.77	0.00	0.00	1.77
Personal deposit accounts	0.00	0.00	1.77	0.00	0.00	1.77
Personal 21-day notice account	0.00	0.00	0.00	0.00	0.00	0.00
Open account	0.54	0.20	0.00	0.05	0.60	1.40
Issue statement	0.66	0.25	0.00	0.06	0.73	1.70
Monitor activity	0.28	0.11	0.00	0.03	0.31	0.73
Set up standing order	0.81	0.31	0.00	0.08	0.90	2.10
Set up direct debit	0.81	0.31	0.00	0.08	0.90	2.10
Close account	0.95	0.36	0.00	0.09	1.05	2.45
Safe custody						
Issue of standard corporate cheque books	1.94	0.73	0.00	0.19	2.15	5.01
Issue of special corporate cheque books	2.62	0.99	0.00	0.26	2.91	6.76
Lodgement of safe custody items	2.47	0.93	0.00	0.24	2.75	6.39
Withdrawal of safe custody items	2.94	1.11	0.00	0.29	3.27	7.60
Temporary withdrawal of safe custody items	3.82	1.44	0.00	0.37	4.25	9.89
Provision of lists of securities held	1.29	0.48	0.00	0.13	1.43	3.33
Provision of valuations of holdings	5.71	2.15	0.00	0.56	6.34	14.75
Registration of death/probates, etc.	4.69	1.77	0.00	0.46	5.21	12.12
Auditors' certificates	6.61	2.49	0.00	0.64	7.34	17.09
Rental charge – per month	0.00	0.00	0.00	0.00	0.00	0.00

Table 9.11 Contd.

Products	Direct unit cost	Premises	Systems	Personnel	Other	Total unit cost
Counter services						
Issue of personal cheque books	1.68	0.63	0.00	0.16	1.87	4.36
Issue of cheque cards	1.35	0.51	0.00	0.13	1.50	3.48
Interview customer	8.10	3.05	0.00	0.79	9.01	20.95
Personal – sterling pay in	0.40	0.15	2.09	0.04	0.44	3.11
Cash dispenser	0.01	0.00	2.09	0.00	0.01	2.11
Sterling withdrawal	0.63	0.24	2.09	0.06	0.70	3.73
Currency pay in	0.79	0.30	4.63	0.08	0.88	6.68
Currency withdrawal	1.27	0.48	4.63	0.12	1.41	7.90
Commercial – sterling pay in	0.95	0.36	2.09	0.09	1.06	4.54
Sterling withdrawal	1.52	0.57	2.09	0.15	1.69	6.02
Currency pay in	1.90	0.72	4.63	0.19	2.11	9.54
Currency withdrawal	3.04	1.15	4.63	0.30	3.38	12.49
Loan services						
Fixed-rate mortgage	0.00	0.00	0.00	0.00	0.00	0.00
Floating-rate mortgage	0.00	0.00	0.00	0.00	0.00	0.00
Personal loan – secured	0.00	0.00	0.00	0.00	0.00	0.00
Personal loan – unsecured	0.00	0.00	0.00	0.00	0.00	0.00
Authorised overdraft	0.00	0.00	0.00	0.00	0.00	0.00
Unauthorised overdraft	0.00	0.00	0.00	0.00	0.00	0.00
Fixed-rate sterling commercial loan	0.00	0.00	0.00	0.00	0.00	0.00
Fixed-rate currency commercial loan	0.00	0.00	0.00	0.00	0.00	0.00
Floating-rate sterling commercial loan	0.00	0.00	0.00	0.00	0.00	0.00
Floating-rate currency commercial loan	0.00	0.00	0.00	0.00	0.00	0.00
Commercial overdraft facility	0.00	0.00	0.00	0.00	0.00	0.00
Open account	0.91	0.34	1.77	0.09	1.01	4.12
Set up direct debit	1.37	0.52	1.77	0.13	1.52	5.30
Input loan application	1.60	0.60	5.62	0.16	1.78	9.76
Obtain credit authorisation	12.91	4.86	5.62	1.26	14.35	38.99
Obtain/verify security	5.90	2.22	0.00	0.58	6.56	15.26
Review facility	8.86	3.34	5.62	0.86	9.84	28.51
Monitor repayments	0.43	0.16	5.62	0.04	0.48	6.72
Debit account for loan fees	1.93	0.73	1.77	0.19	2.15	6.76

Product income	Total volume	Income	Unit cost	Total cost	Profit
Documentary services					
Documentary/clean collections	1334	36 018	10.25	13 677	22 341
Payment of collections	1313	32 825	11.61	15 245	17 580
Discount of bills	35	1260	31.51	1103	157
Sterling advance against bill/cheque purchased	15	705	22.56	338	367
Sterling advance repaid	31	620	9.74	302	318
Negotiation of exchange	35	1505	14.21	498	1007
Negotiation repayments	30	600	5.73	172	428
Currency loan against bill	136	8024	23.08	3139	4885
Outward documentary/clean collection	386	16 212	13.76	5313	10 899
Collection proceeds paid away	412	8652	8.42	3470	5182
Confirmation of letter of credit	226	10 848	13.21	2986	7862
Advising letter of credit without confirmation	443	11 075	12.05	5340	5735
Amendment to letter of credit	550	13 200	8.49	4670	8530
Pay/check documentation presented under letter of credit	483	38 157	39.12	18 897	19 260
Payment of bills at maturity drawn on opening bank	120	8040	34.13	4096	3944
Credit bills negotiated (advances under acceptances)	21	1743	44.30	930	813
Clean reimbursements	430	14 620	13.07	5619	9001
Opening/issuing letter of credit	463	18 983	20.07	9291	9692
Amendment to letter of credit	0	0	11.44	0	0
Check documentation presented under letter of credit	368	16 928	16.47	6063	10 865
Despatch documentation presented under letter of credit	564	14 100	5.61	3167	10 933
Accept draft in respect of documents presented	426	16 188	14.20	6048	10 140
Payment of documents presented under letter of credit	675	32 400	19.72	13 311	19 089

Table 9.12 Parker Bank – profitability report

Product income	Total volume	Income	Unit cost	Total cost	Profit
Foreign exchange					
Travellers' cheques purchased	769	1923	12.26	9430	(7508)
Travellers' cheques sold	934	1401	14.74	13 767	(12 366)
Telegraphic transfer	1891	51 057	13.69	25 885	25 172
Inward remittance	1246	18 690	10.75	13 390	5300
Mail transfer	755	11 325	10.60	8002	3323
Journal entries (intercurrency account transfer)	1899	22 788	10.18	19 323	3465
Journal entries (single-currency account transfer)	390	0	7.63	2977	(2977)
Issue of sterling/dollar bankers' payments/ cheques	1062	26 550	12.72	13 506	13 044
Set up forward deal	214	6634	15.83	3389	3245
Set up spot deal	5791	0	11.40	66 039	(66 039)
Payment transmission services					
Effect payment by bankers' payment/cheque	4041	24 246	3.00	12 135	12 111
Effect payment by CHAPS	6297	31 485	2.79	17 572	13 913
Receive payment by CHAPS	5426	27 130	2.78	15 080	12 050
In-house funds transfer	30 446	0	4.54	138 186	(138 186)
Receipt of payments over £10 000	1372	13 720	2.86	3920	9800
Effect cover payment, etc. by bankers' payment/cheque	370	0	4.42	1636	(1636)
Telegraphic transfer	779	21 033	5.11	3980	17 053
Mail transfer	0	0	4.91	0	0
Issue of draft	65	910	4.21	274	636
Effect payment by BACS	63 504	0	2.66	168 968	(168 968)

Table 9.12 Contd.

Product income	Total volume	Income	Unit cost	Total cost	Profit
Account administration					
Commercial current account	11 210	103 998	1.77	19 798	84 200
Commercial fixed-interest account	8052	160 127	1.77	14 221	145 907
21-day notice account	1422	26 031	1.77	2511	23 520
Personal current accounts	46 521	151 100	1.77	82 161	68 939
Personal high-interest current accounts	8279	99 261	1.77	14 622	84 639
Personal deposit accounts	5049	219 382	1.77	8917	210 464
Personal 21-day notice account	442	9763	0.00	0	9763
Open account	2429	0	1.40	3392	(3392)
Issue statement	40 487	0	1.70	68 753	(68 753)
Monitor activity	80 975	0	0.73	59 046	(59 046)
Set up standing order	2192	0	2.10	4598	(4598)
Set up direct debit	1644	0	2.10	3449	(3449)
Close account	437	0	2.45	1072	(1072)
Safe custody					
Issue of standard corporate cheque books	135	675	5.01	676	(1)
Issue of special corporate cheque books	9	45	6.76	61	(16)
Lodgement of safe custody items	1190	11 900	6.39	7602	4298
Withdrawal of safe custody items	1099	10 990	7.60	8358	2632
Temporary withdrawal of safe custody items	100	500	9.89	989	(489)
Provision of lists of securities held	22	550	3.33	73	477
Provision of valuations of holdings	1	47	14.75	15	32
Registration of death/probates, etc.	14	490	12.12	170	320
Auditors' certificates	123	5781	17.09	2102	3679
Rental charge – per month	5479	13 698	0.00	0	13 698

Table 9.12 Contd.

Product income	Total volume	Income	Unit cost	Total cost	Profit
Counter services					
Issue of personal cheque books	19 089	0	4.36	83 141	(83 141)
Issue of cheque cards	4194	0	3.48	14 613	(14 613)
Interview customer	2118	0	20.95	44 377	(44 377)
Personal – sterling pay in	13 956	0	3.11	43 427	(43 427)
Cash dispenser	29 848	0	2.11	63 125	(63 125)
Sterling withdrawal	15 230	0	3.73	56 744	(56 744)
Currency pay in	1568	7840	6.68	10 469	(2629)
Currency withdrawal	3991	19 955	7.90	31 548	(11 593)
Commercial – sterling pay in	9234	0	4.54	41 966	(41 966)
Sterling withdrawal	214	0	6.02	12 902	(12 902)
Currency pay in	192	1920	9.54	1832	88
Currency withdrawal	426	4260	12.49	5321	(1061)
Loan services					
Fixed-rate mortgage	728	29 674	0.00	0	29 674
Floating-rate mortgage	963	83 074	0.00	0	83 074
Personal loan – secured	672	24 583	0.00	0	24 583
Personal loan – unsecured	395	7287	0.00	0	7287
Authorised overdraft	829	4768	0.00	0	4768
Unauthorised overdraft	516	14 764	0.00	0	14 764
Fixed-rate sterling commercial loan	1027	69 870	0.00	0	69 870
Fixed-rate currency commercial loan	102	6517	0.00	0	6517
Floating-rate sterling commercial loan	4987	508 921	0.00	0	508 921
Floating-rate currency commercial loan	192	12 299	0.00	0	12 299

Table 9.12 Contd.

Product income	Total volume	Income	Unit cost	Total cost	Profit
Commercial overdraft facility	6923	386 347	0.00	0	386 347
Open account	75	41 250	4.12	309	40 941
Set up direct debit	75	0	5.30	398	(398)
Input loan application	75	0	9.76	732	(732)
Obtain credit authorisation	75	0	38.99	2924	(2924)
Obtain/verify security	68	0	15.26	1038	(1038)
Review facility	3856	0	28.51	109 939	(109 939)
Monitor repayments	9066	0	6.72	60 965	(60 965)
Debit account for loan fees	75	0	6.76	507	(507)

Table 9.12 Contd.

Products and services	Standard Tariff	Direct unit cost	Total unit cost	Average profit
Documentary/clean collections	£20 minimum charge	2.33	10.25	9.75
Payment of collections	£20 minimum charge	2.86	11.61	8.39
Discount of bills	£20 standard charge	10.55	31.51	(11.51)
Sterling advance against bill/cheque purchased	£25 minimum charge	4.92	22.56	2.44
Sterling advance repaid	£20 standard charge	2.13	9.74	10.26
Negotiation of exchange	£25 minimum charge	4.67	14.21	10.79
Negotiation repayments		0.58	5.73	(5.73)
Currency loan against bill	£25 minimum charge	5.77	23.08	1.92
Outward documentary/clean collection	£20 minimum charge	3.69	13.76	6.24
Collection proceeds paid away	£20 standard charge	1.62	8.42	11.58
Confirmation of letter of credit	£40 minimum charge	4.28	13.21	26.79
Advising letter of credit without confirmation	£25 standard charge	3.83	12.05	12.95
Amendment to letter of credit	£40 minimum charge	2.46	8.49	31.51
Pay/check documentation presented under letter of credit	£60 minimum charge	13.50	39.12	20.88
Payment of bills at maturity drawn on opening bank	£60 minimum charge	11.57	34.13	25.87
Credit bills negotiated (advances under acceptances)	Charge on application	16.30	44.30	(44.30)
Clean reimbursements	£25 minimum charge	3.42	13.07	11.93
Opening/issuing letter of credit	£40 minimum charge	6.93	20.07	19.93
Amendment to letter of credit	Charge on application	3.60	11.44	(11.44)
Check documentation presented under letter of credit	£40 minimum charge	5.54	16.47	23.53
Despatch documentation presented under letter of credit	£25 standard charge	1.34	5.61	19.39
Accept draft in respect of documents presented	£40 minimum charge	3.86	14.20	25.80
Payment of documents presented under letter of credit	£40 minimum charge	5.99	19.72	20.28
Travellers cheques purchased	£3 minimum charge	2.95	12.26	(9.76)
Travellers cheques sold	£2 minimum charge	3.91	14.74	(13.24)
Telegraphic transfer	£10 minimum charge	3.50	13.69	(3.69)
Inward remittance	£15 minimum charge	2.37	10.75	4.25
Mail transfer	£15 standard charge	2.31	10.60	4.40
Journal entries (intercurrency account transfer)	£10 minimum charge	1.46	10.18	(0.18)
Journal entries (single-currency account transfer)	No charge	1.46	7.63	(7.63)
Issue of sterling/dollar bankers' payments/cheques	£15 minimum charge	3.13	12.72	2.28
Set up forward deal	£10 minimum charge	5.14	15.83	(5.83)
Set up spot deal	Charge on application	3.43	11.40	(11.40)
Effect payment by bankers' payment/cheque	£15 standard charge	0.35	3.00	12.00
Effect payment by CHAPS	£15 standard charge	0.27	2.79	12.21
Receive payment by CHAPS	£5 standard charge	0.27	2.78	2.22
In-house funds transfer	No charge	0.26	4.54	(4.54)
Receipt of payments over £10 000	£10 standard charge	0.30	2.86	7.14
Effect cover payment, etc. by bankers' payment/cheque	£15 standard charge	0.90	4.42	10.58
Telegraphic transfer	£10 minimum charge	1.17	5.11	4.89

Table 9.13   Parker Bank – average profitability report

Products and services	Standard Tariff	Direct unit cost	Total unit cost	Average profit
Mail transfer	£15 standard charge	1.09	4.91	10.09
Issue of draft	£15 minimum charge	0.82	4.21	10.79
Effect payment by BACS	£15 standard charge	0.22	2.66	12.34
Commercial current account	£10 standard charge	0.00	1.77	8.23
Commercial fixed-interest account	£10 standard charge	0.00	1.77	8.23
21-Day notice account	£10 standard charge	0.00	1.77	8.23
Personal current accounts	Charge on application	0.00	1.77	(1.77)
Personal high-interest current accounts	No charge	0.00	1.77	(1.77)
Personal deposit accounts	No charge	0.00	1.77	(1.77)
Personal 21-day notice account	No charge	0.00	0.00	0.00
Open account	Charge on application	0.54	1.40	(1.40)
Issue statement	Charge on application	0.66	1.70	(1.70)
Monitor activity	Charge on application	0.28	0.73	(0.73)
Set up standing order	Charge on application	0.81	2.10	(2.10)
Set up direct debit	Charge on application	0.81	2.10	(2.10)
Close account	Charge on application	0.95	2.45	(2.45)
Issue of stand ard corporate cheque books	£5 standard charge	1.94	5.01	(0.01)
Issue of special corporate cheque books	£10 standard charge	2.62	6.76	3.24
Lodgement of safe custody items	£10 standard charge	2.47	6.39	3.61
Withdrawal of safe custody items	£10 standard charge	2.94	7.60	2.40
Temporary withdrawal of safe custody items	£5 standard charge	3.82	9.89	(4.89)
Provision of lists of securities held	£10 minimum charge	1.29	3.33	6.67
Provision of valuations of holdings	£20 minimum charge	5.71	14.75	5.25
Registration of death/probates, etc.	£20 minimum charge	4.69	12.12	7.88
Auditors' certificates	£30 minimum charge	6.61	17.09	12.91
Rental charge – per month	£3 minimum charge	0.00	0.00	2.50
Issue of personal cheque books	£2 minimum charge	1.68	4.36	(2.36)
Issue of cheque cards	£2 minimum charge	1.35	3.48	(1.48)
Interview customer	No charge	8.10	20.95	(20.95)
Personal – sterling pay in	£0.30 minimum charge	0.40	3.11	(2.81)
Cash dispenser	£0.20 minimum charge	0.01	2.11	(1.91)
Sterling withdrawal	£1 minimum charge	0.63	3.73	(2.73)
Currency pay in	£5 minimum charge	0.79	6.68	(1.68)
Currency withdrawal	£5 minimum charge	1.27	7.90	(2.90)
Commercial – sterling pay in	£1 minimum charge	0.95	4.54	(3.54)
Sterling withdrawal	£2 minimum charge	1.52	6.02	(4.02)
Currency pay in	£5 minimum charge	1.90	9.54	(4.54)
Currency withdrawal	£5 minimum charge	3.04	12.49	(7.49)
Fixed-rate mortgage	Charge on application	0.00	0.00	0.00
Floating-rate mortgage	Charge on application	0.00	0.00	0.00
Personal loan – secured	Charge on application	0.00	0.00	0.00
Personal loan – unsecured	Charge on application	0.00	0.00	0.00
Authorised overdraft	Charge on application	0.00	0.00	0.00
Unauthorised overdraft	£10 minimum charge	0.00	0.00	10.00
Fixed-rate sterling commercial loan	Charge on application	0.00	0.00	0.00
Fixed-rate currency commercial loan	Charge on application	0.00	0.00	0.00
Floating-rate sterling commercial loan	Charge on application	0.00	0.00	0.00
Floating-rate currency commercial loan	Charge on application	0.00	0.00	0.00
Commercial overdraft facility	Charge on application	0.00	0.00	0.00
Open account	Charge on application	0.91	4.12	(4.12)
Set up direct debit	Charge on application	1.37	5.30	(5.30)
Input loan application	Charge on application	1.60	9.76	(9.76)

Table 9.13 Contd.

Products and services	Standard Tariff	Direct unit cost	Total unit cost	Average profit
Obtain credit authorisation	Charge on application	12.91	38.99	(38.99)
Obtain/verify security	Charge on application	5.90	15.26	(15.26)
Review facility	Charge on application	8.86	28.51	(28.51)
Monitor repayments	Charge on application	0.43	6.72	(6.72)
Debit account for loan fees	Charge on application	1.93	6.76	(6.76)

Table 9.13 Contd.

USING ACTIVITY-BASED
COSTING FOR CUSTOMER
PROFITABILITY

INTRODUCTION

One of the major challenges facing all financial institutions is the identification of unprofitable relationships and products. The emphasis is moving away from volumetric sales targets towards profit objectives and so line management are looking for guidance on where to concentrate their limited resources. The primary concern of business managers is to be able to analyse each component of the profit equation (income, costs, business volumes) in terms of customers, customer groups, products and product groups in order to convert lossmakers into profit contributors.

Senior executives of the leading financial institutions have consistently promoted product and customer profitability information as a necessary key strategic input into strategic marketing plans, as well as being an operational tool, enabling management to manage their service and product delivery costs.

The requirements for product and customer profitability information can most effectively be demonstrated by considering the needs of three levels of management: the account officer or client relationship manager, the product manager and the unit manager (say, the branch or divisional manager). Account officers can focus on the reasons for unprofitable customers (price, delivery costs, bad debts, number of products used) and the cross-selling of profitable products. Product managers can identify the relative profitability of products and concentrate marketing/sales resources on the most profitable product/customer combinations. Unit managers can use this information to identify profitable product mixes and motivate account managers to cross-sell.

Profitability measurement and reporting by product and customer is based on the multidimensional analysis of balances, revenues and costs by activities performed in relation to the products and services provided to customers throughout the bank. It should break down departmental barriers and enable management to gain a greater understanding of customer relationships and markets.

Customer profitability reporting identifies and analyses the costs and revenues by customer or customer group. Its applicability depends on the types of customers towards which the business is directed and what the emphasis on marketing and strategic planning is within the organisation.

Customer profitability reporting is generally the last component of profitability reporting to be considered by any organisation because there has been so little emphasis on customer development in the past. As more and more attention has been directed towards managing the customer relationship, however, knowing what the profitability of specific customer groups and individual customers is has increased in importance.

Customer profitability analysis generally builds on product information by taking actual revenues and specific customer relationship-related costs and attaching direct product costs in relation to actual product usage by customer. This enables the analysis of the cross-product contribution and the impact of waived fees and negotiated commissions to be made by customer and customer type. It also means that international and inter-departmental customer relationships can be monitored and compared. It requires data to be collected relating to product usage, average balances, income and costs by individual customer or group of customers.

The income associated with each customer is normally available, although there may be some types of fee or commission income that are not debited to a customer account. These fees or commission payments may be paid by cash or transfer from another financial institution and will therefore be credited directly to 'commissions paid accounts'. In many financial institutions, no record will be maintained of the amount paid by customer. This type of income can generally only be identified by product or service and applied to customer analysis as average fee rates. In these instances, the income per customer can only be estimated, based on the level of activity.

Many financial institutions find it difficult to justify the cost of developing and maintaining customer profitability information for individual customers as this involves the capture and storage of individual transaction analysis from all automated and manual systems within the organisation as well as the maintenance of up-to-date customer profiles. How valuable this information is perceived to be depends to a large extent on how it would be used and this will generally relate to how important the individual customer relationship is to the institution.

DEFINING CUSTOMERS AND CUSTOMER GROUPS

Customers are defined as users of products and services who generate costs and revenues. Customers include external individuals and organisations as well as individuals and functions within other parts of the company. The type and mix of customer will vary by type of activity and market perception of the organisation.

The types of customers could include individuals, commercial organisations, other financial institutions, government, other regulatory bodies and other internal responsibility centres. Which of these customer types exist within the company will depend, in part, on the types of financial services provided. In some organisations, where there are large numbers of customers, analysis of each customer may not be necessary or practical, especially in the retail market. In these circumstances, analysis of customers grouped by common demand patterns instead may be sufficient. How they are grouped will vary by financial institution but should facilitate the recognition of common buying and risk patterns. The following generic customer groups may provide sufficient analysis to enable strategic activity to be directed at particular market sectors:

- other financial institutions
- government agencies
- multinational corporations
- large corporate customers
- middle market customers
- small corporate customers
- high net worth individuals
- ordinary individuals
  - age groups
  - socio-economic groups
  - geographic groups.

Alternatively, an analysis of a specific group of customers, measured by activity, value or profitability potential, may be sufficient to satisfy the information needs that have been identified. The analysis of certain types of customer may have particular relevance for large companies, such as 'global' customer relationships. These are defined as those customers, or related customers (corporate or family groups), who may be serviced by one or more responsibility centres within the institution. These relationships may be important to the organisation as a whole and so their profitability should be monitored. It is sometimes thought that, although the relationship is unprofitable in one unit, it must be profitable in total, but this may not always be the case. Some form of customer profitability analysis is important for all financial institutions, although the level of detail applied will vary by institutional type.

Retail banks and all similar companies with a large number of homogeneous customers are unlikely to be able to justify individual customer profitability, although it may become more common as the level of competition and customer sophistication increase. They may, however, require profitability analysis by customer group. Customer groups can be defined as any identifiable segment of the customer base. Segments may be based on any combination of socio-economic groupings, occupations, geographic location or any other common classification. They may vary by organisation.

The customer base of a private bank is normally small enough to justify the development of individual customer profitability. Fees charged to individual customers should be based on the level of activity necessary to maintain the client relationship and, therefore, the activity-based cost analysis can provide the volume and cost information necessary to derive the appropriate fee rates.

Corporate and wholesale banks are much more likely to require profitability by individual customer because of the higher value of each customer relationship, although this may depend on the number and scale of the customer base. A middle market bank, for example, with a large number of similar small corporate customers may prefer to group the customers by industry and asset base rather than to analyse each individual customer. An international wholesale bank may, however, have a smaller number of international corporate customers serviced by many offices in different locations. In these circumstances, it may be necessary to analyse customer profitability across the global customer relationship for each individual customer in order to balance lossmaking activities in one office with profitable business in another.

Individual customer profitability is generally irrelevant to retail life assurers, although those companies that offer group or corporate life policies where the policy is held by a corporation and relates to a large group of employees, will be interested in the claims history and inherent profitability of the corporate account relationship. Retail life assurance organisations tend to be more interested in segments of the customer base and will normally relate the segment profitability to the actuarial forecasts.

The importance of customer profitability in general insurance, as with life assurance, relates to the types of customer. Retail insurers are only interested in the profitability of segments of the customer base and tend to classify customers by a combination of geographic location and economic grouping. Corporate and specialist insurers, however, may be interested in the profitability of particular accounts.

Customer profitability in reinsurance activity is important in the analysis of the incidence of claims and hence the risk associated with the insurer. Activity-based Costing will assist in the profitability analysis by enabling the costs associated with the administration of the claim to be estimated and these costs to be separated by their cost driver (that is, separating the costs relating to the administering of the claim from those relating to the management of the relationship). It will not, however, provide additional analysis of the claims themselves.

The importance of product costing and customer profitability in investment management depends on the type of clients and the service provided. Those investment management organisations, which focus on the large pension funds and investment trusts, will normally analyse the costs of the components of the services provided and estimate the costs of managing a fund by accumulating the components applicable to the particular characteristics of the portfolio and level of service required. This information will then assist in fee negotiations with individual clients.

Capital markets institutions tend to be one of two types – those organisations that handle individual deals on a discrete basis and are therefore unlikely to require customer profitability, which would normally relate to a number of products or services, and those organisations that provide a relationship-based service (often part of a larger financial institution offering a wider financial relationship) who are interested in full customer profitability and must be able to analyse customers across the range of services offered.

Customers can be classified in many ways to facilitate target marketing and provide a focus for product differentiation. The types of customer segments for which profitability information can be summarised can be defined in at least 13 different ways, as shown in Table 10.1. These segments are not mutually exclusive and may be combined to fit the reporting needs of any organisation, as discussed above.

In large organisations, it is common for information to be analysed in several ways (by customer within geographical areas, by product type and by global customer relationship). In smaller ones, with relatively small numbers of customers, the types of classification may be more specialist and relate to the types of customers and relationships within that particular organisation alone.

IMPORTANCE OF INTERRELATIONSHIPS

The importance of interrelationships between customers may vary significantly between organisations but they should not be ignored. A dissatisfied customer will talk to all of his friends and associates about the fault, whereas a satisfied customer may recommend the level of service to some of his friends. One organisation, for example, analyses its customers by employer and by grade, because they offer personal financial services to high net worth individuals in their key corporate clients and target new customer development on individuals who are promoted to managerial positions in particular industries. Another institution analyses individual customers by family connection to maximise cross-selling opportunities and minimise competition within the customer groups. A small private bank also analyses its customers by membership of clubs and societies to ensure that it manages the key relationships by matching the interests of its customers and account relationship managers.

Interrelationships between customers may be less important in commercial financial services, but maintaining personal contact and ensuring that customers know who to contact with an enquiry will affect the level of customer service and, hence, the way the customer perceives the company.

Classification Type	Examples	
(1) Customer type	High net worth individuals Ordinary individuals Multinational corporations Large businesses Medium-sized businesses Small businesses	Associations Unions Government organisations Partnerships Pension funds Agents/producers
(2) Socio-economic grouping	A,B,C1,C2,D,E	
(3) Profession	Accountant Banker Civil servant Doctor	Landowner Lawyer Journalist Professor
(4) Sex	Male Female	
(5) Age	0–8 19–25 26–35	36–50 50–65 65+
(6) Marital status	Single Married	Divorced Widowed
(7) Salary	£0–20 000 £20–35 000 £35–50 000	£50–100 000 £100 000+
(8) Industrial (standard industry code)	Shipping Oil and energy Chemical Retail Manufacturing Engineering	Telecommunications Leisure industry Food manufacture Banking and finance Government
(9) Geographic	County Region	State Town/city
(10) Size of business	Asset base Number of employees Turnover	Profitability Sales
(11) Products provided	Asset-based products Liability-based products Documentary services Foreign exchange services Capital markets products Investment management services Advisory services Life assurance products Property and casualty insurance products Health insurance products	
(12) Responsibility centre	Customers by responsibility area within the organisations (may be product, location or customer type)	
(13) Account manager	Customers by account manager	

Table 10.1 Types of customer segments

Financial services to commercial customers may be differentiated from the competition by level of service and price, but will, at the very least, require some knowledge of the products and services undertaken for the client and the current status of the account relationship.

CUSTOMER PROFITABILITY IN PRACTICE

In practice, customer profitability analysis can generally be built more efficiently on an Activity-based Costing system, which is designed to analyse activities by product or service offered by the financial institution. As discussed earlier, the costs associated with individual activities may be consolidated by customer where the definition of a generic product is not relevant. This applies particularly to private banking and investment management where activities are combined to provide tailored services by customer or portfolio.

Most operating costs within a financial institution can be attributed to a specific product or service. However, there may be some costs incurred that are driven by the service offered to a particular customer or customer group. These costs must be isolated for customer profitability and the appropriate cost driver identified (see Chapter 5, Determining cost drivers). In order to calculate customer profitability, it is important to be able to measure product usage, income, cost and the associated balances by customer. Product costs can generally be assumed to be standard for a range of customers and can, therefore, be used as the basis of customer cost analysis when related to actual product usage by customer. Income and balances, however, vary significantly by customer and should be identified separately. Income in financial institutions can arise in five ways – interest income, fee or commission income, premiums, trading and investment income. The following paragraphs provide a summary of the types of income and the availability of information by customer. More detail is included in Chapter 6, Calculating costs.

Interest income

Interest is the charge made by the lender to the borrower for the use of the lender's funds over time. Interest is normally shown as two separate items – interest revenue and interest expense. Net interest income is the difference between interest revenue and interest expense and is the spread or contribution to profits and operating costs made by the asset- and liability-related products.

Where products and services need to be identified separately for customer profitability reporting, interest revenue should usually be adjusted for the cost-of-funds (see Chapter 6, Calculating costs). In summary, lending products have gross interest revenue, calculated as the interest received from the customer on the loan, but the funds had to be obtained from a depositor before they could be lent and, consequently, interest expense had to be paid to the depositor for those funds.

Interest income is calculated in relation to the balance on the account. The balance is, however, likely to vary during the reporting period and hence the interest should reflect the actual balances as they change. In practice, most financial institutions calculate interest on the transaction processing systems daily, but may not keep records or the daily balances or calculate the internal funding cost at the same time. Balances are generally stored in financial accounting systems as actual balances at the end of the period. In order to calculate a more accurate interest margin, it is therefore necessary to calculate the average balance. This should be calculated by accumulating daily balances and calculating a daily average debit or credit balance to the end of the reporting period. Some institutions, however, may still use an average of the current and prior period end. This ignores any fluctuation between reporting dates and so may misrepresent the margins reported as return on assets. This generally provides more favourable margins as many customers may try to reduce their borrowing at the period end for reporting purposes. The interest paid by the customer may, therefore, reflect higher balances during the period, but be reported against the lower actual balance at the period end.

Current accounts can be more difficult to analyse as they may fluctuate between debit and credit balances. In order to calculate the interest payable and receivable and the associated cost-of-funds, it is, therefore, necessary to maintain and report both average debit and credit balances for any account that may fluctuate and to calculate the interest payable and receivable on both balances.

Fee- or commission-based income

Fee- or commission-based income is the revenue that is generated by means of charges levied for products or services provided. These services include most credit advisory, foreign exchange and transmission, documentary, advisory and broking services. The increase or decrease in revenue is generally related to the volume of services provided and can be analysed in detail by means of product and customer reporting.

Fees or commissions are also payable by customers for the initiation and management of most funded products in the form of loan, new issue underwriting and arrangement fees. This revenue could be identified separately and reported in conjunction with the spread or yield made on the product.

Fee- or commission-based revenue is usually related to the agreed fee structure of the organisation and is predetermined. Exceptions arise when fees are waived or discounted for particular customers. The profitability reporting must take account of the reduced fees for those customers and the sources of data capture must identify the transactions to which these relate.

Premium income

Insurance premiums are generally stated gross and net of reinsurance and may represent single premiums (to create an annuity, for example) or recurring annual premiums that may be paid weekly, monthly, quarterly or annually. Policies are generally stored by policy holder on the administration systems, although no attempt may be made to combine the different policy types held by any customer. Premiums and any related claims should then be available for profitability reporting and the only problem will be the need to accumulate the profitability of all policy types with the range of other services used by the customer.

Trading income

Trading income is that revenue made by speculative trading in the money markets and exchanges on behalf of the company. Speculative trading can take place in any negotiable instruments, including foreign exchange, certificates of deposit, Eurocurrency, futures, options, stocks, bonds and other securities. Trading income rarely relates to external customers and is performed on behalf of the internal organisation. Trading performed for an external customer will generate fcc income as discussed above.

Investment income

Investment income is the revenue made by holding any negotiable instrument held with the intention of gaining financial advantage in the longer term. The principal source of profit for a life assurance office is the earnings obtained directly or indirectly from investment income. Investment income can be generated for a customer, through investment management and trusts. It can also be generated as part of the profitability of an insurance policy. It is necessary to review not just the premium income net of claims and administrative costs but also the investment income gained on the premiums held in relation to the policy. Insurance premiums are not normally invested by policyholder, but are generally identifiable by policy type. It is therefore necessary to apportion the income generated between the individual customers or policyholders to calculate customer profitability.

In unit-linked business, the policyholders directly benefit from the investment performance and the life office normally receives a management fee defined as a percentage of the fund. The management fee is the principal source of profit on these contracts, though the office will receive jobbing profits if a bid/offer spread is built into the unit price.

Profitability recognition

Customer profitability can be recognised at several points in the financial analysis, depending on the definition of sustaining or overhead costs. As shown in the following case study, income is normally recognisable by customer or customer group, costs may be attributed to customers directly via product utilisation or allocated as a proportion of sustaining or overhead expenses. Hence, contribution to sustaining cost by customer may be an important measure and indeed, is the one used in the case study below.

CASE STUDY: PLATINUM BANK

This case study considers a small segment of a private bank and was developed as a prototype for a larger, longer term profitability measurement and reporting system. The example considers a sample of customer relationships utilising a range of lending, depositary, investment, advisory and custodial services.

Approach

The exercise is discussed in relation to the six phases of development of an Activity-based Costing system as detailed in Chapter 3, The Activity-based Costing process.

Review and confirm requirements

Platinum Bank prefers to analyse its customers by individual customer, account officer, profession, age band and geographic area. The customers in this sample fall within the responsibility of four account officers, or, customer relationship managers and within four geographic areas.

The customer names and account numbers and interrelational information are shown in Table 10.1 in the Appendix to this chapter and are totally fictional. Any similarities to real circumstances are purely accidental.

The organisation chart shown in Figure 10.1 in the Appendix shows the matrix management structure, where the operating areas of the bank are managed by product managers and the client account management activities remain the responsibility of the client service division. The ultimate objective of the financial information strategy is to have full internal transfer pricing between the product management and the client service staff such that the product development and service levels can be focused on client needs and driven by client relationship initiatives.

Define reporting entities
When using Activity-based Costing for customer profitability, products, activities and cost drivers must all be defined in the same way as shown in Chapter 9, Using Activity-based Costing for product costing.

DEFINE PRODUCTS AND TRANSACTIONS
The sample of Platinum Bank customers utilise a range of lending, depositary, investment, advisory and custodial services which are defined at a high level for this prototype of the eventual customer profitability system. The products include:

- floating-rate loans
- high-interest deposits
- interest-bearing current accounts
- investment accounts
- financial advisory services
- safe custody.

AGREE ACTIVITIES
For this exercise, activities are defined at a similar level to that used in Chapter 9, Using Activity-based Costing for product costing. They can then be classified as operational or sustaining as discussed in Chapter 4, Agreeing activities. In Platinum Bank, the classification has been further refined as shown in Table 10.2 in the Appendix to this chapter. Operational costs have been sub-classified as:

- direct
- premises
- IT
- marketing
- customer-specific.

DETERMINE COST DRIVERS
Cost drivers are defined as shown in Chapter 9, Using Activity-based Costing for product costing, but care must be taken in any customer profitability analysis to ensure that customer-specific activities have cost drivers related to the individual customers or types of customers.

IDENTIFY CUSTOMERS AND CUSTOMER GROUPS
Customers are defined as individual customers analysed by profession, age group, geographic location and account officer and reports will be necessary that demonstrate this analysis. This will enable Platinum Bank to focus its marketing activity on particular customer groups in future and to measure the performance of individual account officers in terms of customer type, customer and product profitability.

Commence data collection

As this exercise is a prototype, it is important not just to concentrate on the data required for the cross-section of customers and products within the sample. Data sources were identified for *all* products and customers, incorporating transaction volumes and average balances and the related costs and income.

Develop an Activity-based Costing system

In this case, the system required is for full customer profitability information, rather than just Activity-based Costing. Figure 10.2 in the Appendix shows the data structure diagram for the customer profitability prototype on which this case study is based. It highlights the static data stored by customer to enable reporting to be achieved by individual customer, account officer, profession, age band or geographic area. It also identifies the variable information that must be collected and input to the calculation model for each reporting period. This data includes the balance and income data relating to each customer as well as the product volume information by customer.

Determine costs and revenues

Customer profitability has been derived using Activity-based Costing to calculate the operating costs of the products and services provided to the individual customers as shown in Chapter 9, Using Activity-based Costing for product costing. These costs have then been linked with interest costs and income by customer to develop customer profitability reports.

CALCULATE COSTS

Costs have been analysed at three levels: product-related operating costs driven by product volume, transaction mix and average balances; customer-related costs driven by client relationship management activities; sustaining costs that cannot be assigned to customer relationships or products and services but form part of the basic infrastructure of the organisation.

In this case study, product- and customer-related operating costs include the cost classifications shown in Table 10.2 in the Appendix. This includes premises, IT and marketing costs as, within this organisation, the activities are undertaken within a product-driven organisation with the responsibility for management costs being firmly within the control of the product manager.

ESTIMATE REVENUES

Lending and depositary services are analysed by average balance (calculated on the basis of average daily spot balances) against which interest income and interest expense must be calculated together with the associated loan fees where appropriate.

Platinum Bank pays interest on credit current account balances and charges interest on overdraft balances and these interest figures should also be calculated. To keep the example simple, it is assumed that current accounts remain in credit or debit throughout the period being analysed and therefore an average current account balance can be used to estimate interest payable or receivable. Transaction charges are payable on overdraft accounts. A fee is also charged for the use of an overdraft facility, as can be seen from the analysis, and the fee only relates to facilities of less that £5000 as the interest charges on large facilities are assumed to cover costs.

Investment services offered by Platinum Bank are fee-based products. Fee scales currently relate to the value of the portfolio under management at the reporting date. Platinum Bank are, however, considering a change in their fee rates to take account of the variations in cost in managing portfolios with differing mixes of local and international equities and government stocks. Advisory services are also fee-based, for which fees are charged based on the time spent by the advisor with the customer. Safe custody fees are based on the number of items held and the degree of access required.

Income used in the analysis in Table 10.3 in the Appendix assumes that account officers charge customers according to the standard tariff list. Any waived fees or discounted interest rates must therefore be recorded by the relationship manager and will be assigned to the customer as part of the customer profitability calculation. Any additional expenditure or time spent by the account manager over that normally spent on each customer should also be recorded so that the additional cost can be included in the customer profitability estimate.

Table 10.4 in the Appendix summarises the contribution to sustaining costs, and hence to profitability, by customer, showing the contribution by product for each customer as well as any customer-specific costs. Customer-specific costs have only been recorded against 11 customers. These relate either to waived fees or to additional time and expense on the part of the account relationship manager. They represent a significant portion of the overall cost base assigned to this customer sample, adding a further 18 per cent to the direct product-related costs.

Review results and prioritise recommendations

In Table 10.5 in the Appendix, the customer contribution is analysed by customer and account officer (customer relationship manager), ranking customers by profitability who are the responsibility of each account manager. This report highlights the account officers' performance and any unprofitable relationships. It also identifies circumstances where fees have been waived or additional expenditure incurred for customers, enabling management to review the impact of this practice on overall profitability.

In Table 10.6 in the Appendix, the customer contribution by product within age band is analysed, highlighting the profitability of customers in bands 2 (21–35 years) and 3 (36–50 years) within this particular sample of customers. Product utilisation also varies by age band in this case study. Loan services and depositary services tend to be utilised more heavily by bands 2 and 3, whereas investment services seem to be used mainly by the older customers. Advisory service usage seems to be concentrated at the two ends of the age bands.

If this sample is representative of the customer base within Platinum Bank, then marketing activity should be targeting lending and depositary products at the middle age bands and some action should be taken to improve the profitability of the investment and advisory products and services used by the higher age band customers.

In Table 10.7 in the Appendix, the customer contribution by geographic location is analysed and highlights those geographic areas that appear to attract more profitable customers. As can be seen from the report, customers in the north-eastern and south-eastern areas seem to generate higher profits than those in the north-western and south-western ones. This may be because of the products and services utilised – these profitable customers tend to use the lending and depositary services, which are inherently profitable. Also, it can be seen that many of the customers in the north-western area in this sample seem to use depositary services and this may be a market that could be extended.

In Table 10.8 in the Appendix, the customer contribution by profession is analysed and highlights those professions that appear more profitable from this sample of customers. It also identifies the product distribution by profession by showing the net contribution by product group.

If this sample is representative, scientists and academics appear not to borrow money, although landowners, accountants and directors borrow heavily. Landowners and lawyers also tend to hold deposit accounts, while investment accounts could be held by any profession. Scientists, actors and doctors may pay for advisory services. Profitability seems to be generated by landowners, accountants, lawyers and directors – possibly those professions who are prepared to pay for the private banking services and may not question the fees.

SUMMARY

Profitability measurement and reporting by product and customer is based on the multidimensional analysis of balances, revenues and costs by activities performed in relation to the products and services provided to customers throughout the bank. Its applicability depends on the types of customers to which the business is directed and the emphasis on marketing and strategic planning within the organisation.

Customer profitability reporting is generally the last component of profitability reporting to be considered by any organisation because in the past there has been a lack of emphasis on customer development in the past. As more and more attention has been directed towards managing the customer relationship, profitability of specific customer groups and individual customers has become more important.

The cost of providing the mix of products and services to a customer or type of customer is usually based on product cost information but may be enhanced to reflect those costs that can be attributed directly to individual customers or customer groups.

Customers are defined as the users of the products and services who generate costs and revenues. Customers include external individuals and organisations as well as individuals and functions within other parts of the institution. The type and mix of customer will vary by type of activity and market perception of the organisation.

The types of customers could include individuals, commercial organisations, other financial institutions, government, other regulatory bodies and other internal responsibility centres.

In some organisations, where there are large numbers of customers, analysis by every customer may not be necessary or practical, especially in the retail market. In these circumstances, analysis of customers grouped by common demand patterns may be sufficient. What types of groups will be most useful will vary by financial institution but they should facilitate the recognition of common buying and risk patterns. In large organisations, it is common for information to be analysed in several ways (say, by customer within geographical areas, by product type and by global customer relationship). In smaller institutions, with relatively small numbers of customers, the types of classification may be more specialist and relate to the types of customers and relationships within the organisation.

In practice, customer profitability analysis can generally be built more efficiently on an Activity-based Costing system that is designed to analyse activities by product or service offered by the financial institution. Most operating costs within a financial institution can be attributed to a specific product or service. However, there may be some costs incurred that are driven by the service offered to a particular customer or customer group. These costs must be isolated for customer profitability and the appropriate cost driver identified (see Chapter 5, Determining cost drivers).

In order to calculate customer profitability, it is important to be able to measure product usage, income, cost and the associated balances by customer. Product costs can generally be assumed to be standard for a range of customers and can, therefore, be used as the basis of customer cost analysis when related to actual product usage by customer. Income and balances, however, vary significantly by customer and should be identified separately. Income in financial institutions can arise in five ways: interest income, fee or commission income, premiums, trading and investment income.

APPENDIX: PLATINUM BANK

Customer		Account officer		Customer relationships		
Name	Number	Name	Number	Profession	Geographic area	Age Band
Lee	20486	Vine	120	431	SW	1
James	57620	Vine	120	286	SW	1
Price	10928	Vine	120	309	NE	3
Hall	28541	Vine	120	286	SW	4
Nunn	29856	Vine	120	312	SE	4
Good	69875	Vine	120	257	NE	2
Day	56930	Vine	120	257	SE	3
Lunn	24566	Vine	120	312	NE	3
Page	28943	Vine	120	286	SW	4
White	12394	Vine	120	309	NE	5
Gray	39853	Trout	197	303	NE	2
Jones	94547	Trout	197	183	NW	5
Smith	92847	Trout	197	431	NW	4
Black	75783	Trout	197	312	NE	3
Cray	56749	Trout	197	195	NW	2
Bush	87593	Trout	197	286	NW	1
Noon	97573	Trout	197	303	SE	3
Davis	29745	Trout	197	312	SE	3
Allen	89563	Trout	197	257	SE	2
Johnson	38536	Sage	236	183	SE	1
Freeman	60928	Sage	236	257	NE	3
Cook	97534	Sage	236	195	SW	1
Taylor	39856	Sage	236	303	SE	4
King	38754	Sage	236	257	NE	3
Baker	82583	Sage	236	243	NW	5
Brown	69654	Sage	236	431	SW	4
Crown	65368	Sage	236	243	SW	5
Rose	48486	Sage	236	257	NE	3
Astor	75375	Sage	236	414	SW	5
Howe	57301	Ford	105	303	NE	2
Evans	20597	Ford	105	414	SW	5
Thomas	32984	Ford	105	309	NE	2
Simms	97825	Ford	105	414	SE	4
Rush	10938	Ford	105	309	NW	5
Green	37545	Ford	105	183	NE	1
Turner	29384	Ford	105	213	SE	1
Ellis	47364	Ford	105	243	SE	3

Key

Profession		Age band
183 = Scientist	303 = Accountant	1 = 0 – 20
195 = Academic	309 = Lawyer	2 = 21–35
243 = Civil servant	312 = Director	3 = 36–50
257 = Landowner	414 = Artist	4 = 51–65
286 = Doctor	431 = Actor	5 = 65+

Table 10.1 Platinum Bank – customer information

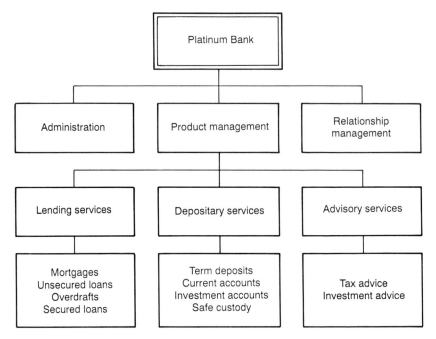

Figure 10.1 Platinum Bank – organisation/product structure

Costs	Loans	Deposits	Current accounts	Investment accounts	Financial advice	Safe custody	Total
Operational activities	1056	194	8602	11 330	1170	245	22 597
Premises costs	333	61	3872	3532	370	84	8252
IT costs	521	103	4836	3259	397	37	9153
Marketing costs	215	45		1435			1695
Total product costs	2125	403	17 310	19 556	1937	366	41 697
Customer-specific costs							7457
Total operating costs							49 154
Sustaining costs at 40 per cent							19 662
Total costs attributable to customer sample							68 816

Table 10.2 Platinum Bank – product- and customer-related costs

Customer		Interest income			Interest expense			Fee income				
Name	Number	Loans	Deposits	Current accounts	Loans	Deposits	Current accounts	Loans	Current accounts	Investment fees	Advisory	Safe custody
Ellis	47364	12 375	0	414	(10 500)	0	(322)	500	87	0	0	0
Evans	20597	0	(90)	72	0	126	(56)	0	66	100	630	0
Green	37545	0	0	-10	0	0	35	0	0	1875	126	0
Howe	57301	48 050	0	0	0	0	0	500	0	2900	252	0
Rush	10938	0	(2500)	0	0	3500	0	0	0	160	0	0
Simms	97825	0	0	0	0	0	0	0	0	5000	0	0
Thomas	32984	22 400	0	-540	-14 000	0	1260	500	0	0	567	0
Turner	29384	16 500	0	-38	0	0	133	500	0	0	0	31
Astor	75375	0	0	0	0	0	0	0	0	1260	0	0
Baker	82583	0	0	-180	0	0	420	0	0	500	0	0
Brown	69654	0	0	-2950	0	0	4130	0	0	600	315	21
Cook	97534	0	0	-1240	0	0	2170	0	0	0	0	0
Crown	65368	0	(500)	-38	0	700	133	0	0	0	252	42
Freeman	60928	5775	(14 625)	-26	-4900	16 380	91	500	30	0	126	0
Johnson	38536	0	(2500)	2700	0	3500	(2100)	0	81	0	0	0
King	38754	15 180	0	1206	-12 880	0	(938)	500	0	1900	252	76
Rose	48486	38 750	0	-2550	-35 000	0	3570	500	0	0	0	0
Taylor	39856	3298	0	3060	-2716	0	(2380)	388	31	0	0	20
Allen	89563	0	0	(4)	0	21 420	14	0	0	0	0	55
Black	75783	13 530	0	(960)	(11 480)	0	1680	500	120	0	441	0
Bush	87593	63 525	0	144	(5390)	0	(112)	500	0	0	378	0
Cray	56749	0	(1000)	(252)	0	1400	882	0	0	0	126	0
Davis	29745	10 230	(500)	9	(8680)	700	(7)	500	73	0	0	0
Gray	39853	20 000	0	(414)	(17 500)	0	1449	500	0	0	0	0
Jones	94547	0	(500)	0	(12 600)	700	0	0	0	1740	126	0
Noon	97573	14 850	0	(2)	0	0	7	500	0	0	0	105
Smith	92847	0	0	0	0	0	0	0	0	1500	189	0
Day	56930	14 025	0	1062	(11 900)	0	(826)	500	95	0	0	0
Good	69875	50 325	(11 500)	225	(4270)	14 000	(175)	500	105	1500	0	0
Hall	28541	0	0	0	0	0	0	0	0	1000	0	0
James	57620	0	(1500)	45	0	2100	(35)	0	96	0	0	0
Lee	20486	0	0	540	0	0	(420)	0	66	0	567	0
Lunn	24566	5016	0	(210)	(4256)	21 000	490	500	0	0	0	0
Nunn	29856	5115	0	2700	(4340)	0	(2100)	500	23	0	0	0
Page	28943	0	0	(30)	0	0	105	0	0	0	378	0
Price	10928	0	(11 500)	216	0	14 000	(168)	0	58	0	0	0
White	12394	0	0	(378)	0	0	882	0	0	4500	0	61

Table 10.3 Platinum Bank – product- and customer-related income

Customer Name	Customer Number	Account officer	Net contribution to customer-specific and sustaining costs						Product contribution	Customer specific costs	Total operating contribution
			Loans	Deposits	Current accounts	Investment accounts	Advisory services	Safe custody			
Howe	57301	Ford	5021	0	(545)	666	149	0	5291	(888)	4403
White	12394	Vine	0	0	293	3370	0	0	3663	0	3663
Thomas	32984	Ford	3186	0	345	0	0	0	3531	0	3531
Lunn	24566	Vine	1151	2219	(28)	0	0	8	3342	0	3342
Rose	48486	Sage	4126	0	521	867	0	8	5522	(2476)	3046
King	38754	Sage	2682	0	(206)	0	149	0	2625	0	2625
Good	69875	Vine	1127	2469	(711)	229	0	0	3114	(500)	2614
Gray	39853	Trout	2882	0	(327)	0	0	0	2556	0	2556
Freeman	60928	Sage	1244	1724	(534)	0	74	5	2513	(167)	2346
Price	10928	Vine	0	2469	(171)	0	0	7	2305	0	2305
Black	75783	Trout	2410	0	2	0	0	6	2418	(137)	2281
Turner	29384	Ford	2888	0	(252)	0	335	0	2971	(1067)	1904
Day	56930	Vine	2496	0	(618)	0	0	0	1878	0	1878
Ellis	47364	Ford	2252	0	(462)	0	0	0	1790	0	1790
Noon	97573	Trout	2597	0	(887)	0	0	12	1722	0	1722
Allen	89563	Trout	0	2264	(818)	0	0	2	1448	0	1448
Nunn	29856	Vine	1163	0	157	0	0	0	1320	0	1320
Davis	29745	Trout	1938	169	(390)	0	74	0	1791	(699)	1092
Johnson	38536	Sage	0	969	77	0	0	0	1046	0	1046
Taylor	39856	Sage	852	0	145	0	0	0	997	0	997
Green	37545	Ford	0	0	0	833	74	0	907	0	907
Jones	94547	Trout	0	169	0	345	74	0	588	0	588
Rush	10938	Ford	0	969	0	(421)	0	0	548	0	548
Hall	28541	Vine	0	0	0	285	0	0	285	0	285
Astor	75375	Sage	0	0	0	213	0	3	216	0	216
Brown	69654	Sage	0	0	511	(181)	186	0	516	(315)	201
Lee	20486	Vine	0	0	(186)	0	335	0	149	0	149
Smith	92847	Trout	0	0	0	(1)	112	0	111	0	111
Cray	56749	Trout	0	369	(502)	0	223	0	90	0	90
Cook	97534	Sage	0	0	38	0	0	2	40	(78)	(38)
Page	28943	Vine	0	0	(268)	0	223	0	(45)	0	(45)
James	57620	Vine	0	569	(638)	0	0	0	(69)	0	(69)
Crown	65368	Sage	0	169	(539)	0	149	0	(221)	0	(221)
Bush	87593	Trout	1316	0	(891)	0	260	0	685	(1061)	(376)
Simms	97825	Ford	0	0	0	(464)	0	0	(464)	0	(464)
Evans	20597	Ford	0	5	(291)	(483)	372	0	(397)	(69)	(466)
Baker	82583	Sage	0	0	(532)	(279)	0	0	(811)	0	(811)
									53 968	(7457)	46 511

Total operating contribution

Less sustaining costs apportioned at 40 per cent of operating costs (19 662)

Total profit before tax 26 849

Table 10.4 Platinum Bank – product and customer profitability contribution calculation

Input data						
Customer	Product	Average balance	Interest income	Interest expense	Fees and commissions	Product volumes

Static data				
Customer	Account officer	Customer relationships	Product	Operating cost

Calculated data				
Contribution margin by:	Account officer	Product	Customer	Customer relationship
Account officer				
Product				
Customer				
Customer relationship				

Figure 10.2 Platinum Bank – data structure

Account officer	Customer		Product contribution by customer	Customer-specific costs		Total operating contribution	
	Name	Number		Waived fees	Direct costs		
Ford	Howe	57301	5291	752	136	4403	12 152
	Thomas	32984	3531			3531	
	Turner	29384	2971	1067		1904	
	Ellis	47364	1790			1790	
	Green	37545	907			907	
	Rush	10938	548			548	
	Simms	97825	464)			(464)	
	Evans	20597	(397)		69	466)	
Sage	Rose	48486	5522	2476		3046	9407
	King	38754	2625			2625	
	Freeman	60928	2513		167	2346	
	Johnson	38536	1046			1046	
	Taylor	39856	997			997	
	Astor	75375	216			216	
	Brown	69654	516	315		201	
	Cook	97534	40		78	(38)	
	Crown	65368	(221)			(221)	
	Baker	82583	(811)			(811)	
Trout	Gray	39853	2556			2556	9511
	Black	75783	2418		137	2281	
	Noon	97573	1722			1722	
	Allen	89563	1448			1448	
	Davis	29745	1791	699		1092	
	Jones	94547	588			588	
	Smith	92847	111			111	
	Cray	56749	90			90	
	Bush	87593	685	1061		(376)	
Vine	White	12394	3663			3663	15 440
	Lunn	24566	3342			3342	
	Good	69875	3114	500		2614	
	Price	10928	2305			2305	
	Day	56930	1878			1878	
	Nunn	29856	1320			1320	
	Hall	28541	285			285	
	Lee	20486	149			149	
	Page	28943	(45)			(45)	
	James	57620	(69)			(69)	
Total operating contribution			53 968	6870	587	46 511	46 511
Less sustaining costs apportioned at 40 per cent of operating costs							(19 662)
Total profit before tax							26 849

Table 10.5 Platinum Bank – customer contribution by account officer

Customer Name	Number	Age band	Net contribution to customer-specific and sustaining costs						Product contribution	Customer-specific costs	Total operating contribution
			Loans	Deposits	Current accounts	Investment accounts	Advisory services	Safe custody			
Turner	29384	1	2888	0	(252)	0	335	0	2971	(1067)	1904
Johnson	38536	1	0	969	77	0	0	0	1046	0	1046
Green	37545	1	0	0	0	833	74	0	907	0	907
Lee	20486	1	0	0	(186)	0	335	0	149	0	149
Cook	97534	1	0	0	38	0	0	2	40	(78)	(38)
James	57620	1	0	569	(638)	0	0	0	(69)	0	(69)
Bush	87593	1	1316	0	(891)	0	260	0	685	(1061)	(376)
Howe	57301	2	5021	0	(545)	666	149	0	5291	(888)	4403
Thomas	32984	2	3186	0	345	0	0	0	3531	0	3531
Good	69875	2	1127	2469	(711)	229	0	0	3114	(500)	2614
Gray	39853	2	2882	0	(327)	0	0	0	2556	0	2556
Allen	89563	2	0	2264	(818)	0	0	2	1448	0	1448
Cray	56749	2	0	369	(502)	0	223	0	90	0	90
Lunn	24566	3	1151	2219	(28)	0	0	0	3342	0	3342
Rose	48486	3	4126	0	521	867	0	8	5522	(2476)	3046
King	38754	3	2682	0	(206)	0	149	0	2625	0	2625
Freeman	60928	3	1244	1724	(534)	0	74	5	2513	(167)	2346
Price	10928	3	0	2469	(171)	0	0	7	2305	0	2305
Black	75783	3	2410	0	2	0	0	6	2418	(137)	2281
Day	56930	3	2496	0	(618)	0	0	0	1878	0	1878
Ellis	47364	3	2252	0	(462)	0	0	0	1790	0	1790
Noon	97573	3	2597	0	(887)	0	0	12	1722	0	1722
Davis	29745	3	1938	169	(390)	0	74	0	1791	(699)	1092
Nunn	29856	3	1163	0	157	0	0	0	1320	0	1320
Taylor	39856	4	852	0	145	0	0	0	997	0	997
Hall	28541	4	0	0	0	285	0	0	285	0	285
Brown	69654	4	0	0	511	(181)	186	0	516	(315)	201
Smith	92847	4	0	0	0	(1)	112	0	111	0	111
Page	28943	4	0	0	(268)	0	223	0	(45)	0	(45)
Simms	97825	4	0	0	0	(464)	0	0	(464)	0	(464)
White	12394	4	0	0	293	3370	0	0	3663	0	3663
Jones	94547	5	0	169	0	345	74	0	588	0	588
Rush	10938	5	0	969	0	(421)	0	0	548	0	548
Astor	75375	5	0	0	0	213	0	3	216	0	216
Crown	65368	5	0	169	(539)	0	149	0	(221)	0	(221)
Evans	20597	5	0	5	(291)	(483)	372	0	(397)	(69)	(466)
Baker	82583	5	0	0	(532)	(279)	0	0	(811)	0	(811)

Table 10.6 Platinum Bank – customer contribution analysis by age band

| Customer | | | Net contribution to customer-specific and sustaining costs | | | | | | Product contribution | Customer-specific costs | Total operating contribution |
Name	Number	Geographic area	Loans	Deposits	Current accounts	Investment accounts	Advisory services	Safe custody			
Howe	57301	NE	5021	0	(545)	666	149	0	5291	(888)	4403
White	12394	NE	0	0	293	3370	0	0	3663	0	3663
Thomas	32984	NE	3186	0	345	0	0	0	3531	0	3531
Lunn	24566	NE	1151	2219	(28)	0	0	0	3342	0	3342
Rose	48486	NE	4126	0	521	867	0	8	5522	(2476)	3046
King	38754	NE	2682	0	(206)	0	149	0	2625	0	2625
Good	69875	NE	1127	2469	(711)	229	0	0	3114	(500)	2614
Gray	39853	NE	2882	0	(327)	0	0	0	2556	0	2556
Freeman	60928	NE	1244	1724	(534)	0	74	5	2513	(167)	2346
Price	10928	NE	0	2469	(171)	0	0	7	2305	0	2305
Black	75783	NE	2410	0	2	0	0	6	2418	(137)	2281
Green	37545	NE	0	0	0	833	74	0	907	0	907
Jones	94547	NW	0	169	0	345	74	0	588	0	588
Rush	10938	NW	0	969	0	(421)	0	0	548	0	548
Smith	92847	NW	0	0	0	(1)	112	0	111	0	111
Cray	56749	NW	0	369	(502)	0	223	0	90	0	90
Bush	87593	NW	1316	0	(891)	0	260	0	685	(1061)	(376)
Baker	82583	NW	0	0	(532)	(279)	0	0	(811)	0	(811)
Turner	29384	NW	2888	0	(252)	0	335	0	2971	(1067)	1904
Day	56930	SE	2496	0	(618)	0	0	0	1878	0	1878
Ellis	47364	SE	2252	0	(462)	0	0	0	1790	0	1790
Noon	97573	SE	2597	0	(887)	0	0	12	1722	0	1722
Allen	89563	SE	0	2264	(818)	0	0	2	1448	0	1448
Nunn	29856	SE	1163	0	157	0	0	0	1320	0	1320
Davis	29745	SE	1938	169	(390)	0	74	0	1791	(699)	1092
Johnson	38536	SE	0	969	77	0	0	0	1046	0	1046
Taylor	39856	SE	852	0	145	0	0	0	997	0	997
Simms	97825	SE	0	0	0	(464)	0	0	(464)	0	(464)
Hall	28541	SW	0	0	0	285	0	0	285	0	285
Astor	75375	SW	0	0	0	213	0	3	216	0	216
Brown	69654	SW	0	0	511	(181)	186	0	516	(315)	201
Lee	20486	SW	0	0	(186)	0	335	0	149	0	149
Cook	97534	SW	0	0	38	0	0	2	40	(78)	(38)
Page	28943	SW	0	0	(268)	0	223	0	(45)	0	(45)
James	57620	SW	0	569	(638)	0	0	0	(69)	0	(69)
Crown	65368	SW	0	169	(539)	0	149	0	(221)	0	(221)
Evans	20597	SW	0	5	(291)	(483)	372	0	(397)	(69)	(466)

Table 10.7 Platinum Bank – customer contribution analysis by geographic area

Customer Name	Number	Profession	Net contribution to customer-specific and sustaining costs						Product contribution	Customer-specific costs	Total operating contribution
			Loans	Deposits	Current accounts	Investment accounts	Advisory services	Safe custody			
Johnson	38536	183	0	969	77	0	0	0	1046	0	1046
Green	37545	183	0	0	0	833	74	0	907	0	907
Jones	94547	183	0	169	0	345	74	0	588	0	588
Cray	56749	195	0	369	(502)	0	223	2	90	0	90
Cook	97534	195	0	0	38	0	0	0	40	(78)	(38)
Ellis	47364	243	2252	0	(462)	0	0	0	1790	0	1790
Crown	65368	243	0	169	(539)	0	149	0	(221)	0	(221)
Baker	82583	243	0	0	(532)	(279)	0	0	(811)	0	(811)
Rose	48486	257	4126	0	521	867	0	8	5522	(2476)	3046
King	38754	257	2682	0	(206)	0	149	0	2625	0	2625
Good	69875	257	1127	2469	(711)	229	0	0	3114	(500)	2614
Freeman	60928	257	1244	1724	(534)	0	74	5	2513	(167)	2346
Day	56930	257	2496	0	(618)	0	0	0	1878	0	1878
Allen	89563	257	0	2264	(818)	0	0	2	1448	0	1448
Hall	28541	286	0	0	0	285	0	0	285	0	285
Page	28943	286	0	0	(268)	0	223	0	(45)	0	(45)
James	57620	286	0	569	(638)	0	0	0	(69)	0	(69)
Bush	87593	286	1316	0	(891)	0	260	0	685	(1061)	(376)
Howe	57301	303	5021	0	(545)	666	149	0	5291	(888)	4403
Gray	39853	303	2882	0	(327)	0	0	0	2556	0	2556
Noon	97573	303	2597	0	(887)	0	0	12	1722	0	1722
Taylor	39856	303	852	0	145	0	0	0	997	0	997
White	12394	309	0	0	293	3370	0	0	3663	0	3663
Thomas	32984	309	3186	0	345	0	0	0	3531	0	3531
Price	10928	309	0	2469	(171)	0	0	7	2305	0	2305
Rush	10938	309	0	969	0	(421)	0	0	548	0	548
Lunn	24566	312	1151	2219	(28)	0	0	0	3342	0	3342
Black	75783	312	2410	0	2	0	0	6	2418	(137)	2281
Turner	29384	312	2888	0	(252)	0	335	0	2971	(1067)	1904
Nunn	29856	312	1163	0	157	0	0	0	1320	0	1320
Davis	29745	312	1938	169	(390)	0	74	0	1791	(699)	1092
Astor	75375	414	0	0	0	213	0	3	216	0	216
Simms	97825	414	0	0	0	(464)	0	0	(464)	0	(464)
Evans	20597	414	0	0	(291)	(483)	372	0	(397)	(69)	(466)
Brown	69654	431	0	5	511	(181)	186	0	516	(315)	201
Lee	20486	431	0	0	(186)	0	335	0	149	0	149
Smith	92847	431	0	0	0	(1)	112	0	111	0	111

Table 10.8 Platinum Bank — customer contribution by profession

11 USING ACTIVITY-BASED COSTING FOR OPERATIONAL COST MANAGEMENT

INTRODUCTION

Any organisation must aim to maximise its profitability in either the short or longer term. In order to achieve this, it must be able to manage its cost base. Managing the cost base can be performed in a variety of ways. Traditionally the costs were managed by dividing the organisation into cost centres and controlling the costs within each cost centre through the use of regular reporting of actual expenditure. Many reports would compare expenditure for the period against the same period for the previous year, the previous period or some form of budget of expected expense. Reports would be produced at least once each year and probably quarterly or monthly, although some organisations do produce reports on a weekly basis.

As markets become increasingly competitive and profit margins are squeezed, the need to control and reduce costs focuses attention on the means of cost management within the organisation. Every financial institution that I know of has undertaken some form of cost-reduction exercise within the last 12 months. In most instances, cost-reduction initiatives consist of a directive from a managing director or a finance director stating that costs will be held at last year's levels (a cost reduction in line with inflation) or will be reduced by a fixed percentage. Those cost centre managers who have seen these kinds of initiatives in the past will have padded their budgets to ensure reductions can be achieved without damaging the infrastructure of their departments. Other managers, who have managed their costs down already will suffer potentially damaging reductions in service levels that may affect the delivery capability of the organisation as a whole.

Managing the cost base by activity, using Activity-based Costing as the basis of analysis and control, provides a means of looking at the expenditure from a new direction. The focus on activities instead of cost centres reduces the emphasis on cost centres and hence on the domains of cost centre managers. It can form the basis of cost/benefit analysis, which facilitates decision making based on the value placed on an activity within the organisation and the costs that it incurs. The following sections look at Activity-based Costing as the basis of activity-based management, activity-based budgeting, performance management and cost reduction and include a practical example of cost reduction in an insurance company.

USES OF THE INFORMATION

Activity-based Costing information can be used in financial institutions as the basis for a variety of tools that will assist senior managers in the management of the cost base. It can be used as the basis of a regular means of managing the cost base by activity throughout the organisation. It may include the need to set targets or budgets for activities and costs, but tends to focus on longer term improvements in the delivery of activities that enable the institution to move towards its corporate goals through the monitoring of productivity, capacity utilisation, efficiency and effectiveness. It may therefore be used as the basis of an activity-based budgeting system, but can also be used simply as the basis of a one-off cost reduction exercise.

Activity-based management

Cost reduction is only one element within the wider framework of cost management. Traditionally cost reduction tends to be a short, sharp initiative that may only have a short-term effect because the underlying causes of the problems have not been addressed. An activity-based cost reduction exercise, however, should provide the basis for better ongoing cost management, but will not replace existing methods of cost management. Ways of managing the cost base depend on ongoing planning and control of all aspects of the business. Costs are an integral part of the business infrastructure and any decision made by management will inevitably involve expenditure in either the long or short term. Implementing a new cost management system may have far-reaching effects, changing the way in which performance is measured within the organisation as a whole.

The objective of activity-based cost management is to determine the importance and costs of activities within the value chain, giving management the opportunity to focus resources strategically to realise maximum value and continuously improve the effectiveness of costs. Activity-based cost management utilises Activity-based Costing as the basic component of financial management information that assists the operational control of the business by focusing attention on the key cost drivers and the factors that influence the day-to-day dynamics of the cost base.

Activity-based budgeting

Activity-based budgeting differs from traditional budgeting in that it concentrates on the factors that drive the costs, not just historical expenditure.

The volume of activity, for example, will be a key driver of the costs within any operations function and the quality of customer service will have a significant effect on the costs associated with customer liaison. Figure 11.1 demonstrates the linkage between Activity-based budgeting (the baseline) and the development of an activity-based budget.

The strategic objectives can drive the budgetary targets and determine the volume of activities to be performed. The budgets are then derived from the activities using estimated cost rates.

Activity-based budgeting is often compared to zero-based budgeting and, in some ways, is based on similar concepts. Zero-based budgeting requires that expenditure above a zero base be justified and that costs be estimated for differing levels of output and service. Activity-based budgeting, however, assumes an ongoing operation, justifying expenditure on the basis of activities performed in relation to the predetermined drivers and places responsibility for cost control on the manager with responsibility for the control of the driver. Activity-based budgeting separates the analysis of cost/benefit and value of activities from the more mechanistic budgeting exercise, reducing the complexity of the budgetary process and concentrating attention on the *management* of the business not simply on the *costs* incurred.

Performance management

Performance management combines objective setting, cost control and responsibility by setting people-related targets or key performance

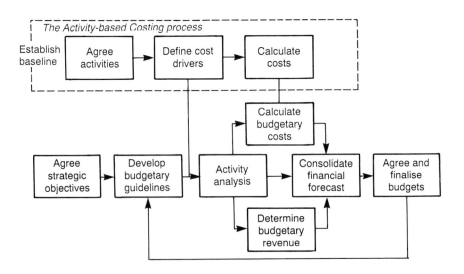

Figure 11.1 Developing an Activity-based budget

indicators and monitoring activity against the indicators on a regular basis. Performance can be influenced by using these key performance indicators as the basis of regular reporting, identifying those areas where individual managers can control or influence behaviour towards the achievement of corporate objectives. The control of cost in a key component of any performance measurement system and activity-based analysis can be used to focus attention on the areas of cost over which the individual has responsibility.

Performance can be measured in relation to both long-term and short-term goals. For example, a manager may have responsibility for the development of a new market (which may take years to become profitable) and may also have short-term profit targets relating to existing business. Key performance indicators based on activity analysis enable both types of performance to be measured by focusing attention on the factors that influence the behaviour. In this example, the key performance indicators may relate to the amount of time and investment made in the new market as well as the volume, quality and profitability of existing business.

Cost-reduction initiatives

Using Activity-based Costing as the basis of a one-off cost-reduction exercise provides a means by which management can identify duplicate or extraneous activities and evaluate the benefit to the organisation of the activities performed throughout the organisation. Analysis by activity also allows a fundamental rethink of the way the institution is organised and how it operates and may result in radical reorganisation.

The primary benefit of using activity-based costs rather than any other form of costing lies in the essence of the technique itself. Activity-based Costing focuses on activities not responsibilities and so are seen as less threatening to the managers of the various functions under review. It depersonalises the cost review and enables management to value the activities undertaken in relation to the level and/or quality of service provided and factors that cause costs to be incurred.

Implementing cost reduction in practice requires strong commitment from senior management and sponsorship at board level. Without this kind of commitment, the initiative is likely to flounder when politically complex decisions must be taken relating to reorganisation and redundancy.

ACTIVITY-BASED MANAGEMENT

The objective of activity-based cost management is to determine the importance and costs of activities within the value chain, giving management the opportunity to focus resources strategically to realise maximum value and continuously improve the effectiveness of costs. Activity-based cost management combines the cost analysis described above with the product and customer analysis described in Chapters 9 and 10.

Activity-based management may include activity-based budgeting, but may simply include activity targets that monitor productivity, efficiency and effectiveness on an ongoing basis. Costs may be monitored and controlled both through the existing budgetary systems (to monitor costs by department in the traditional way) and also through the cost per unit of activity (to focus on efficiency and effectiveness). Productivity will be monitored in volume and quality terms in parallel to cost analysis based on consistent definitions of activities.

Activity-based analysis, therefore, forms the basis of activity-based management, as described above. Key concepts in activity-based management include all those discussed in Chapter 3, The Activity-based Costing process, and expanded in Chapters 4, 5, 6 and 7. In particular, attention must be focused on the definition of products, activities, and customers, the classification of activities and the calculation of both cost and contribution.

Defining products and services

Definitions of products and services are frequently not established unless some form of product costing or profitability analysis has already been performed. Each functional area of the organisation is likely to have a different perspective on the issue of product definition. For reporting purposes, it is important to agree on product definitions that can be supported by the tracking of clearly identifiable income and costs, but that also provide adequate sales and marketing information to the end users. Another associated issue is the need to construct a product coding convention that supports the grouping of individual products into product families (such as, deposits, investments and advisory services) in order to satisfy product grouping reporting requirements.

Defining activities

The process of defining activities for activity-based cost management involves pinpointing the principal activities throughout the organisation and defining them on a consistent basis and the subsequent definition of sub-activities that are capable of being assigned to products and customers. It is important that common activities are defined and the definitions agreed prior to any analysis being undertaken, so as to avoid confusion and facilitate comparisons. Definition should be undertaken at two levels – first, of the principal activities that are performed in the department (normally no more than 12 in each department) and, second, the detailed sub-activities, which form the components of the principal activities, and either relate to different products or are affected by different cost drivers. The emphasis of the activity analysis for activity-based cost management normally rests on the examination of sub-activities at product and customer level throughout the organisation and summarises it to identify any opportunities there may be to reduce, eliminate or improve the individual activities performed. Those activities that are identified in this process enable the detailed analysis of operational activities, such as transaction processing and customer relationship management, and for there to be less emphasis placed on the sustaining activities except for cost reduction purposes.

Defining customers and customer groups

Customers are the users of the products and services that generate costs and revenues. Customers include external individuals and organisations as well as individuals and functions within other parts of the company. The type and mix of customer will vary depending on the types of activities that the organisation carries out and how it is perceived in the market. In some organisations, where there are large numbers of customers, analysis by every customer may not be necessary, or practical, especially in the retail market. In these circumstances, analysis of customers grouped by common demand patterns may be sufficient. The groups will, of course, vary by financial institution but should facilitate the recognition of common buying and risk patterns. The generic customer groups given in Chapter 10, Using Activity-based Costing for customer profitability, may provide sufficient information to pinpoint particular market sectors that are worth developing.

Alternatively, an analysis of a specific group of customers, measured by activity, value or profitability potential, may be sufficient where the information need is known. The analysis of certain types of customer may have particular relevance in large institutions, but some form of customer profitability analysis is important to all financial institutions, although the level of detail necessary will vary depending on the type of institution.

Classifying activities

The classifications are explained in detail in Chapter 4, Agreeing activities, but briefly, all principal activities identified by any department should be identifiable as fundamental or discretionary and as operational or sustaining. A fundamental activity is one that *must* be done, either to fulfil a legal requirement or because the business will cease to function if the activity is not performed. Discretionary activities are those activities that are not fundamental and may not vary with the level of business undertaken.

Within the basic categories of fundamental and discretionary, activities should be further classified as sustaining or related to the provision of products or services. Sustaining activities are those non-product-related activities that are performed to stay in business (such as financial accounting). These activities are generally fundamental in nature but can include such discretionary activities as corporate advertising as this is not related to a product or product group but undertaken to maintain the corporate image in the market-place.

Operational activities can be either fundamental or discretionary. How they are classified will determine, to some extent, how the analysis can be used. When Activity-based Costing is used to reduce costs or improve efficiency, the classification of the activities will facilitate the search for ways in which reductions or efficiency improvements can be made. When operational activities are classified as fundamental in a cost-reduction initiative, they are therefore eliminated from the cost/benefit analysis and any cost reductions that may be identified are then limited to what might be achieved by means of the efficiency improvements identified during the opportunity search exercise. If operational activities are classified as discretionary, then they may be reviewed in value terms as part of the cost/benefit exercise but will make the exercise more complex and time consuming. In general, those core activities that are unlikely to change may be considered fundamental and the operational activities to which changes and enhancements could be made may be considered discretionary.

Calculating costs

The calculation of the costs of activities will be performed as discussed in Chapter 6, Calculating costs. The type of costs used as the basis of the calculations will depend on the scope of the activity-based management. It is likely to be actual costs to enable cost efficiency to be monitored on a regular basis. This requires a strong degree of structure and discipline to be built into the analysis to ensure that actual costs can be recalculated regularly on a consistent basis without allocation of indirect or sustaining costs as part on the ongoing cost management system. Budgets may be calculated on the basis of activity-based budgeting, but this is not essential if the existing budgeting system is understood and accepted by the management team.

Calculating contribution

Cost analysis by activity is sufficient to enable cost-reduction and cost/benefit initiatives to be worked through, but for product and customer reporting it is necessary to analyse the sources and types of revenue streams as well as the cost base (income analysis is reviewed in detail in Chapters 6 and 9). Activity-based Costing assists in the identification of non-interest-related costs but can only be used to support the analysis of income and interest costs if the products have been defined and the volume of activity has been ascertained.

The identification and tracking of income by product is one of the most fundamental issues to be resolved in activity-based management. If the amount of information at the product level is limited, other options of tracking income will need to be identified.

In practice, most financial institutions will be able to track premiums, fees and interest that are debited or credited to customer accounts as they can be linked to products via the account number. However, income collected by means of cheque or cash (where an account number and hence a product cannot be clearly identified) requires either a change in procedures or the implementation of manual tracking processes. In many cases, it will not prove cost-effective to try and track this income by product as it usually represents no more than 1 per cent of total income. This income should therefore be recorded as a pool item, say, against a non-existent product. The entries for this product are essential in order to achieve a full reconciliation of total income to the total income figures in other profitability systems.

Costs of funds and the related earnings credits are prime cost components of all depositary and lending products. These costs usually vary over time and may have a significant impact on the price and profitability of the product base. Implementing a funds transfer pricing system, therefore, can be a major task in itself.

The combination of income analysis and Activity-based Costing provides a powerful management tool for the appraisal of product and customer profitability. Its amalgamation with activity-based budgeting ensures that management have effective control of the organisation and provides a management tool that mirrors organisational restructuring easily by linking activities to responsibility only at the reporting level.

Over the past few years, it has become common practice to allocate all sustaining costs back to operating functions on sophisticated bases. This practice has a tendency to focus attention on the allocation *process* and not on the *management* of the underlying costs. Activity-based Costing, however, concentrates the mind on the analysis of activities and reviews sustaining costs by means of direct cost management without the need to allocate costs to operating functions. Where full absorption costs are required for certain types of product analysis, then sustaining costs may be apportioned on an appropriate basis. This does not, however, enable them to be managed any more effectively and should be avoided whenever possible. It is much better to define a target return that includes the contribution to sustaining costs and a relevant profit margin which can then be used by product and customer management as the basis for pricing and fee negotiation.

ACTIVITY-BASED BUDGETING

As the concept of activity-based management becomes more common, the need to extend Activity-based Costing to the budgeting process becomes obvious, linking resources to cost drivers at the planning stage. Business unit goals can be linked directly to corporate objectives so that managers become accountable for managing their costs. As shown in Figure 11.1 earlier, the strategic objectives can drive the budgetary objectives and determine the volume of activities that need to be performed. The budgets are then derived from the activities using estimated cost rates. The steps involved are as follows.

Establish a baseline

In any activity-based budgeting system, it is necessary to first establish the activity-based cost baseline. This uses the standard Activity-based Costing approach described in Chapter 3, The Activity-based costing process, and defines the linkages between activities, cost drivers and basic resource utilisation. This can then be used as the basis of an activity-based budgeting system.

The baseline may be an established Activity-based Costing system or an isolated exercise, but will form the foundation of the initial budgetary process, ensuring consistency with actual data.

Develop budgetary guidelines

The budgetary guidelines will be based on the strategic goals of the organisation and should link the objectives to the value chain and the associated cost drivers in order to determine the volume of products and services, the quality and service standards and operational emphasis within the budgetary period.

Activity analysis

The budgetary guidelines will provide the quantitative and qualitative cost drivers that will then enable the volume of activities to be estimated for the period. This will be achieved using the activity-based cost baseline as a point of reference with which to link the cost drivers back to the underlying activities.

Calculate budgetary costs

The costs can then be calculated based on the activity levels estimated above and the cost rates identified in the activity-based cost baseline can be adjusted to take account of any known changes (such as inflation or any planned efficiency improvements).

Determine budgetary revenue

In parallel to the cost calculations, when the budgetary guidelines have been agreed, the revenue budgets can be determined, based on the estimated product and service volumes and the anticipated prices and margins.

Consolidate the financial forecast

The whole process of calculating costs and revenue and establishing budgetary guidelines may be iterative as the need to forecast adequate profits becomes paramount. The balance between cost and revenue will depend on the degree to which short-term volume drivers are balanced by the longer term qualitative investments.

Agree/finalise the budgets

When the values of the cost and revenue drivers have been balanced in such a way that adequate returns can be generated, the budgets can be agreed and finalised by activity within responsibility. As the budgets are derived by cost driver, they will be defined by the factors that cause the costs to be incurred and should, therefore, be controllable within the areas of responsibility.

Budgetary reporting

When the budgets have been finalised, they can be used as the basis for monthly reporting. Management performance can be measured based on actual expenditure in relation to the cost drivers and can be related to volume, value and quality of delivery. Activity-based budgeting can, therefore, form the basis of the type of cost management defined above.

PERFORMANCE MANAGEMENT

The objectives of activity-based performance management are likely to include the need to motivate management to focus attention on the improvement of productivity and cost management by means of improvements in efficiency and effectiveness and prioritisation of activities that drive the organisation towards its corporate goals. The basis of any performance management system should be the key performance indicators. A key performance indicator is a quantifiable measure of an activity that the manager must do well. Indicators will generally relate to activities and should incorporate measures that focus on financial performance, staff management, risk management, quality and customer service. The essence of a good performance management system depends on effective activity analysis and the identification of drivers that enable quantifiable measures to be agreed; there will thus be a strong connection between drivers and key performance indicators.

The agreement of key performance indicators is not normally part of an Activity-based Costing exercise, but will be linked to activity-based analysis in that the indicators agreed will be related to cost drivers (such as volumes, values, quality, time and level of service) and must be measurable to enable performance to be monitored. The regular reporting will therefore require a strong Activity-based Costing system that is capable of generating the volume and value data necessary to support the performance management.

COST-REDUCTION INITIATIVES

Activity-based cost-reduction initiatives analyse costs by *activity* not *department* and are therefore seen as less threatening than traditional cost-reduction techniques by the managers within the organisation. The process of Activity-based Costing is explained in more detail in Chapter 3, The Activity-based Costing process, but, in summary, for activity-based cost-reduction initiatives, all of the phases shown in Chapter 3 and repeated in Figure 11.2 need to be performed. The following paragraphs discuss the practicalities in more detail.

Review and confirm requirements

The requirements for a cost-reduction initiative will focus on the sponsorship of senior management, the commitment of management at all levels and the scope of the exercise.

Define reporting entities

The process involves noting the principal activities throughout the organisation and defining them on a consistent basis. It is important that common activities are defined and the definitions agreed prior to any analysis being undertaken so as to avoid confusion and enable true comparisons to be made. The emphasis of the cost-reduction initiative normally rests on the analysis of common activities throughout the organisation and the finding of opportunities to reduce, eliminate or improve the individual activities performed. The process of identifying activities enables more detailed and fruitful analysis of common activities such as training, secretarial support, management reporting etc., to be made and to reduce the usual emphasis on the operational activities.

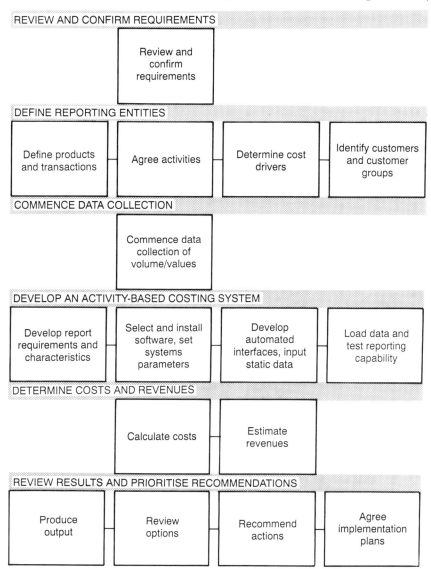

REVIEW AND CONFIRM REQUIREMENTS

Review and confirm requirements

DEFINE REPORTING ENTITIES

Define products and transactions

Agree activities

Determine cost drivers

Identify customers and customer groups

COMMENCE DATA COLLECTION

Commence data collection of volume/values

DEVELOP AN ACTIVITY-BASED COSTING SYSTEM

Develop report requirements and characteristics

Select and install software, set systems parameters

Develop automated interfaces, input static data

Load data and test reporting capability

DETERMINE COSTS AND REVENUES

Calculate costs

Estimate revenues

REVIEW RESULTS AND PRIORITISE RECOMMENDATIONS

Produce output

Review options

Recommend actions

Agree implementation plans

Figure 11.2   The Activity-based Costing process

The activities can then be used as the core of the analysis. Each activity must classified. The classifications are explained in detail in Chapter 4, Agreeing activities, but in brief, all principal activities identified by any department should be identifiable as fundamental or discretionary. It is important to stress that the classification is subjective and is used only as an aid to the search for opportunities for reducing costs or improving efficiency. The classification of an activity is an art not a science and may vary for different companies. For example, staff training may be viewed as absolutely fundamental in one organisation but be discretionary in another.

A fundamental activity is one that must be done, either because it is a legal requirement (such as meeting regulatory reporting requirements) or because the business will cease to function if the activity is not performed (such as maintenance on transaction processing systems). Fundamental activities must be performed at some level and management must decide on the level of effort and associated expenditure that are necessary.

Discretionary activities are those activities that are not fundamental and may not vary with the level of business undertaken. They can be eliminated without affecting the basic fabric of the organisation.

Commence data collection

Having agreed the common definitions of activities throughout the organisation, it is then necessary to identify the time spent on the various activities in each department. Some activities will be specific to individual departments, while others will be common and may occur in a number of departments. For cost-reduction initiatives, it is not normally necessary to go into more detail than principal activities and time allocation is normally limited to units of one tenth of a man year.

Develop an Activity-based Costing System

In any cost reduction initiative, there will inevitably be a large volume of data to be analysed. Activities must be measured and costs estimated, consistency applied and data integrity maintained. There are several proprietary software packages used by consultants who specialise in this type of work and some packages on the market can be used without the need for external consultants. They do, however, call for skills and experience if they are to be used effectively.

Determine costs and revenues

Costing, as we have seen, is the process of identifying, measuring, assigning and analysing the expenses associated with items that are to be costed. Costs within a financial institution can be of several basic types, including interest costs, claims, commissions paid, operating costs and overhead or support costs. Interest costs, for example, are usually those within financial institutions that can be attributed directly to a fundamental activity related to a product or group of products. Claims costs can also be attributed to a fundamental activity that is related to a particular policy type or group of policies. Commissions may include insurance commissions paid to agents and brokers, trading commissions paid to securities or foreign exchange traders or brokers, payments commissions paid to members of the clearing organisations, commissions paid to credit agencies and commissions or fees paid to research organisations who specialise in economic or industrial research. In general, all commissions paid can be assigned to fundamental activities. Operating costs within a financial institution will normally include all direct costs relating to the provision of products and services to customers or other parts of the organisation. These costs may be identifiable by organisational unit and can be assigned to the activities performed within the operational area. Overhead or support costs may include all costs that are not directly attributable to fundamental activities and will, therefore, be classified as sustaining activities and which traditional cost accounting would apportion to products and services according to some standard allocation practice.

Costs can be based on a variety of time frames. Historical, actual, budgeted, forecast and long-term expenditure projections of costs are all cost bases that may be used in cost-reduction initiatives. Any cost analysis should include all the costs of doing business in order to demonstrate that integrity of the cost base has been maintained. It is important, however, not to cloud the analysis by arbitrarily allocating costs just to ensure recon- ciliation to the financial accounts. The balance between the need to include all costs and what information is needed for decision-making can be achieved by means of reconciling statements and sub-totals that highlight the key results.

Review results and prioritise recommendations

In parallel to the costing exercise, the value of each discretionary activity to the organisation can be determined. This involves obtaining consensus within the organisation as to the value to be placed on each activity in relation to the strategic goals of the organisation. Activities should be ranked in relation to each other. For example, does the organisation value market research more than management accounting? Is training more important than staff counselling?

The values given to the discretionary activities can then be used to develop a cost/benefit matrix that enables management to focus attention in different ways on the activities which fall under its various headings (an example of a cost benefit matrix can be seen in Figure 11.4 in the Appendix to this chapter.

Management should initially focus on those high-cost, low-value activities that could be eliminated, reduced, improved or automated to reduce the cost and increase the value placed on the activity. Those identified as high-cost, high-benefit activities should also be reviewed in order to identify any ways in which costs can be reduced or improvements could be made in the efficiency and effectiveness of the activities.

Alternatively management should consider the low-cost, high-benefit activities that could be promoted, increased or enhanced to increase the value of the activity to the organisation at minimal cost. Finally, management may review the low-cost, low-benefit activities in order to determine whether these activities should be performed at all or, conversely, whether the value of the activities can be improved.

The process of reviewing the activities identified on the cost/benefit matrix and the finding of opportunities for reducing costs, improving efficiency, for automation, elimination, promotion and enhancement is one of the most important steps in a cost-reduction initiative. It is important to involve the management and staff of the organisation in the identification of opportunities to change both the fundamental and discretionary activities performed within their environment and to ensure their commitment to the implementation of the recommendations.

This opportunity search can be performed in two ways – by interviewing those involved in actually performing the activities and by discussions between groups of senior or middle management within the organisation. The manager responsible for the delivery of the activity or group of activities should discuss with his peers or users the value of the activity and the benefits derived. The group may decide that the level of service provided is too high and should be reduced, therefore resulting in reduced costs. Alternatively, they may decide that the activity can be undertaken more efficiently in another manner. One should not underestimate the value of asking the individuals undertaking the activities to suggest ways in which efficiency or effectiveness could be improved. They are closer to the tasks and often have good ideas that have never been voiced.

The opportunity search may also identify ways in which the organisation should be reorganised or restructured to optimise the work flow and eliminate the duplication of activities performed in different departments.

When all the opportunities have been identified, they should be classified by cost/benefit and priority to enable an implementation plan to be produced. It is very easy to develop the opportunities in theory, but it is important that the exercise is completed and the benefits achieved. The implementation plan must, therefore, be agreed and the implementation monitored against the plan on a regular basis.

CASE STUDY: IMPERIAL INSURANCE

Imperial Insurance is a small insurance company that undertook a cost reduction exercise last year to reduce costs by 10 per cent across the company. This exercise was relatively successful, in that budgeted costs were reduced by 8 per cent and, at the end of the year, the average overrun was only 2 per cent. A net reduction of approximately 6 per cent across the company was achieved. Unfortunately, last year there was a high number of claims, with the subsidence claims from a series of dry summers exceeding expectations by 300 per cent. The executive must now reduce costs in line with income and would like to aim for a reduction of 15 per cent.

In my experience, even in organisations that have already tried to reduce costs by traditional means, reductions in costs using Activity-based Costing of between 10 and 20 per cent are achievable with better savings being possible with an experienced team.

The Managing Director of Imperial Insurance has recently been to a seminar where a speaker was talking about Activity-based Costing and he feels that this may be the way to solve his problem.

The process

The steps involved in the project are shown in Figure 11.2 earlier in this chapter.

Review and confirm requirements
The Managing Director is prepared to sponsor the project and the Board of Directors feel that his approach may work better than the traditional approach to cost reduction undertaken last year. The project will be organised by the Finance Director and a Steering Committee consisting of a senior manager from each of the key business areas (Underwriting, Actuarial Services, Administration, Sales and Marketing and Management). An organisation chart of Imperial Insurance is shown in Figure 11.3 in the Appendix to this chapter. The project will include all activities within Imperial Insurance and no costs will be excluded from the analysis.

Defining reporting entities
The first step in the process involves the definition of and agreement on common activities throughout the company. After some discussion, the Steering Committee agreed a list of 37 principal activities (to be subdivided if necessary, in the key business areas). The list is given as Table 11.1 in the Appendix.

The Steering Committee then completed an activity analysis for their key business areas, detailing the activities performed in each area and the man time spent on each activity. The Personnel Manager was made responsible for ensuring that the total time allocation equated to the establishment figures (a summary of the analysis is given in Table 11.2 in the Appendix).

Commence data collection

The identified activities can then be used as the core of the analysis. Each activity must be costed and classified. The classifications for cost reduction initiatives are limited to fundamental or discretionary (Table 11.3 in the Appendix shows the classification finally agreed by the Steering Committee).

Develop an Activity-based Costing System

As in any cost-reduction initiative, there will inevitably be a large volume of data to be analysed. Activities must be measured and costs estimated, consistency applied and data integrity maintained. Imperial Insurance decided not to purchase one of the proprietary software packages, but to develop their own in-house database. This required a significant amount of man time to design and develop. It does, however, link into their existing accounting system to obtain cost data directly.

Determine costs and revenues

In parallel to the classification exercise, the Finance Director was given the task of estimating the costs of each activity identified. This had to include all costs within Imperial Insurance. Claims costs are costs that can be attributed to fundamental activities and, in Imperial Insurance, would be related to the claims investigation activity. Commissions may include insurance commissions paid to agents and brokers and, in this exercise, would be included in the cost of sales. Commissions or fees paid to research organisations who specialise in economic or industrial research would be charges to economic or market research as appropriate. Operating costs within Imperial Insurance may be identifiable by organisational unit and can be assigned to the activities performed within the operational area. Sustaining costs may include all costs in the management function in Imperial Insurance.

Review results and prioritise recommendations

As with any Activity-based Costing exercise, the most important phase of the project is the final phase, in which the results are reviewed and action taken.

PRODUCE OUTPUT
The cost analysis for Imperial Insurance is shown in Table 11.4 in the Appendix. It details the costs calculated for each activity within each key

business area and the total expenditure on the activity in the organisation as a whole.

REVIEW OPTIONS
When the activities had been classified (in parallel to the estimation of costs and revenues), the value of each discretionary activity to the organisation could be determined. This involved obtaining consensus within the organisation as to the value placed on each activity in relation to the strategic goals of the organisation. The strategies of Imperial Insurance are:

- to provide returns to the shareholders that match any in the industry
- to maintain or improve market share without reductions in quality or profitability
- to be a high-quality producer of premium policies
- to recruit and retain high-quality, motivated staff
- to maintain the social and environmental status of the company.

The management group and the Steering Committee ranked the activities within Imperial Insurance as shown in Table 11.5 in the Appendix.

The value of the discretionary activities was then used to develop a cost/benefit matrix, as shown in Figure 11.4 in the Appendix. The process of reviewing the activities identified on the cost/benefit matrix and the identification of opportunities for reducing costs, improving efficiency, automation, elimination, promotion and enhancement is one of the most important steps in the cost-reduction initiative. The whole management team got involved in the identification of opportunities to change both the fundamental and discretionary activities performed within their environment and to ensure their commitment to the implementation of the recommendations (the opportunities they found are shown in Table 11.6 in the Appendix).

RECOMMEND ACTION
When all the opportunities had been identified, they were classified by cost/benefit and priority to enable recommendations to be proposed to the management.

AGREE IMPLEMENTATION PLANS
Finally, when the recommendations had been accepted, an implementation plan was agreed in which the opportunities for cost reduction and improvements in efficiency could be actioned. A regular monitoring mechanism was built into the Activity-based Costing system to enable changes in actual costs to be monitored during the implementation.

SUMMARY

Any organisation must aim to maximise its profitability in either the short or longer term. In order to achieve this, it must be able to manage its cost base. As markets become increasingly competitive and profit margins are squeezed, the need to control and reduce costs focuses attention on the means of cost management within the organisation. Most financial institutions have undertaken some form of cost-reduction exercise within the last 12 months. Managing the cost base by activity (using Activity-based Costing as the basis of analysis and control) provides a means of looking at the level of expenditure from a new direction. The focus on *activities* instead of *cost centres* reduces the emphasis on cost centres and, hence, on the domains of cost centre managers. It can form the basis of cost/benefit analysis, which facilitates decision making based on the value placed on an activity within the organisation and the costs that it incurs.

Activity-based Costing analyses can be used in financial institutions as the basis for a variety of information tools that will assist senior managers in the management of the cost base. It can be used as the basis of activity-based management, including or excluding activity-based budgeting. It can be used simply as a replacement budgeting system. It can also be used as a core component of a performance management system and alternatively, can be used as the basis of an isolated cost-reduction initiative.

Cost reduction is only one element within the wider framework of cost management. An activity-based cost-reduction exercise should provide the springboard for better ongoing cost management, but will not replace existing methods of cost management. Ways of managing the cost base depend on ongoing planning and control of all aspects of the business. Costs are an integral part of the business infrastructure and any decision made by management will inevitably involve expenditure in either the long or short term. Implementing a new cost management system may have far-reaching effects, changing the way in which performance is measured within the organisation as a whole.

APPENDIX: IMPERIAL INSURANCE

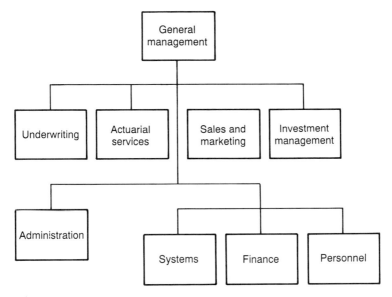

Figure 11.3 Imperial Insurance – organisation chart

Activities	Activities
1 Accounts payable	20 Personnel appraisal/counselling
2 Actuarial services	21 Policy administration
3 Advertising and promotions	22 Policy inception
4 Audit	23 Premium accounting
5 Claims administration	24 Property management
6 Claims investigation	25 Public relations
7 Compliance	26 Recruitment
8 Computer operation	27 Regulatory reporting
9 Data maintenance	28 Reinsurance
10 Economic research	29 Sales
11 Filing and archiving	30 Secretarial support
12 Financial accounting	31 Security
13 General management	32 Strategic planning
14 Investment management	33 Systems development
15 IT research	34 Taxation services
16 Litigation	35 Training
17 Management accounting	36 Treasury management
18 Market research	37 Underwriting/risk assessment
19 New product development	

Table 11.1 Imperial Insurance – list of activities

Activities	Underwriting	Sales/Marketing	Actuarial	Administration	Investment Management	Management	Total
1 Accounts payable				4.5		3.2	7.7
2 Actuarial services			15.0	2.0		3.0	20.0
3 Advertising and promotions		2.6					2.6
4 Audit						0.7	0.7
5 Claims administration			1.9	8.9		0.7	11.5
6 Claims investigation			7.4				7.4
7 Compliance	0.3					2.3	2.6
8 Computer operation		0.5		3.1		9.3	12.9
9 Data maintenance				2.5		4.8	7.3
10 Economic research	0.3	0.5	0.8			0.5	2.1
11 Filing and archiving	1.1	3.3	0.9	1.4	0.8	0.3	7.8
12 Financial accounting						1.5	1.5
13 General management	5.4	3.1	2.0	1.0	2.0	3.0	16.5
14 Investment management					18.4		18.4
15 IT research		0.4				1.7	2.1
16 Litigation			0.5			2.0	2.5
17 Management accounting	0.8	0.6	1.3	0.8	1.8	4.2	9.5
18 Market research	1.3						1.3
19 New product development	3.6	1.9					5.5
20 Personnel appraisal/counselling	1.2	2.9	1.8	0.9	1.1	0.5	8.4
21 Policy administration	3.8		3.8	14.3			21.9
22 Policy inception	4.2	8.4	2.7	6.2		0.3	21.8
23 Premium accounting			4.7	5.2		3.1	13.0
24 Property management					5.6		5.6
25 Public relations		1.6	1.8		1.4	0.8	5.6
26 Recruitment	0.7	1.6	0.4	0.7	0.3	1.8	5.5
27 Regulatory reporting						2.5	2.5
28 Reinsurance	6.4						6.4
29 Sales		65.0	4.2			4.9	74.1
30 Secretarial support	7.6	3.3	8.5	3.6	6.8	12.4	42.2
31 Security		0.3				8.5	8.8
32 Strategic planning	0.4	0.2	1.6		0.2	3.6	6.0
33 Systems development	0.8	1.9		2.1		12.8	17.6
34 Taxation services						1.3	1.3
35 Training	0.5	2.4	0.7	1.8	0.5	0.3	6.2
36 Treasury management					2.1	3.5	5.6
37 Underwriting/risk assessment	5.6						5.6
Total	44.0	100.5	60.0	59.0	41.0	93.5	398.0

Table 11.2 Imperial Insurance – activity analysis

Activities	Fundamental	Discretionary
1 Accounts payable	★	
2 Actuarial services	★	
3 Advertising and promotions		★
4 Audit	★	
5 Claims administration	★	
6 Claims investigation		★
7 Compliance	★	
8 Computer operation	★	
9 Data maintenance	★	
10 Economic research		★
11 Filing and archiving		★
12 Financial accounting	★	
13 General management		★
14 Investment management	★	
15 IT research		
16 Litigation	★	★
17 Management accounting		★
18 Market research		★
19 New product development		★
20 Personnel appraisal/counselling		★
21 Policy administration	★	
22 Policy inception	★	
23 Premium accounting	★	
24 Property management	★	
25 Public relations		★
26 Recruitment		★
27 Regulatory reporting	★	
28 Reinsurance	★	
29 Sales	★	
30 Secretarial support		★
31 Security		★
32 Strategic planning		★
33 Systems development		★
34 Taxation services	★	
35 Training		★
36 Treasury management	★	
37 Underwriting/risk assessment	★	

Table 11.3 Imperial Insurance – activity classification

Activities	Underwriting	Sales/Marketing	Actuarial	Administration	Investment Management	Management	Total
1 Accounts payable	0	0	0	99	0	154	253
2 Actuarial services	0	0	630	44	0	144	818
3 Advertising and promotions	0	65	0	0	0	500	565
4 Audit	0	0	0	0	0	34	34
5 Claims administration	0	0	80	196	0	34	309
6 Claims investigation	0	0	311	0	0	0	311
7 Compliance	11	0	0	0	0	110	122
8 Computer operation	0	13	0	68	0	446	527
9 Data maintenance	0	0	0	55	0	230	285
10 Economic research	11	13	34	0	0	24	81
11 Filing and archiving	41	83	38	31	27	14	233
12 Financial accounting	0	0	0	0	0	72	72
13 General management	200	78	84	22	68	144	595
14 Investment management	0	0	0	0	626	0	626
15 IT research	0	10	0	0	0	82	92
16 Litigation	0	0	21	0	0	96	117
17 Management accounting	30	15	55	18	61	202	380
18 Market research	48	0	0	0	0	0	48
19 New product development	133	48	0	0	0	0	181
20 Personnel appraisal/counselling	44	73	76	20	37	24	274
21 Policy administration	141	0	160	315	0	0	615
22 Policy inception	155	210	113	136	0	14	630
23 Premium accounting	0	0	197	114	0	149	461
24 Property management	0	0	0	0	190	0	190
25 Public relations	0	40	76	0	48	38	202
26 Recruitment	26	40	17	15	10	86	195
27 Regulatory reporting	0	0	0	0	0	120	120
28 Reinsurance	237	0	0	0	0	0	237
29 Sales	0	1625	176	0	0	235	2037
30 Secretarial support	281	83	357	79	231	595	1626
31 Security	0	8	0	0	0	408	416
32 Strategic planning	15	5	67	0	7	173	267
33 Systems development	30	48	0	46	0	614	738
34 Taxation services	0	0	0	0	0	62	62
35 Training	19	60	29	40	17	14	179
36 Treasury management	0	0	0	0	71	168	239
37 Underwriting/risk assessment	207	0	0	0	0	0	207
Total	1628	2513	2520	1298	1394	4488	13 841

Table 11.4 Imperial Insurance – cost analysis

Discretionary Activity Ranking		
Activities	Discretionary	Ranking
6 Claims investigation	★	1
32 Strategic planning	★	2
3 Advertising and promotions	★	3
33 Systems development	★	4
19 New product development	★	5
17 Management accounting	★	6
20 Personnel appraisal/counselling	★	7
35 Training	★	8
18 Market research	★	9
25 Public relations	★	10
30 Secretarial support	★	11
26 Recruitment	★	12
15 IT research	★	13
10 Economic research	★	14
31 Security	★	15
11 Filing and archiving	★	16

Table 11.5 Imperial Insurance – ranking of discretionary activities in order of value

OPPORTUNITIES FOR CHANGE
1 Review the cost of secretarial support to either improve the effectiveness or reduce the cost of the service provided.
2 Review the cost of providing security services (compare the costs of external/internal services.
3 Investigate the cost of systems development, although the benefits are perceived to be high, the costs should be reduced if at all possible.
4 Reduce the cost of advertising and promotions, consider ways of making the investment in marketing more effective.
5 Consider ways of reducing the cost of management accounting by reducing the number of reports required or further automation.
6 Consider the cost/benefit of market research, it may be worth increasing the investment if the benefit can be increased at the existing cost/benefit ratio.

Table 11.6 Imperial Insurance – opportunities for change

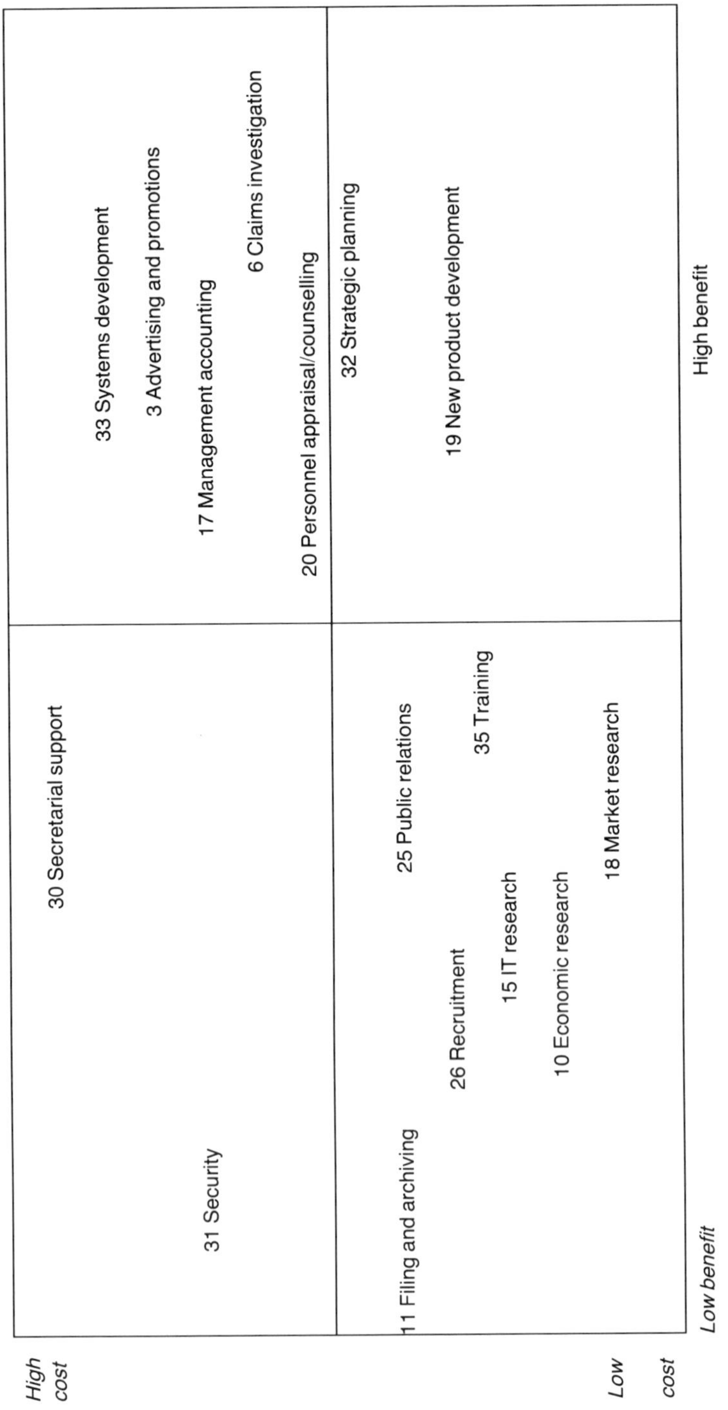

Figure 11.4 Imperial Insurance – cost/benefit analysis

INDEX

Notes:
1. Captions of Figures and Tables are indexed alphabetically under 'figures' and 'tables' respectively.
2. Subjects of Summaries are indexed alphabetically under 'summaries'.